JERUSALEM:
CITY OF PROPHECY

Dr. Don V. Bailey (D. Min)

WESTBOW
PRESS®
A DIVISION OF THOMAS NELSON
& ZONDERVAN

WestBow Press books may be ordered through booksellers or by contacting:

WestBow Press
A Division of Thomas Nelson & Zondervan
1663 Liberty Drive
Bloomington, IN 47403
www.westbowpress.com
1 (866) 928-1240

ISBN: 978-1-5127-1990-1 (sc)

Library of Congress Control Number: 2015918862

Print information available on the last page.

WestBow Press rev. date: 11/30/2015

ACKKNOWLEDGEMENTS

I am deeply grateful and acknowledge my debt to the following publishers for permission to quote from their copyrighted works: Abingdon Press, Nashville, TN—Strong's Exhaustive Concordance of the Bible, #1964, #2411, #3485, #3724 (1890); Brentwood Press, Columbus, GA [Permission granted by the author's family]—Lee A. Gore: Confrontation (1990); Canterbury Press, Canterbury, England, Oremus Hymnal [Hymns Ancient and Modern]—Bernard of Morlaix: Jerusalem the Golden (1983); CIA World Fact Book, Washington, DC—Guide to Country Profiles [Military] (2008); Dallas Seminary, Dallas, TX—Lewis Sperry Chafer: Systematic Theology, Vol. 5 (1948); Dictionnaire des sciences médicales, Paris—par une société de médicins et de chirurgiens, Volume 29 (1818); Emeth Publications, Whittier, CA—Charles Lee Feinberg: Is the Virgin Birth in the Old Testament? (1967); Fleming H. Revell Company, New York—W.E. Blackstone: Jesus is Coming (1932); Grace Theological Journal, Winona, IN—James D. Price: Rosh: An Ancient Land Known to Ezekiel, Vol. 6, 1, Spr., 85-68 (1999); Harvest House Publishers, Eugene, Oregon—Randall Price: In Search of Temple Treasures (1994); Hebrew Christian Testimony to Israel, London—David Baron: The Visions and Prophecies of Zechariah (1951); Henry Holt and Company, New York—Joan Comay: The Temple of Jerusalem (1975); Journal of the Evangelical Society, Lynchburg, VA—Robert W. Thurston: Are "Babylon" and "Diaspora" Literal or Figurative? JETS 17:3 [Summer] 175 (1974); Kregel Publications, Grand Rapids, MI—William Whiston: Josephus' Complete Works (1960); Sir Robert Anderson: The Coming Prince (1963); Leavitt and Allen Publishers, New York—Albert

Barnes: The Prophet Isaiah, Vol. I (1863); Mennonite Publishing House, Scottdale, PA—J. B. Smith: A Revelation of Jesus Christ (1961); Moody Press, Chicago—Wilbur M. Smith: The Biblical Doctrine of Heaven (1968); Wilbur M. Smith: Moody Monthly "Jerusalem in Prophecy," 60:30-33, 43-54 (June 1960); Our Hope Publication Office, New York—A.C. Gaebelein: The Annotated Bible. Vol. 5 (n.d.); Princeton University Press, Princeton, NJ—James B. Pritchard: Ancient Near Eastern Texts Relating to the Old Testament (1969); Stackpole Books, Mechanicsburg, Pa—Chaim Herzog, Mordechai Gichon: Battles of The Bible (1997); The Macmillan Company, New York—H.E. Dana and Julius R. Mantey: A Manuel Grammar of the Greek New Testament (1927, 1955); J. Gresham Machen: New Testament Greek for Beginners (1961); The Soncino Press, London—Rabbi Dr. S. Fisch: Ezekiel, Hebrew Text & English Translation With An Introduction And Commentary (1950); Tyndale House Publishers, Inc., Wheaton, IL—Henry Morris: The Revelation Record (1983); WM. B. Eerdmans Publishing Company, Grand Rapids, MI—J. Howard Kitchen: Holy Fields (1955); Keil-Delitzsch: Commentary on the Old Testament, Vols. 9,10 (1975); Kenneth S. Wuest: In These Last Days (1957); Wordsworth Editions Ltd, Hertfordshire, England—The Works of Lord Byron (1994); Zondervan Publishing Company, Grand Rapids, MI—John F. Walvoord: The Nations in Prophecy (1967); Dwight Pentecost: Things to Come (1966); R.C.H. Lenski: Commentary on the Holy Scriptures: The Interpretation of St. John's Revelation, Vol.12 (1960).

Also, my appreciation goes to the many authors and publishers of the works listed in the Bibliography and Reference Lists who are not mentioned above. The knowledge I have gained from them through the years has been invaluable.

All charts in this book were devised and illustrated by the author, unless otherwise indicated.

Dedicated to the memory of Dr. E. W. Bullinger,
Rightly divider of the Word of Truth, par-excellence.

PREFACE

My love for the city of Jerusalem and its people began at the end of WWII when, as a boy in the mountains of Kentucky, I would hear radio reports of how the Nazis were persecuting and murdering the Jewish people, and accounts of how the Jews were escaping from the Holocaust and fleeing to Jerusalem, their only home. As the years passed, the more I learned about Jerusalem. My love grew stronger for her and for her people.

I became chaplain of a hospital in 1968 where most of the patients were Jewish, and for 25 years I ministered to God's beloved people, hearing first-hand accounts of persecution and evil from hundreds of survivors of the Holocaust. They are a large part of the reason I have written this book.

The late Dr. Wilbur Smith wrote an article, Jerusalem in Prophecy, 1968, stating, "The Librarian of Dallas Theological Seminary, where more thesis [sic] on prophetic subjects have been written during the last thirty years than perhaps any Seminary in America, tells me that no thesis has ever been written there on the subject Jerusalem in prophecy."[1] Various works on Jerusalem have been written and published since he wrote that statement, but I have found none that have concentrated exclusively on the deliverances and destructions of that city. Challenged by Dr. Smith's words, I decided to take a different approach to Jerusalem in prophecy—trace her deliverances and destructions from King David's deliverance of the citadel, Jebus, from the Jebusites to the far-off distant future when Christ will deliver Jerusalem into the hands of God the Father (I Cor. 15:24-28). My purpose is not to write a history of

Jerusalem, but to address those parts of her history relating to prophecy, hence the title of this work, Jerusalem: City of Prophecy.

This book is divided into four parts: Part One consists of chapter I and deals with the derivation and descriptive names of Jerusalem and their prophetic indicatives. It presents and explains the different appellations of Jerusalem, and how they shed light on the fact that she is, indeed, the outstanding city of prophecy among all the cities of the earth.

Part Two comprises chapters II through V. Chapter II addresses fulfilled prophecies of the deliverances and destructions of Jerusalem during the Old Testament period and covers relative events from Shishak, King of Egypt, through the reign of the Babylonian King, Nebuchadnezzar.

Fulfilled prophecies of the deliverance and destruction of Jerusalem during the Intertestamental Period are addressed in chapter III and include the sparing of Jerusalem by Alexander the Great and the cruelties of Antiochus Epiphanes during the Maccabean revolt.

Chapter IV addresses fulfilled prophecies of the destructions and deliverances of Jerusalem during New Testament times, and treats the destruction of the city by Titus the Roman, forerunner of "the prince who is to come" (Dan. 9: 26).

Chapter V deals with fulfilled prophecies of the destructions and deliverances of Jerusalem during the present age. It includes the destruction of the city by Hadrian and the closing of the New Testament Period followed by events during the Present Age, i.e., events and actions not cited in Scripture, but prophetic in general covering the period cited by Luke, "... Jerusalem will be trampled underfoot by the Gentiles until the times of the Gentiles are fulfilled" (Lk. 21:24).

Part Three, chapters VI through VIII follow and spotlight *unfulfilled* prophecies of the deliverances and destructions of the city.

Unfulfilled prophecies of the deliverances and destructions of Jerusalem during the time impinging the Tribulation age, dealt with in chapter VI, present a vivid description of the destruction of the Godless forces of Russia and her allies who attempt Jerusalem's destruction.

Chapter VII, Excursus of II Thessalonians 2: The Restrainer Recast, comprises arguments that identify the Antichrist and the Restrainer of "the lawless one" in II Thessalonians 2:1-12.

Chapter VIII, Unfulfilled Prophecies of the Deliverances and Destructions of Jerusalem during the Tribulation Period, brings to light the actions of the Antichrist against the city.

Chapter IX looks to the very end (the far-off distant future) of prophecy at which point the Son of Man delivers the Kingdom into the hands of His Father, beyond which there is no revelation except for the revelation of the beginning of the ages upon the ages that will never end.

Part Four, Jerusalem in the Light of Poetry: A Prophetic Incentive, consists of chapter X and presents many of the well-known poems and hymns of plaint and praise about the city's destructions and deliverances, from the writing of the Psalms to the present.

I have deliberately chosen not to address the different views and arguments on the Millennium. They have been discussed *ad nauseam* in other works and, in my opinion, it would be a waste of the reader's time to rehash materials already available in abundance. Those who differ with my view on the Millennium should consult specific works that explain all of the millennial views in detail. I have included those works in the reference list at the end of this book.

Two noted Bible scholars who influenced me to write this work were the late Dr. Wilbur M. Smith, a student of prophecy, to whom I referred above, and the late Dr. E.W. Bullinger who suggested in his outstanding, Commentary on Revelation, that a recasting of the view of the Holy Spirit as the Restrainer be considered. Without his supposition I would not have taken up the challenge to discover the solution to two of the most difficult verses in the Bible, II Thessalonians 2: 6-7. The result is chapter VII, Excursus of II Thessalonians 2: The Restrainer Recast.

HONORARY MENTION

Sincere appreciation to my three granddaughters: Hayden, Bailey, and Peyton Fantino. Hayden and Bailey were a tremendous help in answering questions, typing and emailing information to the publisher.

Peyton helped in various ways, e.g., bringing food to my office when I was famished, and dusting my office when the dust settled too deep.

And also, many thanks to my good friend Matt Moore for his technical expertise whenever computer issues arose.

CONTENTS

PART ONE
The Name of Jerusalem: A Prophetic Indicative

PART TWO
Fulfilled Prophecies of the Deliverances and Destructions of Jerusalem During the Old Testament Period Through the Present Age

PART THREE

*Unfulfilled Prophecies of the Deliverances and Destructions of Jerusalem
During the Time Impinging the Tribulation Through the Ages of the Ages*

PART FOUR

The Name of Jerusalem: A Poetic Incentive

PART ONE

The Name of Jerusalem:
A Prophetic Indicative

INTRODUCTION

Historically, there have been many beautiful cities, but none whose beauty in God's eyes surpasses that of the city of Jerusalem. To her enemies she is an object of ridicule and hatred, but to God she always has been and always will be His precious one, which is why she can be characterized as the most prophetic city of the world, foretelling His plan and purpose for a sin-wracked planet. Jerusalem is the only city on Earth where God has chosen to inscribe His name. It was outside her walls, where on a cruel cross, God would choose from before the foundation of the world His redeemed ones in His Son, Jesus the Messiah.

The name Jerusalem (city of peace) is prophetic of the perfect peace of the heavenly city, New Jerusalem, which is to come that will be the eternal dwelling place of God's chosen ones from every city and nation on Earth. Everything implied in the name, Jerusalem, has already been accomplished in one fashion or another during her long and difficult history. Investigation into the origin of the name, Jerusalem, reveals that it always has been a *prophetic indicative*; this will be discussed in Chapter I.

CHAPTER I

The Derivation and Descriptive Names of Jerusalem

I. THE DERIVATION OF THE NAME OF JERUSALEM

The derivation of the name Jerusalem is uncertain but certainly predates Israel's invasion of the Promised Land. Whether the name was given by aboriginals, the Canaanite inhabitants (Jebusites), or by God Himself is difficult to determine.

1. THE ABORIGINAL

Archaeology has uncovered evidence of human activity at the site of the future city of Jerusalem as early as 5000 to 4000 B.C.,[1] indicating that aboriginals who were near descendants to Adam migrated there roughly 2000 years after Adam's death (Gen. 5:5). Whoever named the site would have done so between the lives of Adam and Abraham, for it is not until the time of Abraham that we find the first biblical reference to the name—Salem (Gen. 14:18). God instilled in Adam the wisdom and intellectual capacity to ascribe names to Eve and to the animals. Any one of his descendants could have named the ancient community, but there is no evidence to show the site had a name until after the aboriginals were driven away.

2. THE JEBUSITES

The aboriginal inhabitants were expelled between 4000 B. C. and 3000 B.C., and subsequently the site was occupied by the Hittites. Later it was captured by the Jebusites, a dominant tribe among the Old Testament Canaanites. At that time, according to the Egyptian Tel El-Amarna Tablets (1480 B.C.-1460 B.C.), the city was known as Jerusalem and the king of Jerusalem had a Hittite name. Kitchen states: "...the history of the city must be carried back 5000 years. Excavations have found occupation by Canaanite cave dwellers as early as 3000 B.C., and by 1900 B.C. the city Ur-salim was known on the Egyptian records, at the time of the Tel El-Amarna correspondence 500 years later..."[2] Masterman agrees that the name Jerusalem is not mentioned until 1450 B.C., where it appears on the Tel El-Amarna Tablets in the form Ur-Salim. Along with that he mentions the form Ur-sa-li-immu found on Assyrian monuments of the 8th century B.C.[3] That the Egyptians were very much aware of Ur-salim is confirmed by inscriptions found on fragments of Middle Kingdom pottery bowls dating to the latter part of the Twelfth or Thirteenth Dynasties (19th-18th centuries B.C.). In James B. Pritchard's book, Ancient Near Eastern Text Relating to the Old Testament, Line 27 of one inscription is given as, "...the Ruler of Jerusalem [Ur-salim], Yaqar-'Ammu, and all the retainers who are with him; the Ruler of Jerusalem, Setj-'anu, and all the retainers who are with him..." Quoting Pritchard more fully: "In the Middle Kingdom period the Egyptians practiced the magical cursing of their actual or potential enemies. In the Berlin Museum are fragments of pottery bowls that had been inscribed with the names of such foes and then smashed. In the Cairo and Brussels Museums, inscribed figurines carry the same kind of curse. As they smashed such pottery, so they thought to break the power of their enemies. The exorcised elements were Nubians, Asiatics, Libyans, hostile Egyptians, and evil forces."[4] Among the Asiatic princes were the rulers of Jerusalem mentioned above, Yaqar-'Ammu and Setj-'anu.

The Egyptian records show that the Pharaohs' influence had spread into Palestine during Egypt's Middle Kingdom. The site of Jerusalem had been named long before Abraham left Ur of the Chaldeas. The following account of Abraham supports the dates of Kitchen and

Masterman. Abraham lived in Ur of the Chaldea's between 2000 and 1500 B.C. The Hebrews did not enter servitude in Egypt until around 1400 B.C., meaning that Abraham's defeat of Chedorlaomer and the kings that were with him and his meeting with Melchizedek (Gen. 14:1-24) occurred sometime between 1500 B.C.-1400 B.C., probably around 1450 B.C. Melchizedek ("my righteous king" or "king of righteousness") was a Canaanite chieftain. Ur-salim was well known by 1900 B.C.; it was named long before Melchizedek came on the scene, when Abraham met him on the way from doing battle with the kings of the plains. It had been ruled as Ur-salim by at least two previous Canaanite chieftains, Yaqar-'Ammu and Setj-'Anu. While he had nothing to do with the naming of the site of Jerusalem, Melchizedek is mentioned relative to the very first appearance of the name of Jerusalem in the Bible.

> "Then after his return from the defeat of Chedorlaomer and the kings who were with him, the king of Sodom went out to meet him at the valley of Shaveh (that is, the King's Valley). And Melchizedek king of Salem brought out bread and wine; now he was a priest of God Most High. He blessed him and said, "Blessed be Abram of God Most High, Possessor of heaven and earth; And blessed be God Most High, Who has delivered your enemies into your hand." He gave him a tenth of all" (Gen. 14:16-20).

It is safe to assume that Ur-salem is the original form of Jerusalem. George Adam Smith has the following to say concerning the derivation of the name:

> What the etymology of Yerushalem may be it is almost impossible to descry. Various derivations have been suggested, some ludicrous, none satisfactory. The latter half of the word is taken as meaning peace or security; but while the early rabbis and earliest Christian writers interpreted the first part as vision or fear, modern etymologists have been divided between the possession

and the foundation--of peace or security. The resemblance of the first part of the name, Yeru, to the imperfect of the verb, and the compositionof instances of the latter with a divine title in so many of the Palestinian place-names, suggests a similar derivation for Yeru-shalem: as if it were from the very Yarah; and should mean Shalem or Shalman, founds; or rather, since this meaning for yarah is not certainly possible, Shalem casts the lot. On the whole, however, shalem is more probably a noun peace or an adjective perfect or secure. Yeru might be either a verb, he (the god) casts a perfect or peaceful (lot), or a noun, as if secure lot. Therefore, since the original form of Jerusalem was Ur-salim, which no doubt existed before the Hebrews took the land, it seems possible, if not probable, that the earliest form of the Hebrew "Yerushalem" was simply a transliteration of the salim of "Yeru" corresponding to Ur and "shalem" to salim.[5]

The earliest source of information in the Bible occurs in the Old Testament during the time of Joshua. Joshua 10:1 has Yerushalaim. However, Masterman says:

> The most ancient Bib. form is, yerushalem, shortened in Psa. 76:2 (cf Gen. 14:18) to Salem, but in Mt we have it vocalized: yerushalaim. In Jer. 26:18; Est. 2:6; 2 Ch. 25:1; 32:9, we have yerushalayim, a form which occurs on the Jewish coins of the revolt and also in Jewish literature; it is commonly used by modern Talmudic Jews. The form with the ending aim or ayim is interpreted by some as being a dual, referring to the upper and lower Jerus, but such forms occur in other names as implying special solemnity; such a pronunciation is both local and late.[6]

The LXX (Septuagint) has Ierousalhm (Ierousalem), which reflects the earliest Hebrew pronunciation. Luke and Paul have Ierousalhm (Hierousalem) in their writings. The remainder of the New Testament seems to have ta Ierosoluma (ta Hierosoluma). The LXX reflects the earliest Hebrew pronunciation (Ierousalem = Yerushalem) and it is from this that the English spelling Jerusalem is derived:

> The English spelling of the name Jerusalem—which is common to many modern languages—as derived by the Authorized Version of 1611 A. D., through the Vulgate, from the Greek Ierousalem, and approximates to what was in all probability the earlier pronunciation in Hebrew, Yerushalem.[7]

3. GOD

The Egyptians may have been first to record the name; but any commentary beyond that is pure conjecture unless one accepts the possibility that God named it in His own mysterious way. Even though the name Jerusalem has been applied to an earthly site, it corresponds to another city on a much higher plain having the same name, its prototype, heavenly Jerusalem. That is the city for which Abraham looked. He sought it but probably did not know it by name; only that God was its builder and maker (Heb. 11:10). It was, of course, the same city to which Jesus alluded as "a place for you" (Jn. 14:2). Later in Revelation 21:2, 10 John would describe the city as "the holy city New Jerusalem" and Paul would refer to it as "the Jerusalem from above, which is free, our mother" (Gal. 4:26, NASB). How did John and Paul know the city to have those names? There is only one answer. God revealed it to them. Revelation comes only from God. If the truth of the matter is known, God revealed the name Jerusalem to the individual who first named the site in the distant past. His purpose was to present her as a city having a prophetic name that would in the end merge with the heavenly city, New Jerusalem. This will be discussed in chapter IX.

II. THE DESCRIPTIVE NAMES OF JERUSALEM

Jerusalem as a name is mentioned in the Bible no less than 800 times, and the New Jerusalem two times (Rev. 21:2, 10, NKJV). No other city on earth has had so many different names applied to it. The following appellations have been used in Scripture to describe it:

1. JEBUS

The name, Jebus, whose prime root is boos, means trodden hard, threshing-place, fastness, or waterless hill. Because of the characteristics of the site, the Jebusites may have named it when they took the city from the Hittites. The term Jebus is first mentioned in Judges 19:10-11, following the patriarchal period. Some believe that the Hebrews named it for the Jebusites who dwelt there (Josh. 11:3; 15:8; 18:16, 28; Jgs. 19:10-11; I Chron. 11:4-5). While either of the above may be true, it also is possible that it was named for one Jebus who was, according to Gen. 10:15-16, the third son of Canaan, perhaps chieftain of the tribe.

2. ARIEL

The name Ariel, used in Ezekiel 43:15-16, probably means altar-hearth of God. In II Samuel 23:20 and I Chronicles 11:22, it is the name of a Moabite, but in Isaiah 29:1 God applies it to Jerusalem. Although the name Ariel is mentioned five times in Isaiah 29:1, 2 and 7, the name Jerusalem is mentioned nowhere within that text. However, there are two inferences pointing to the fact that God is addressing Jerusalem. In v1, "the city where David once camped!" is no doubt Jerusalem and v8 equates Ariel with Mount Zion, another name for Jerusalem (see 9. Holy Mountain of God).

Isaiah 29 is a pronouncement of divine judgment upon Jerusalem, the place where the temple altar was located and sacrifices were offered and the place where she herself will one day become Ariel, the burning altar and sacrifice. The fire of judgment that is to fall on the city will not come from Sennacherib (who never subjugated the city), but will come in the far-distant future when all nations are gathered against her (Zech. 14). Thus, the name Ariel is prophetically characteristic for Jerusalem.

3. CITY OF DAVID

David was born and raised in Bethlehem, but Bethlehem would not be the city from which he would rule Israel; neither would he reign from Hebron where he was anointed king. Following his anointing, David and his men went up to Jerusalem and took her from the Jebusites, who had held the city for 200 years, after Joshua's conquest of Canaan, c. 1250 B.C. David's conquest is interesting:

Now the king and his men went to Jerusalem against the Jebusites, the inhabitants of the land, and they said to David, "You shall not come in here, but the blind and lame will turn you away"; thinking, "David cannot enter here." Nevertheless, David captured the stronghold of Zion, which is the city of David. David said on that day, "Whoever would strike the Jebusites, let him reach the lame and the blind, who are hated by David's soul, through the water tunnel." Therefore they say, "The blind or the lame shall not come into the house." So David lived in the stronghold and called it the city of David. And David built all around from the Millo and inward" (II Sam. 5:6-9).

When David and his army arrived at the city, the inhabitants taunted him by telling him that even the blind and the lame could defend Jebus against him. Initially, David was not altogether successful; he was able to take only the citadel and could not gain access to the city as a whole. Then he discovered a way into the city, a shaft (ronzt = tzinor = gutter, water tunnel, watercourse) and an improvised geological fissure through which water was drawn from the spring below the city. He promised a high command to whomever would lead the assault. Joab accepted David's challenge and he and the men under his command maneuvered their way through the steep fifty-foot water shaft, gaining access to the city and surprising the inhabitants.

David realized that God had delivered a most valuable possession into his hands. He saw that the city was so strategically situated it would, in the future, meet the needs of his kingdom. Standing on a ridge it was defensible. The water supply afforded via the water tunnel (tzinor), which ran from the cisterns, would be sufficient in the event of siege. It was located in the center of the country with easy access to main arterial roads and the Great (Mediterranean) Sea, vital routes for trade with other countries. "And David dwelt in the stronghold, and called it the city of David. And David built round-about from Millo and inward. David became greater and greater, for the Lord God of hosts was with him" (II Sam. 5:9, 10).

The name City of David is mentioned 33 times in the Old Testament and 2 times in the New Testament; however, the 2 New Testament references speak of Bethlehem (Lk. 2:4, 11), David's birthplace and hometown, not Jerusalem. Joseph went to Bethlehem with Mary to register for the census and while they were there she gave birth to Jesus (v4). When the angels appeared to the shepherds, they said: "...For today in the city of David there has been born for you a Savior, who is Christ the Lord" (v11,).

Later Jesus would refer to Psalm 110: "If David then calls him 'Lord,' how is He his son?" (Matt. 22:45). Because Jesus was David's Lord and son (descendant), Jesus would be known as the greater David, but only in the sense that He, like David, was born in Bethlehem, the City of David, and when He returns to Earth "the Lord God will give Him the throne of His father David..." (Lk. 1:32, NASB), and He will rule from Jerusalem as did David. The name, city of David, is a prophetic characteristic of Jerusalem and may be an appellation during the millennial reign of Christ, especially if, as some believe, David is to rule as vice regent. Walvoord writes:

> ....References to this concept are found in Jeremiah 30:9; 33:15-17; Ezekiel 34:23-24; 37:24-25; Hosea 3:5, with more indirect references in Isaiah 55:3-4, and Amos 9:11....
>
> ....That by David is meant the resurrected David who shares with Christ as prince some of the government duties of the millennial kingdom. It should be clear from many scriptures that the reign of Christ is shared with others. As Newell has written: 'David is not the son of David. Christ, as Son of David, will be King; and David, His father after the flesh, will be prince, during the Millennium. In the light of the many prophecies which promise saints the privilege of reigning with Christ,

it would seem most logical that David the king raised from the dead should be given a place of prominence in the Davidic kingdom of the millennial reign of Christ. As indicated in Revelation 19:16, Christ is 'KING OF KINGS AND LORD OF LORDS.' This would certainly imply other rulers [cf. Isa. 32:1 Ezek. 45:8-9; Matt. 19:28; Lk. 19:12-27].[8]

4. CITY OF GOD

The name, City of God, is referenced in Psalm 46:4 and Psalm 87:3 where it is to be identified with Zion. Just as the city of David is one and the same with Zion and Jerusalem, so too is "the city of God." Psalm 48:1, 8 has "the city of our God." The writer to the Hebrews applies the name to the Jerusalem from above, which is to come: "But you have come to Mount Zion and to the city of the living God [italics mine], the heavenly Jerusalem, and to myriads of angels" (Heb. 12:22, NASB). In Revelation 3:12 Jesus uses the name, City of God, when he tells John to write to the angel of the church in Sardis: "'He who overcomes, I will make him a pillar in the temple of My God, and he will write upon him the name of My God, and the name of the city of My God [italics mine], the new Jerusalem, which comes down out of heaven from My God and My new name."

Similar to the "city of God" are the names "the city of the Lord of Hosts" (Psa. 48:8) and "the city of the Lord" (Psa. 101:8; Isa. 60:14). Certainly the city belongs to the Lord; it is His unique possession. But the inhabitants of Jerusalem have a greater sense of security knowing that He is the Lord of Hosts, with all the power of the armies of heaven at His disposal. Everyone who enters its gates must be without fault and blameless before the Lord (Psa. 101), and so they will be, in the day when He rules in the earthly Jerusalem for 1000 years, and in the heavenly Jerusalem to come.

5. CITY OF THE GREAT KING

Jerusalem has been ruled by great kings (David, Solomon, Hezekiah, Josiah), but a greater king will be her ultimate ruler. Even though "God is

King of the whole earth" (Psa. 47:7) and His Son is "...KING OF KINGS AND LORD OF LORDS" (I Tim. 6:16; Rev. 17:14; 19:16), of no other city is it said that He is King, except the city of Jerusalem (Psa. 48:2).

Jerusalem was a proud city, when in the past she acknowledged God, but her history is sad testimony to an inconsistent track record of sin and rebellion, culminating in complete rejection of Him as her king. When her King came to her "meek and lowly and riding on a donkey," (Zech. 9:9) she failed to recognize Him, rejected Him, and those in authority "...cried out 'Away with Him, crucify Him!'" Pilate said to them, 'Shall I crucify your King?' The chief priests answered, 'We have no king but Caesar'" (Jn. 19:15). He was nailed to a cross like a common criminal, but they got the inscription right: Matthew 27:37 has "'THIS IS JESUS KING OF THE JEWS'"; Mark 15:26 simply reads "'THE KING OF THE JEWS'"; Luke 23:38 records "'THIS IS THE KING OF THE JEWS'"; and John 19:19 adds one word to the placard without contradicting either of the former three, "'JESUS THE NAZARENE, THE KING OF THE JEWS."

Christ was buried, arose on the third day, and later ascended back to Heaven and sat down at the right hand of the Father where He awaits the day when He will come with the armies of Heaven to "...shatter kings in the day of His wrath" (Psa. 110:5). "And on His robe and on His thigh He has a name written, "KING OF KINGS AND LORD OF LORDS" (Rev. 19:16). On that day His feet will touch down on the Mount of Olives (Zech. 14:3-4), after He has fought for His people, and He will march triumphantly through the Eastern Gate into Jerusalem, the city of the great King. The people of Jerusalem will look upon Him whom they have pierced (Zech. 12:10; Rev. 1:7), along with the great entourage of saints and angels who return with Him (Rev. 19:13, 14), raising their voices in unison and singing, "Lift up your heads, O gates, And be lifted up, O ancient doors, That the King of glory may come in! Who is the King of glory? The Lord strong and mighty, The Lord mighty in battle. Lift up your heads, O gates, and lift them up, O ancient doors, That the King of glory may come in! Who is this King of glory? The Lord of Hosts, He is the King of glory [Selah]" (Psa. 24:7-10).

6. CITY OF JUDAH

Judah, son of Jacob and Leah, was the forbearer of the tribe of Judah. After the Exodus and entrance into the Promised Land under the leadership of Joshua, the land was divided among the tribes and the territory that became Judah's inheritance was the Negev to the south, the Shephelah (the lowland between the central highlands and the Mediterranean Sea), the mountains of Judah ("hill-country"), and the Dead Sea area. Judah's inheritance contained thirty-eight towns. Two hundred years later that number rose to thirty-nine when Jebus (the Jerusalem site) fell to David (Josh. 15:20-63; II Sam. 5:6-9).

Though Bethlehem was David's birthplace and became Jesus' home, it was considered "too little to be among the clans of Judah" (Mic. 5:2). Jerusalem, however, would become the city of Judah, when King David moved his capital from Hebron to Jerusalem. It will be the chief city of Judah throughout the Millennium, when Christ "the Lion that is from the tribe of Judah..." comes to rule from what will then be known as the capital-city of the world. Then Judah will be praised (Gen. 49:8-10: Rev. 5:5).

7. CITY OF TRUTH

Jerusalem has been a place of lies, deception and intrigue from the time of David. False prophets led the people astray, religious leaders could not be trusted to speak the truth, and the people themselves were full of lies and deceit. God raised up prophets to cry out against dishonesty and falsehood, but they were ignored and periodic judgments ensued. While the city lay in ruins, Daniel, the great prophet of the captivity, lamented and confessed that they had not given attention to God's truth (Dan. 9:13). Jerusalem did not learn her lesson, rejecting the One who was "...the way, and the truth, and the life'" (Jn. 14:6). Again, judgment fell and Jerusalem fell, as Jesus said she would (Matt. 24:1, 2; Mk. 13:1, 2; Lk. 19:41-44).

Isaiah prophesied that in the future his people would make a covenant with death and Sheol to escape calamity. They would put their trust in falsehood and hide in its security (Isa. 28:14, 15). In Daniel's

70-week prophecy, after Messiah is put to death the covenant is made with the "...prince who is to come" at the beginning of the 70ᵗʰ week. In the middle of that week, the prince will break the covenant, causing the re-instituted sacrifices to cease. "...On the wing of abominations," says Daniel, this one comes "who makes desolate..." by instigating a pogrom against the Jewish people (Dan. 9:26-27). This one's "...coming is in accord with the activity of Satan, with all power and false [lying] wonders and with all deception of wickedness for those who perish, because they did not receive the love of the truth so as to be saved" (II Thess. 2:9, 10).

It is tragic that God must use the man of lies to discipline His people for a whole history of lies and deception, but He knows that will be the only way to bring them to the truth. When they are faced with utter annihilation, He will come and deliver them from their last persecutor. The Lord will destroy him with the breath of His mouth and the brightness of His coming, "sweep away the refuge of lies," and cancel "the covenant of death" and their "pact with Sheol" (Dan. 9:27; Isa. 28:17-18; II Thess. 2:8; Rev. 19:19, 20).

The Chapter for which this part of the study is named is taken from the great Minor Prophet, Zechariah, where the word truth is mentioned 5 times: "Thus says the Lord, 'I will return to Zion and will dwell in the midst of Jerusalem. Then Jerusalem will be called the City of Truth...I will be their God in truth and righteousness...'" He then tells the inhabitants to: "speak the truth to one another; judge with truth and judgment for peace in your gates...so love truth and peace" (Zech. 8:3, 8, 16, 19 [italics mine]). While Messiah's presence on earth will make a difference, it still will be necessary to remind the inhabitants to speak the truth in love. That city does not compare with the city that shall come for "...no one who practices...lying, shall come into it, but those whose names are written in the Lamb's book of life" (Rev. 21:27). The truth—and nothing but the truth—will be spoken.

8. THE HOLY CITY

The word holy, relative to the name of Jerusalem, is mentioned for the first time in Nehemiah 11:1 and again in v18. By what right does a city filled with lies, hypocrisy, and rebellion deserve to be called holy? There is nothing inherent in the name Jerusalem itself that would indicate holiness, and certainly not in the character of the inhabitants. The reason she lay in shambles during Nehemiah's day was that a Holy God had judged her for her sins. Why then should she be called the holy city?

A Holy God chose to put His Name there. There has been no other city chosen for His name's sake other than Jerusalem. In the book of Deuteronomy, beginning with Chapter 12, there are at least 20 references to the "place" where God would choose to put His name—long before Jerusalem was ever named. I Kings 11:36 specifically names "...Jerusalem, the city where I have chosen for Myself to put My name." Though she has been judged time-and-time again through the centuries, and even though God said, "...I will cast off Jerusalem [italics mine], this city where I have chosen, and the temple of which I said, 'My name shall be there'" (II Kgs. 23:27); God will choose her again (Zech. 1:17; 2:12). His name will be in the earthly city and the holy city, New Jerusalem, where all will see it—"...and His name shall be on their foreheads" (Rev. 22:4).

God directed both David (who didn't) and Solomon (who did) to build Him a Temple that would be the place of worship for Israel. There He would dwell in the holy of holies, in a thick cloud (the sheki-nah) over the mercy seat, atop the Ark of the Covenant, overshadowed by the out-stretched wings of two cherubim. There He would meet with the priests (representatives of the people) and instruct them in the way of guidance, holiness, and sacrifices for sin (II Chron. 1-8:1). Earthly Jerusalem was called the holy city because the Holy God of heaven and earth was there in His temple in the midst of His people, but when John observed the holy city, new Jerusalem, descending out of heaven, he saw "...no temple in it, for the Lord God, the Almighty, and the Lamb, they are its temple" (Rev. 21:22).

9. HOLY MOUNTAIN OF GOD

The mountain of God includes Zion and Ophel, two eminences on which the city of Jerusalem was built, and the mountain of Moriah. The Psalmist described Jerusalem as being the "holy mountain of God" which is "Beautiful in elevation, the joy of the whole earth..." and calls her "...Mount Zion in the far north..." (Psa. 48:1-2). Zion probably means, sunny or protected height, and is the southeastern hill of the city, rising between the Kidron and Tyropean valleys. After David captured it from the Jebusites, it was named "the city of David" (Josh. 15:63; II Sam. 5:7; I Kgs. 8:1; II Kgs. 19:21, 31; I Chron. 11:5), which generally meant Jerusalem, but occasionally referred to Israel, the Church of God, and the heavenly city, New Jerusalem (Psa. 51:18; 87:2, 5; 149:2; Isa. 33:14; Joel 2:1; Heb. 12:22; Rev. 14:1).

As one can see from the above references, Zion is prophetic in character, from the first mention of the name to the last, culminating in the splendor of the Zion from above (Heb. 12:22). All of God's people are moving toward that city and singing: "We're marching to Zion, Beautiful, beautiful Zion; We're marching upward to Zion, The beautiful city of God."[9]

On the southern slope of the temple hill is the Ophel (hill, mound) spur. It lies between the Tyropoeon and Kedron valleys. The city David took from the Jebusites (II Sam. 5:6-9) was on the lower end of the plateau on which the city of Jerusalem stands. The first reference to Ophel is II Chronicles 27:3, when Jotham extended its walls. At a later date, Manasseh encircled it, and the city of David, with walls (II Chron. 33:14). After the return of the exiles under the leadership of Nehemiah, those who served in the Temple made repairs to the Ophel area and lived there (Neh. 3:26, 27; 11:21).

Mount Moriah is located at the very top of the mountain of the Lord where God chose to put His name; the place Abraham saw in the land of Moriah, and the exact spot where he would bind his only son Isaac and offer him in obedience as a sacrifice (Gen. 22:2). There, at the command of the angel of the Lord (I Chron. 22:18-30), King David purchased a threshing floor from the Jebusite, Ara-unah, to build an altar. David did not take the land or accept the land as a gift. He bought it for fifty shekels of silver so that no one could contest ownership in the future. It fell to Solomon to build the first Temple on what is now known as the Temple Mount (II Sam. 24:15-24; II Chronicles 3:1). Presently, the illegally built Mosque of Omar (the Dome of the Rock) houses the great stone of Abraham, which is thought to be where the Holy of Holies sat. In his book, In Search of Temple Treasures, Randall Price quotes Dan Bahat:

There is no doubt that the Dome of the Rock is the Temple itself, and in my opinion, the Holy of Holies. Some others believe that this was the place of the altar of sacrifice, but I think that this is impossible; it won't fit with the natural features of the mountain. It is an axiom that the rock, which can be seen in the middle of the Dome of the Rock, is nothing but the rock of the Holy of Holies, the top of Mount Moriah, the place when Abraham...attempted to sacrifice Isaac.[10]

According to prophecy the Temple will be rebuilt in that very place (it must be, otherwise Scripture would not prophesy its future desecration). It should be kept in mind, however; that the Temple in which the Antichrist sets up the "abomination of desolation," spoken of by Daniel and Jesus (Dan. 9:27, 11:31; 12:11; Matt. 24:15), is not the final house of worship; it is one of two that will be built. The other is the temple spoken of by Ezekiel (Ezek. 40-47), the millennial temple.

The very next Temple will be funded and built by the Jews themselves and plans are underway at the present time to bring that about. Some believe that this must be accomplished in order to bring back Messiah. While it is true that Jesus does not return until after this Temple is built, rebuilding this temple does not bring Him back. His return is prompted by the nations coming against Jerusalem to destroy the city and the people of Israel. A topographical change of the land (Zech. 14:4-11) will provide an escape route for the remnant remaining. "Then the Lord will go forth and fight against those nations, as when He fights on a day of battle" (Zech. 14:3). Another topographical change of the land is vital to accommodate the measurements of Ezekiel's Temple; the mountain of the house of the Lord must be raised very high and enlarged to accommodate a larger temple, the one the Lord Himself will build (Isa. 2:1-4; Ezek. 40-47; Zech. 1:16; 12-15). One of the most sublime passages in the Book of Isaiah says, "Now it will come about that In the last days, The mountain of the house of the Lord Will be established as the chief of the mountains, And will be raised above the hills; And all the nations will stream to it. And many peoples will come and say, 'Come, let us go up to the mountain of the Lord, To the house of the God of Jacob; That

He may teach us concerning His ways, And that we may walk in His paths.' For the law will go forth from Zion, And the word of the Lord from Jerusalem" (Isa. 2:2, 3).

10. PERFECTION OF BEAUTY

Ironically, the name, Perfection of Beauty, appears in Jeremiah's Lamentations, which describes the pathetic condition of Jerusalem after her reduction by Nebuchadnezzar. Her beauty had become no more than a question on the lips of those gloating over her misery and appearance: "Is this the city of which they said, 'The perfection of beauty, A joy of all the earth'?" (Lam. 2:15). Jerusalem's beauty was God-given and Ezekiel recorded the process by which God beautified her. He found her as a newborn baby, born in the land Canaan, of the Amorites and Hittites. He cleansed and clothed her, bedecked her with the finest jewelry, and she became the envy of the nations around her and the joy of the earth (Ezek. 16).

Even today, some of the original splendor that God had bestowed upon her shines through and around her scars. The Jerusalem of antiquity is there, beautiful in a way that time has not erased. Comay describes it well:

> The ancient landscape round the city has a bleak and indefinable beauty. The light is incredibly sharp and clear, the sky luminous except when shrouded by winter rains. As the harshness melts into soft shades of orange and mauve, before the swift dark comes and the rush of stars. These hills have a brooding quality, and one can believe that here the Hebrew prophets of old talked to God.
>
> Yet the air of serenity is belied by thirty-three centuries of turbulent history. At times Jerusalem's buildings and ramparts burgeoned into splendor, under Solomon, Herod, Constantine and Suleiman. At other times the city was reduced to rubble, with the blood of its slaughtered citizens flowing down the gutters. The

Jewish sages said: 'Ten parts of beauty were allotted
the world at large, and these Jerusalem assumed nine
measures and the rest of the world but one...ten parts
of suffering were visited upon the world – nine for
Jerusalem and one for the world.'[11]

The coming millennial Jerusalem (Isa. 52:1-10) will outshine the city
in her present condition, but it will in no way compare to the heavenly
Jerusalem, which John describes as coming down from God out of
heaven in dazzling splendor (Rev. 21, 22).

11. SALEM

As previously mentioned, this was the name of the site when Abraham
met Melchizedek (Gen. 14:17-20), and if those men existed, Salem
was a literal place. There are those who interpret "Salem" in the title
"Melchizedek king of Salem" (v18) as describing the character of
Melchizedek as opposed to the place (Ur-Salem) to which the pharaohs
referred in the Tel el Amarna Tablets. They also confuse Salem with
Salim, near Aenon, the place where John the Baptist baptized (Jn. 3:23),
but the Psalmist confirms the ancient name, for Jerusalem was Salem:
"God is known in Judah; His name is great in Israel. His tabernacle is
in Salem; His dwelling place is in Zion" (Psa. 76:1, 2). Here Salem is
connected with and is one and the same with Zion and is in no way to
be identified with the Salim of John 3:23. Unger states: "It is doubtless
the name of Jerusalem (Psa. 76:2). The name appears as Ur-salem ('City
of Peace') in the Amarna Letters and is ...Jerusalem [italics mine]."[12]

Salem means peaceful but no one could describe a place of so much
violence and grief as peaceful. The city has known periods of peace
over the centuries, but they were relatively brief and uneasy. Some say
the term Melchizedek, king of Salem, characterized the state of the
city during his rule. True or not, the city was called Salem long before
Melchizedek came on the scene, and from the time of man's earliest
occupation of the site, the city has known violence and war. Anyone
familiar with the city's tumultuous history must come to one conclusion:
the name Jerusalem (the city of peace), is the very root of its prophetic

destiny, looking forward to the time when her blessed Messiah, The Prince of Peace, will come and deliver her from the warring nations of the world. But even that millennial peace will be enforced with a "rod of iron" (Psa. 2:9) and will end with rebellion of the nations against her (Rev. 20:7-9). True peace will not come until the earthly Jerusalem is purged by fire and the heavenly Jerusalem appears (this will be discussed in chapter IX).

12. THE THRONE OF JEHOVAH

When God will have brought His people to Zion in the future "At that time they shall call Jerusalem 'The Throne of the LORD' (Jehovah) [italics and parenthesis mine] and all nations will be gathered to it, to Jerusalem..." (Jer. 3:17). A study of all the references to *the* throne of God reveals six facts:

One. His throne was established from of old (Psa. 93:2). "From of old" (before the worlds began) is the same phrase used by Micah of the One who would be born in Bethlehem: "His goings forth are from long ago, from days of eternity" (Mic. 5:2). Humanly speaking, its foundation was conceived in the mind of God, however; the beginning of His throne on the earth was when He directed David to buy the Jebusite's threshing floor and promised that His throne would begin, when his son Solomon built the temple. (II Sam. 7-16).

Two. Jesus ultimately will sit on His throne. "The LORD has sworn to David, A truth from which He will not turn back; 'Of the fruit of your body I will sit upon your throne'" (Psa. 132:11). The "fruit" of which God speaks is the virgin's child and son promised in Isaiah 7:14 and is the "...Wonderful Counselor, Mighty God, Eternal Father, Prince of Peace," of whom he prophesied, who would govern from the throne of David (Isa. 9:6, 7). Zechariah says: "Behold, a man whose name is the Branch, for He will branch out from where He is...He will build the temple of the LORD...and sit and rule on His throne." Thus, He will be a priest on His throne... (Zech. 6:12, 13). Luke records the words of the angel who identifies not only the virgin but also the exact name of the person (the "fruit"): "...you shall name Him Jesus...and the Lord God will give Him the throne of His father David..." (Lk. 1:31, 32). Peter says that David was a prophet in that he looked ahead and prophesied of the resurrection of Christ, his descendant, who would sit on his throne. (Acts 2:29-32).

Three. His throne will be located on the exact spot where Abraham attempted to offer Isaac as a sacrifice (Gen. 22:1-18), where David told Solomon to erect the temple, II Sam. 7:16, and where God told Ezekiel the Temple would stand during the Millennium: "...this is the place of My throne and the place of the soles of my feet, where I will dwell among the sons of Israel forever" (Ezek. 43:7, NASB). "...The place of the soles of My feet..." refers to the One who walked there over two thousand years ago, and who will return again to rule from the temple mount.

Four. Fear and awe will fill the hearts of the peoples of the earth when He returns to Jerusalem and sits on His throne to judge the twelve tribes of Israel and the nations (Ezek. 20:33-38; Dan. 7:9-14; Matt. 19:28; 25:31-46). Throughout history men and nations have shirked their responsibility toward God and one another. They must, and will, answer to the judge of the earth. Never again will the cry of help be heard in the streets. Violence will have disappeared and the law and justice will be upheld (Hab. 1:2-4).

Five. Judgment and righteousness will characterize His throne (Psa. 9:7, 8). He is "Wonderful Counselor," the only sovereign capable of settling the differences between nations (Isa. 9:6, 7). Isaiah speaks of the disarmament that will take place: "For the law will go forth from Zion, And the word of the LORD from Jerusalem. And He will judge among the nations, and will render decisions for many peoples; And they will hammer their swords into plow-shares, and their spears into pruning hooks. Nation will not lift up sword against nation, And never again will they learn war." (Isa. 2:3-4).

Six. His throne will last forever (Psa. 45:6; Heb. 1:8). Any nation opposing Him will be put down with speedy judgment. No power in the universe will dethrone Him. They will be as dust on the balance (Isa. 40:15) and whisked off by the breath of His mouth. He alone deserves the title KING OF KINGS AND LORD OF LORDS. "Thy throne, O God, is forever and ever" (Psa. 45:6, KJV). His throne will last for the ages abiding (the age of the Millennium, the first phase of His kingdom, and the age during which time He will rule throughout the great age of the second phase of His kingdom in the heavenly Jerusalem (see chapter

IX for a complete explanation). Then God the Son will relinquish the Kingdom to God the Father. The Son will become subject to God the Father, and God shall be "all in all" (I Cor. 15:24-28).

While the name Jerusalem is not mentioned specifically in the foregoing references, the context of each refers to Jerusalem and is, in one way or another, prophetic in character.

PART TWO

*Fulfilled Prophecies of the
Deliverances and Destructions of
Jerusalem During the Old Testament
Period Through the Present Age*

INTRODUCTION

Many prophetic utterances in the Old Testament are related to the deliverances and destructions of Jerusalem that already have come to pass. Some were fulfilled during Old Testament times (deliverances and destructions from Shishak, Rezin and Pekah, Sennacherib, and Nebuchadnezzar). Others found their fulfillment during the Intertestamental Period, the silent time during which no prophetic voice was heard. That period came to a close with John the Baptist, "the voice of one crying in the wilderness." However, Daniel prophesied fulfillments that occurred during the Old Testament period, namely those having to do with Alexander the Great and the wars of the Maccabees (Dan. 7-8, 11). The wars of the Maccabees brought the cruelties of Antiochus Epiphanes to an end, delivered Jerusalem, and cleansed the desecrated Temple.

One outstanding prophecy was fulfilled during New Testament times following Israel's rejection of Jesus, the Messiah. Luke records Jesus' own words concerning Jerusalem's destruction by the Roman general, Titus: "But when you see Jerusalem surrounded by armies, then recognize that her desolation is near...and they will fall by the edge of the sword, and will be led captive into all the nations; and Jerusalem will be trampled underfoot by the Gentiles until the times of the Gentiles are fulfilled" (Lk. 21:20, 24).

The Gentiles would trample Jerusalem from that time to the present age. The Roman Emperor Hadrian would destroy the city and events not specifically prophesied would occur, but their fulfillment fell within the range of the prophecy of the times of the Gentiles: General Allenby's deliverance of Jerusalem from Muslim dominance, and the Six Day War which resulted in the city's deliverance and reunification by Israel herself. An examination of these fulfilled prophecies will prove the exact accuracy of God's Word.

CHAPTER II

*Fulfilled Prophecies of the Destructions
and Deliverances of Jerusalem During
the Old Testament Period*

Jerusalem experienced three deliverances and one destruction during this period. The deliverances are: (1) deliverance from Shishak, (2) deliverance from Rezin and Pekah, (3) deliverance from Sennacherib, and (4) the total destruction of the city by Nebuchadnezzar (which will be discussed later in the chapter).

I. DELIVERANCE FROM SHISHAK

First Kings 14:25-27 and II Chronicles 12:1-9 give an account of this event. The latter informs us that after Rehoboam established his kingdom and became strong, he and Israel disregarded the law of Jehovah, resulting in God allowing Shishak to invade the fortified cities of Judah, even Jerusalem. The Chronicler writes:

> And it came about in King Rehoboam's fifth year, because they had been unfaithful to the Lord, that Shishak king of Egypt came up against Jerusalem with 1,200 chariots and 60,000 horsemen. And the people who came with him from Egypt were without number: the Lubim, the Sukkiim and the Ethiopians. He captured the fortified cities of Judah and came as far as Jerusalem.

Then Shemaiah the prophet came to Rehoboam and the princes of Judah who had gathered at Jerusalem because of Shishak, and he said to them, "Thus says the Lord, 'You have forsaken Me, so I also have forsaken you to Shishak.'" So the princes of Israel and the king humbled themselves and said, "The Lord is righteous." When the Lord saw that they humbled themselves, the word of the Lord came to Shemaiah, saying, "They have humbled themselves so I will not destroy them, but I will grant them some measure of deliverance, and My wrath shall not be poured out on Jerusalem by means of Shishak. " But they will become his slaves so that they may learn the difference between My service and the service of the kingdoms of the countries." So Shishak king of Egypt came up against Jerusalem, and took the treasures of the house of the Lord and the treasures of the king's palace. He took everything; he even took the golden shields that Solomon had made. (II Chron. 12:2-9)

Egyptian records at Karnak have identified Shishak as Sheshonk or Sheshenq I, a warlike prince who desired to conquer all of Asia. On this occasion he took advantage of the weak and sinful condition of Israel and came against Jerusalem. Egypt had not troubled the Israelites since God's defeat of the Egyptian army at the Red Sea. When the kingdom became divided and the more powerful part of the nation under Jeroboam separated from Judah, Shishak, aware of Judah's weakness, invaded the southern part of Palestine about 921 B.C. and destroyed many cities in Judah, Israel and Edom (I Kgs. 14:25-28). Dr. Wilbur Smith has the following to say about Shishak's invasion:

There is scarcely a more pitiful statement in the whole of Judah's recorded history, from her entrance into Palestine to the time of Nebuchadnezzar's invasion, than that which depicts the spoiling of Solomon's temple by Shishak, who in the Egyptian records is called Sheshonk I, and all this within five years of Solomon's death.[1]

It was indeed a pitiful sight, however; if the people had not repented, the city of Jerusalem would have been utterly destroyed, and a more pitiful state would have resulted. God gave this prophecy of deliverance from utter destruction through the prophet, Shemaiah, and though the people were taken in servitude, destruction was diverted from the city. The fact that this event took place is without question. Shishak himself has recorded it and confirmed it on the south wall of the Temple of Amon at Karnak in Egypt.[2]

II. DELIVERANCE FROM REZIN AND PEKAH

The passages of Scripture relating to the deliverance of Jerusalem from Rezin and Pekah are II Kings 15:37; 16:5-10 and the great prophecy found in Chapters 7-9 of the book of Isaiah.

Rezin, king of Syria who reigned in Damascus, and Pekah, son of Remaliah the king of Israel, formed an alliance against Assyria. Efforts to persuade Ahaz King of Judah to join them in this alliance were unsuccessful. Having failed through diplomatic means, they turned to force, and together went to war against Ahaz and the city of Jerusalem: "And his heart trembled, and the heart of his people, as the trees of the forest tremble with the wind." (Isa. 7:1, 2). God sent Isaiah to Ahaz and the people with comforting news of deliverance: Then the Lord said to Isaiah, "Go out now to meet Ahaz, you and your son Shear-jashub, at the end of the conduit of the upper pool, on the highway to the fuller's field, and say to him, 'Take care and be calm, have no fear and do not be fainthearted because of these two stubs of smoldering firebrands, on account of the fierce anger of Rezin and Aram and the son of Remaliah.' Because Aram, with Ephraim and the son of Remaliah, has planned evil against you, saying, "Let us go up against Judah and terrorize it, and make for ourselves a breach in its walls and set up the son of Tabeel as king in the midst of it," thus says the LORD GOD: "It shall not stand nor shall it come to pass." For the head of Aram is Damascus and the head of Damascus is Rezin (now within another 65 years Ephraim will be shattered, so that it is no longer a people), and the head of Ephraim is Samaria and the head of Samaria is the son of Remaliah. If you will not believe, you surely shall not last." (Isa. 7:3-9)

God wanted Ahaz to know that He would protect Jerusalem from impending destruction and told him to "ask a sign" that He would indeed keep His word. Barnes has an interesting comment on the foregoing:

A sign. A demonstration that shall confirm the promise now made, and that shall be evidence that Jerusalem shall be safe. The word used here, and translated sign-oth – means a flag, or standard, Num. 2:2; a memorial or pledge of a covenant, Gen. 17:11; 6:17; any pledge, token or proof of a divine mission, Judges 6:17; or a miracle wrought in attestation of a divine promise or message. That which Isaiah had spoken seemed highly improbable to Ahaz, and he asked him to seek a proof of it, if he doubted, by any prodigy or miracle. It was customary for miracles or prodigies to be exhibited on similar occasions. See Ch. 38:7, where the shadow on the dial of this same Ahaz was carried backward ten degrees in proof of what the prophet Isaiah had spoken.[3]

Ahaz would not ask (v12) so God, unasked, provided this prophetic assurance: "Therefore the Lord Himself will give you a sign: Behold a virgin shall be with child and bear a son, and she will call His name Immanuel. He will eat curds and honey at the time He knows enough to refuse evil and choose good, the land whose two kings you dread will be forsaken" (Isa. 7:14-16). This portion of Scripture has been the subject of many debates and a few comments about it are warranted.

Does this prophecy relate to the deliverance of Jerusalem during the time of Ahaz or does it await future fulfillment by Messiah? The prophecy has a double application: It was applicable for the then present time and it looked forward to the distant future when the son of the virgin would come and deliver his people from their last enemy.

A close examination of the text reveals that Ahaz was faced with a present problem. An invasion by Rezin king of Syria and Pekah king of Samaria and Israel was imminent. Ahaz and the people were in great fear and he went to meet Isaiah "at the end of the aqueduct of the upper pool on the road to Washerman's Field" to see if there was any means of defense. Isaiah assured him there was no cause to fear. How would Messiah's future coming help the present situation? God pledged that He would help at that time, with the then problem and that in a very short time the two threatening kings, Rezin and Pekah, would be thwarted.

"Thus says the LORD GOD: "It shall not stand nor shall it come to pass" (Isa. 7:7).

The prophecy may refer to an immediate fulfillment during the time of Ahaz, but the argument for a Messianic interpretation comes from Chapter 8:8 and Chapter 9:1-7. The verses in Chapter 9 are certainly connected to this event but do not apply to Isaiah's son or any other born at that time. This passage is Messianic because Isaiah spoke of God's assurances to Ahaz that the land would be safe from the present invasion and he described a future, more glorious demonstration of protection—Jerusalem's ultimate and final deliverance by Messiah.

If the prophecy had its basic fulfillment during the time of Ahaz, why should Ahaz be interested in a future deliverance? Feinberg presents us with a satisfactory answer:

> To many fulfillment centuries later would be worthless to Ahaz and his contemporaries in their distress. But the exact opposite is true. Ahaz and his courtiers were fearful of the extinction of the Davidic dynasty and the displacement of the king by a Syrian pretender. However, the longer the time needed to fulfill the promise to the Davidic house, the longer that dynasty would be in existence to witness the realization of the prediction. It is well stated by Alexander: "...The assurance that Christ was to be born in Judah, of its royal family, might be a sign to Ahaz, that the kingdom should not perish in his day; and so far was the remoteness of the sign in this case from making it absurd or inappropriate, that the further off it was, the stronger the promise of continuance of Judah, which it guaranteed."[4]

Isaiah's words to Ahaz may have kept him from joining the Syrian/Samarian alliance, but they did not prevent him from appealing to Tigleth-pileser of Assyria for help. When Isaiah told Ahaz that Tigleth-pileser was marching toward Jerusalem, and word reached Rezin and Pekah, a hasty retreat was made from the city and the blow Isaiah predicted soon fell, not only on Rezin and Pekah, but also on their kingdoms.

The Assyrians fell upon Damascus and Rezin was defeated in a decisive battle and took refuge in his capitol. Another part of the Assyrian army descended upon the other districts of Syria and Samaria and city after city fell to them. A list of those cities can be found in II Kings 15:29.

The remaining King Pekah was left with a third of his former kingdom. He became unpopular with his subjects and later was assassinated by Hoshea. The Bible states that "...Hoshea the son of Elah made a conspiracy against Pekah the son of Remaliah, and struck him, and put him to death, and became king in his place" (II Kings 15:30).

The wording of Isaiah 9:14 and 10:9-11 is conclusive proof that Isaiah's prophecy was given before the fall of Damascus, Syria and Samaria. Deliverance of Jerusalem was contingent upon this. Once again, God in His love and mercy saved the city from destruction by delivering her from her enemies, but more was yet to come.

III. DELIVERANCE FROM SENNACHERIB

The next great deliverance was from the hand of the Assyrian, Sennacherib. Prophecies relating to Sennacherib's siege are numerous. Dr. Wilbur Smith said:

> I believe there are more long parallel accounts of Sennacherib's siege of Jerusalem in the Old Testament than any other single event in Israel's history, with the possible exception of the destruction of Jerusalem under Nebuchadnezzar. (The siege, which occurred in 701 B.C., is recorded in II Kings 18:13-19:37, in II Chron. 32:1-21; Isa. 36:1, 37:38 – a total of 143 verses.)[5]

Isaiah 29:1-7 refers to the same event. Here, God addresses Jerusalem as Ariel and states that He is the One who will lay siege to her. Sennacherib thought it was his own doing, but God, who controls the reins of the hearts of kings (Ezek. 1:1-4), moved him to come up against Jerusalem (Isa. 29:1-7). In the future, Gog, who leads the northern alliance, also will think it is his own doing, when he comes against the mountains of Israel (see chapter VI).

The city where David once pitched his tent became a place of heartbreak and distress. God described the calamity of Sennacherib's siege as an event He Himself brought about. The words of the inhabitants of Jerusalem would cry out from the dust of the earth and it would be as though the dust itself would whisper as a result of their suffering. But the nations would become likewise, only dust driven away by the wind. The end would be like a dream, a vision in the night (Isa. 29:1-7).

Isaiah 31:4-5 promised deliverance of Jerusalem from the Assyrian and likened God to shepherds who protect their flocks from lions, and birds that hover to protect. The writer of II Kings 19:32-34 said that after Sennacherib laid siege to the city he would not come into the city nor build up a mound against it. The great deliverance and how God accomplished it is described in Isaiah 37:36, 37, "Then the angel of the LORD went out and struck 185,000 in the camp of the Assyrians; and when men arose early in the morning, behold, all these were dead. So Sennacherib king of Assyria departed, and returned home and lived at Nineveh."

What is the meaning of the word angel in verse 37? All one can be sure of is that angel in the original (Hebrew) is (Malekh) and means messenger of God, so in this case a messenger was sent forth to execute the judgment of Jehovah.

The Jewish historian Josephus ascribes the destruction of Sennacherib's army to pestilence, quoting Herodotus as saying that "'a multitude of mice gnawed to pieces in one night both the bows and the rest of the armor of the Assyrians; and that it was on that account that the king, when he had no bows left, he drew off his army from Pelsium.'" He further states:

> Now when Sennacherib was returning from his Egyptian war to Jerusalem, he found his army under Rabshakeb his general in danger (by a plague) for God had sent a pestilential distemper upon his army; and on the very first night of the siege, a hundred fourscore and five thousand, with their captains and generals, were destroyed. So the king was in great dread, and in a terrible agony at this calamity; and being in great fear

for his whole army, he fled with the rest of his forces to his own kingdom, and to his city Nineveh; and when he had abode there a little while, he was treacherously assaulted, and died by the hands of his older sons, Adrammelech and Seraser, and was slain in his own temple, which was called Araske...And this proved to be the conclusion of this Assyrian expedition against the people of Jerusalem.[6]

The information that Josephus sets forth does not conflict with Scripture and confirms Isaiah. The army of Sennacherib was destroyed. From the foregoing account, it would seem that the destruction was directed and controlled by an angelic being who was able to cause great hordes of mice to overrun the army of Sennacherib, carrying with them destruction and plague. Nevertheless, no matter how God did it, the people of Jerusalem saw a great deliverance that day and another enemy "bit the dust."

Sennacherib provides his own account of the invasion of Judah and the siege of Jerusalem on a clay prism found in Mosul, Iraq in 1880 and presently housed at the Oriental Institute of Chicago (although Unger states it is in the British Museum (see Sennacherib, Unger's Bible Dictionary). The inscription reads:

"Because Hezekiah, king of Judah, would not submit to my yoke, I came up against him, and by force of arms and by the might of my power I took forty-six of his strong fenced cities; and of the smaller towns which were scattered about, I took and plundered a countless number. From these places I took and carried off 200,156 persons, old and young, male and female, together with horses and mules, asses and camels, oxen and sheep, a countless multitude; and Hezekiah himself I shut up in Jerusalem, his capital city, like a bird in a cage, building towers round the city to hem him in, and raising banks of earth against the gates, so as to prevent escape...[7]

Henry H. Halley has the following comment concerning Sennacherib's siege of Jerusalem: "While no Assyrian king would ever record a defeat, such as Sennacherib's army received before the walls of Jerusalem, II Kin. 19:35, 36, it is significant that he did not claim to have taken Jerusalem. It is indeed a most remarkable confirmation of Biblical history."[8]

There are two reasons Sennacherib did not claim victory: 1) a good portion his army lay dead at the base of the walls of Jerusalem, and 2) he ran when he heard that Pharaoh Tirhakah was approaching. "So Sennacherib King of Assyria broke up camp and withdrew. He returned to Assyria and stayed there" (II Kings 19:35, 36)), where later he was assassinated by his two sons (see Lord Byron in chapter X).

Herzog and Gichon furnish an interesting comment in their Battles of the Bible:

> His retreat was so sudden that it seemed a miracle in the eyes of his generation... An important factor in holding out against Sennacherib was certainly the high morale of the defenders. We do not wish to deny that belief in divine aid and counsel strengthened the Judeans in their desperate fight for survival, but we do wish to stress the decisive part played by Rehoboam's fortifications in making this miracle possible. Sennacherib's offensive power that I should remove it from before my face . . .." And remove it from His face, he did. was severely curtailed, his heirs avoided becoming entangled in a war in the Judean heartland and Judah was able to survive for another 115 years, until its conquest in 587 B.C. by Nebuchadnezzar.[9]

As seen from the above, more than one factor could have contributed to the downfall of Sennacherib's army. God repeatedly promised that Sennacherib would not enter the city (II Kgs. 19:32-34). He moved the heart of Rehoboam to fortify the city because in His omniscience He knew the outcome from eternity.

IV. DESTRUCTION BY NEBUCHADNEZZAR

God was faithful in watching over and protecting His beloved city from Shishak, from Rezin and Pekah who formed the alliance of Syria and Ephraim, and from Sennacherib, but her utter destruction was inevitable. God warned His people before they entered the Promised Land that their cities would be destroyed (Deut. 31:14-24). God's patience was wearing thin, as sensed in Chapter 32, verse 31 of the prophet Jeremiah: "For this city hath been to Me a provocation of Mine anger and of My wrath from the day that they built it even unto this day; that I should remove it from before My face..." Before looking at the prophecies concerning the destruction of Jerusalem, a chronological list of events that occurred during the last days of Jerusalem is provided as follows:

606 B.C. Jerusalem first taken by Nebuchadnezzar (Dan. 1:2, 2)

605 B.C. King Jehoiakim made tributary to Nebuchadnezzar (II Kgs. 24:1a; II Chron. 36:6; Jer. 25:1ff)

602 B.C. Nebuchadnezzar sends a Chaldean army against Jehoiakim (II Kgs. 24:1b, 2)

598-597 B. C. Jehoiachin deported along with ten thousand Jews (II Kgs. 24:10-16; II Chron. 36:9, 10; Jer. 29:1, 2)

588-587 B.C. Zedekiah is persuaded by Egypt to rebel against Nebuchadnezzar (Ezek. 17:3-21), while Jeremiah pleads with him to surrender to Babylon (Jer. 34:1-6). The final siege of Jerusalem begins on the tenth day of the tenth month, January (II Kgs. 25:1; Jer. 39:1, 52:4)

586 B.C. On the ninth day of the fourth month, July, the walls are breached (II Kgs. 25:4-7; Jer. 39:1-7; 52:5-11). On the seventh day of the fifth month, Nebuchadnezzar himself came to Jerusalem, and in the days that followed the city was utterly destroyed and the buildings burned with fire (II Kgs. 25:8-21; II Chron. 36:13-21; Jer. 39:8; 52:12-27)

582 B.C. A small group of some 745 Jews were deported (Jer. 52:30)

562 B.C. The death of Nebuchadnezzar after a reign of 43 years.[10]

Following are references to the prophecies unfulfilled and fulfilled concerning the destruction of the city by Nebuchadnezzar:

Prophecies unfulfilled:

II Kings 21: 11-15; 22; 16,17; 23:27; II Chronicles 34; 24, 25; Isaiah 27:11; 64:11, 12; Jeremiah 1:14-15; 4:7; 9:11; 13:9, 18; 15:2-5, 14; 16:2, 9; 17:3; 19:8; 20:5; 21:7-10; 34:1-3, 22; 38:1-3, 28-31; Ezekiel 7:22, 27; 9:7; 11:8-10, 25; 12:10-16, 20; 21:23; 24:2, 9, 24-26.

Prophecies fulfilled:

II Kings 24; 25:1-10; I Chronicles 6:15; II Chronicles 36; Jeremiah 39:1-4, 8, 9; 51:50- 51; 52:4-29; Lamentations 1-5; Ezekiel 33:21; Daniel 1:1-2.

Second Kings 22:16, 17 is probably the first of the prophetic utterances on the destruction of Jerusalem. The city persistently indulged in the sins of idolatry and the grossest of iniquities and God pronounced judgment upon her through the prophetess Huldah: "Thus says the Lord God of Israel, 'Tell the man who sent you to me, thus says the Lord, "Behold I bring evil on this place and on its inhabitants, even all the words of the book which the king of Judah has read, because they have forsaken Me and have burned incense to other gods that they might provoke Me to anger with all the work of their hands, therefore My wrath burns against this place, and it shall not be quenched"' (II Kgs. 22:15-17). Even though God chose Jerusalem as the place to put His name, He vowed to cast her off (II Kgs. 23:37).

Isaiah, the great prophet of salvation, looked 150 years into the future and saw her destruction (Isa. 3). Jeremiah, the weeping prophet, prophesied of Her impending doom with tears streaming down his face and later he saw his beloved city in shambles (Lam.; Jer. 9:1, 9-11). He looked toward the North Country and saw a symbolic boiling pot. God told him that He would bring the peoples of the north down against all the cities of Judah (Jer. 1:13-15). In Jeremiah 4 God told him to sound the alarm because judgment was on the way. Evil soon would be at the gates like a lion come up from the thicket. The cities would be laid waste (vv5-7). He was told to run through the streets to find one just man and, if he could, God would pardon the city (Jer. 5:1).

The first major prophecy of destruction was uttered during the reign of Josiah (Jer. 6:1-8, 22-26):

> "Flee for safety, O sons of Benjamin, from the midst of Jerusalem! Now blow a trumpet in Tekoa And raise a signal over Beth-haccerem; For evil looks down from the north, And a great destruction. "The comely and dainty one, the daughter of Zion, I will cut off. " Shepherds and their flocks will come to her, They will pitch their tents around her, They will pasture each in his place. "Prepare war against her; Arise, and let us attack at noon. Woe to us, for the day declines, For the shadows of the evening lengthen! "Arise, and let us attack by night And destroy her palaces!" For thus says the Lord of hosts, "Cut down her trees And cast up a siege against Jerusalem. This is the city to be punished, In whose midst there is only oppression. "As a well keeps its waters fresh, So she keeps fresh her wickedness. Violence and destruction are heard in her; Sickness and wounds are ever before Me. "Be warned, O Jerusalem, Or I shall be alienated from you, And make you a desolation, A land not inhabited." (Jer. 6:1-8).

> Thus says the Lord, "Behold a people is coming from the north land, And a great nation will be aroused from the remote parts of the earth. "They seize bow and spear; They are cruel and have no mercy; Their voice roars like the sea, And they ride on horses, Arrayed as a man for the battle Against you, O daughter of Zion!" We have heard the report of it; Our hands are limp. Anguish has seized us, Pain as of a woman in childbirth. Do not go out into the field And do not walk on the road, For the enemy has a sword, Terror is on every side. O

daughter of My people, put on sackcloth And roll in
ashes; Mourn as for an only son, A lamentation most
bitter. For suddenly the destroyer Will come upon us
(Jer. 6:22-26).

Even as Jeremiah spoke, Nebuchadnezzar was approaching the city
gates. It was in the tenth year of the reign of King Zedekiah of Judah,
who didn't much care for Jeremiah prophesying that Nebuchadnezzar
would destroy Jerusalem and take him (Zedekiah) to Babylon where he
would be until God would settle with him (Jer. 37:5-10); so he locked
him up in the court of the prison which was in the king's house (Jer.
32:1-5).

God made it clear that the deliverance He gave Jerusalem from
Nebuchadnezzar's first siege would not be offered this time. The
approach of Pharaoh Necho's army caused Nebuchadnezzar to lift his
siege, but the Egyptian would provide no protection for Jerusalem. The
Lord said that he (Pharaoh Necho) would return to Egypt, leaving the
city vulnerable to the Chaldean army. The prophecy was so sure that,
even if all of the attacking army of the Chaldeans was smitten, the
wounded would rise up and put the torch to the unfaithful city (Jer. 37:5-
10). The remainder of the book of Jeremiah is devoted to intermittent
prophecies of the approaching destruction of the city.

The next great prophetic book that continually warned of Jerusalem's
destruction is Ezekiel, who prophesied Jerusalem's fall before he and the
Jews were carried away captive to Babylon. His four parables depicting
the city's fall are well known: the parable of the tile (4:1-7) on which
was to be drawn the plan of the siege; the parable of the knife (5:1-7),
emblematic of Nebuchadnezzar's army sweeping everything clean as
a razor; the parable of the man clothed in white linen who slays the
inhabitants of the city (Chapter 9); and the parable of the boiling pot
which describes the destruction of Jerusalem (Chapter 24). Everything
the prophet spoke concerning the city's utter destruction came to pass
and was fulfilled to the letter.[11]

Second Kings 25:1-17 gives a vivid picture of Nebuchadnezzar's
treatment of the city:

And it came to pass in the ninth year of his reign, in the tenth month, in the tenth day of the month that Nebuchadnezzar king of Babylon came, he and all his army, against Jerusalem, and encamped against it; and they built forts against it round about. So the city was besieged unto the eleventh year of King Zedekiah. On the ninth day of the fourth month the famine was sore in the city, so that there was no bread for the people of the land. Then a breach was made in the city, and all the men of war fled by night by the way of the gate between the two walls, which was by the king's garden (now the Chaldeans were against the city round about); and the king went by the way of Arabah.

But the army of the Chaldeans pursued after the king, and overtook him in the plains of Jericho; and all his army was scattered from him. Then they took the king, and carried him up unto the king of Babylon to Riblah; and they gave judgment upon him. And they slew the sons of Zedekiah before his eyes, and put out the eyes of Zedekiah, and bound him in fetters, and carried him to Babylon. (II Kings 25:1-7, KJV)

Here the account must be interrupted with the reminder that God, indeed, kept His promise that He would settle with Zedekiah because Zedekiah imprisoned Jeremiah for prophesying against him and Jerusalem. Second Kings continues: "Now in the fifth month, on the seventh day of the month, which was the nineteenth year of king Nebuchadnezzar, king of Babylon, came Nebuzaradan the captain of the guard, a servant of the king of Babylon, unto Jerusalem. And he burnt the house of Jehovah, and the king's house; and all the houses of Jerusalem, even every great house, burnt he with fire (II Kings 25:8, 9 KJV). God does not make idle threats as is seen in the following passage:

And all the army of the Chaldeans, that were with the captain of the guard, brake down the walls of Jerusalem round about. And the residue of the people that were left in the city, and those that fell away, that fell to the king of Babylon, and the residue of the multitude, did Nebuzaradan the captain of the guard carry away captive. But the captain of the guard left of the poorest of the land to be vinedressers and husbandmen. And the pillars of brass that were in the house of Jehovah, and the bases and the brazen sea that were in the house of Jehovah, did the Chaldeans break in pieces, and carried the brass of them to Babylon. And the pots, and the shovels, and the snuffers, and the spoons, and all the vessels of brass wherewith they ministered, took they away. And the fire pans, and the basins, that which was of gold, in gold, and that which was of silver, in silver, the captain of the guard took away. The two pillars, the one sea, and the bases, which Solomon had made for the house of Jehovah, the brass of all these vessels was without weight. The height of one pillar was eighteen cubits, and a capital of brass was upon it; and the height of the capital was three cubits, with network and pomegranates upon the capital round about, all of brass: and like unto these had the second pillar with network (II Kings 25:10-17).

With the exception of the destruction by Titus the Roman, no such devastation of the city has been repeated. Smith reminds us of Donald Wiseman's remarkable discovery of previously misplaced cuneiform tablets in the British Museum's collection, "Chronicles of the Chaldean Kings (626-656 B.C.)." On these tablets are inscribed, in brief, events of Nebuchadnezzar's reign and, although Josephus and other historians have given considerable attention to these exploits, only in recent years do we have the Babylonian monarch's contemporary statement of the destruction:

In the seventh year of his rein, Nebuchadnezzar began his march to the west, in December, 598 B.C. The Cuneiform record is brief and reads as follows: 'In the seventh year, the month Kislev, the king of Akkad mustered his troops, marched to Hatti-land, and encamped against [i.e., besieged] the City of Judah, and on the second day of the month of Adar he seized the city and captured the king. He appointed there a king of his own choice [lit., heart], received its heavy tribute and sent [them] to Babylon.' The date of this conquest, as Wiseman says, 'is now known precisely for the first time, namely, the second of Adar (15/16th March, 597 B.C.).[12]

God's Word was fulfilled again. Throughout the book of Lamentations Jeremiah grieves for the desolate and lifeless city (1:1). He pictures her as a weeping woman with tears streaming down her cheeks (1:2) and asks passersby if they care for what has befallen her at the hand of the Lord (1:2). In Lamentations 2:11, he describes his emotions as he mourns over the hopeless condition of the small children and infants.

Long after Jeremiah and the inhabitants of Jerusalem were carried away to Babylon, the horror remained in their hearts and minds. All joy was gone. They sat along the banks of the rivers of Babylon, weeping for their sins against God and longing for Jerusalem (Psa. 137:1, 2, 5, 6).

God brought His servant, Nebuchadnezzar, against Jerusalem (Jer. 25:9), but He, nevertheless, held him responsible for his attitude toward and actions against the Jews. Rather than acknowledge God as the One who granted him success, he attributed his accomplishments to himself: "The king reflected and said, 'Is this not Babylon the great, which I myself [italics mine] have built as a royal residence by the might of my power and for the glory of my majesty?'" For the sins of pride and arrogance God sentenced him to the life of a beast in the field. Nebuchadnezzar recounts his humiliating experience in Daniel 4.

Nebuchadnezzar's illness cannot be identified with certainty. Some scholars think he suffered from lycanthropy. One medical source has: "LYCANTHROPY ... from [ly'kos], lupus, wolf; [an'thro-pos], homo, man. This name was given to the sickness of people who believe themselves to be changed into an animal, and who imitate the voice or cries, the shapes or manners of that animal. These individuals usually imagine themselves transformed into a wolf, a dog or a cat; sometimes also into a bull, as in the case of Nebuchadnezzar."[13] He ate grass as the cattle of the field.

A period of 156 years elapsed between the destruction of Jerusalem by Nebuchadnezzar and the close of Old Testament history (586-430 B.C.), during which time Babylon was destroyed by the Medes and Persians (Dan. 5). The Jews had been in captivity for 70 years, when by the decree of Cyrus the Persian, they were allowed to return to Jerusalem and rebuild the temple (II Chron. 36:22, 23; Ezra 1:1-4). Later, under the leadership of Nehemiah, during the reign of Artaxerxes I Longimanus, the wall of the city was rebuilt (c. 445 B.C.).

CHAPTER III

Fulfilled Prophecies of the Deliverances
and Destructions of Jerusalem During
the Intertestamental Period

The intertestamental period began between 450 B. C. and 430 B.C. with the close of the book of Malachi and lasted until the beginning of the New Testament era (c. 6 B.C.-4 B.C.). Prophecy was fulfilled by one deliverance and one destruction during this period: deliverance of Jerusalem from Alexander the Great and destruction of Jerusalem by Antiochus Epiphanes.

I. DELIVERANCE FROM ALEXANDER THE GREAT

The deliverance of Jerusalem from Alexander The Great is one of the marvelous events in recorded history, though its prophecy is found in only one verse of Scripture, "And I will encamp about My house against the army, that none pass through or return; and no oppressor shall pass through them any more: for now have I seen with Mine eyes" (Zech. 9:8). This verse appears in one of the greatest prophetic Chapters of the Bible. Chapter 9 is a prophetic account of the victories of Alexander the Great over Damascus, Sidon, Tyre and Gaza, which fell before the lightning speed of the "he-goat" from the west (Dan. 8:5a), but the God of Israel diverted Alexander from the Holy Land and no harm came to Jerusalem. David Baron, the great Hebrew Christian scholar, comments on verse 8:

But while Israel's enemies in the north and south have occasion to tremble at the approach of the army, God Himself would be the shield and the protector of His people and His dwelling place in their midst. "And I will encamp about My house vechanithi lebhethi: (or 'for'—i.e., on account, or for the protection of My house) because of the army" (which is most probably the correct reading, though some, by a slight alteration of the first vowel, would read (matsabhah), instead (mitsabhah) and translate: "I will encamp about, or for, My house, as a garrison, or guard"), "because (or 'on account') of him who passeth through or returneth; and no oppressor shall pass through them anymore, for now have I seen with mine eye.[1]

The phrase "him who passeth through" refers to Alexander when he came near Jerusalem on his way to subdue the city of Tyre and the Philistine strongholds. To paraphrase Josephus: After the death of Philip, king of Macedonia, his son Alexander inherited the throne. He crossed the Hellspont into Asia. Darius the Persian, fearing that Alexander would ride roughshod over all of Asia, crossed the Euphrates River and engaged Alexander in battle at Cilicia. Darius was defeated and fled back to Persia. Alexander took Damascus, Syria and laid siege to Tyre. In a letter to Juddua, the high priest of Jerusalem, Alexander requested provisions and whatever else the high priest had been favoring Darius with in order to help him defeat Tyre, telling him that he should become a friend to the Macedonians. The high priest replied that he owed allegiance to Darius. Juddua's reply angered Alexander, whereupon he sent word back to the high priest that once he had taken Tyre and the Philistine strongholds (Gaza was one), he would return to chastise the city of Jerusalem. Juddua the high priest had a dream wherein God told him not to worry. He related the dream to the people and told them not to worry, to decorate the city and dress in white robes. When Alexander returned and approached the City, tradition has it that the people of Jerusalem positioned themselves on the walls of the city and waited in silence to see what Alexander would do. Quoting Josephus:

As the Greek king approached the city, the high priest and the people went out to meet him. The Phoenicians and the Chaldeans who were with Alexander thought they would have a heyday by putting the priest to death, and torturing the people, as Alexander had promised them, but something had happened in the meantime. Alexander too had a dream. When he saw the high priest arrayed in purple robes, the golden mitre on his head on which was written, "Holiness to The LORD," and the other priests in white robes and the people in their white garments coming out to meet him, Alexander surprised all who were with him. He adored the name that was on the head plate of the high priest and saluted him. The people in turn saluted Alexander, but his army and officers were critical of him and thought he had lost his mind for showing so much respect for God and His representative.[2]

Josephus relates the words of Alexander's General, Parmenio, and the king's response:

However, Parmenio alone went up to him, and asked him how it came to pass that when all others adored him, he should adore the high priest of the Jews? To whom he replied, "I did not adore him, but that God who hath honored him with his high priesthood; for I saw this very person in a dream, in this very habit, when I was at Dios in Macedonia, who, when I was considering with myself how I might obtain the dominion of Asia, exhorted me to make no delay, but boldly to pass over the sea thither, for that he would conduct my armies, and would give me the dominion over the Persians; whence it is, that having seen no other in that habit, and now seeing this person in it, and remembering that vision, and the exhortation which I had in my dream, I believe that I bring this army under the divine conduct,

and shall therewith conquer Darius, and destroy the
power of the Persians, and that all things will succeed
according to what is in my own mind. And when he had
said this to Parmenio, and had given the high priest his
right hand, the priests ran along by him, and he came
into the city; and when he went up into the temple, he
offered sacrifice to God, according to the high priest's
direction, and magnificently treated both the high priest
and the priests.[3]

According to Jewish tradition, Messiah would ride into their midst
on a great white charger, and the Jews of Jerusalem would have accepted
Alexander as their Messiah had he allowed them to do so. However,
immediately following Zechariah's prophecy in Chapter 9:8, there
is another prophecy of supreme importance. In verse 9, God speaks
through the prophet and says, "Rejoice greatly, O daughter of Zion;
shout, O daughter of Jerusalem: behold, thy king cometh unto thee; he
is just, and having salvation; lowly, and riding upon an ass, even upon
a colt the foal of an ass." Clearly, God in this verse is telling His people
how to recognize their Messiah. He would not come mounted on a white
charger, but He would be a humble man riding a donkey. Later, when
Jesus directed His disciples to obtain a donkey for Him to ride (Matt.
21:1-4), He in effect was saying to His people, "I am the One. I am the
Messiah." Zechariah prophesied Messiah would come on a donkey.
That prophecy was fulfilled, and John witnessed it (Jn. 12:12-18); "And
the multitudes that went before Him, and that followed, cried, saying,
Hosanna to the son of David: Blessed is He that cometh in the name
of the Lord; Hosanna in the highest." In the Book of Revelation John
describes Messiah's return with clouds (1:7), and seated on a white horse
(the way His people expected Him to come the first time, because they
blindly overlooked the fifty-third chapter of Isaiah):

And I saw heaven opened, and behold, a white horse,
and He who sat on it is called Faithful and True, and in
righteousness He judges and wages war. His eyes are a
flame of fire, and on His head are many diadems; and

He has a name written on Him which no one knows except Himself. He is clothed with a robe dipped in blood, and His name is called The Word of God. And the armies which are in heaven, clothed in fine linen, white and clean, were following Him on white horses. From His mouth comes a sharp sword, so that with it He may strike down the nations, and He will rule them with a rod of iron; and He treads the wine press of the fierce wrath of God, the Almighty. And on His robe and on His thigh He has a name written, "KING OF KINGS, AND LORD OF LORDS." (Rev. 19:11-16)

Alexander could have trashed Jerusalem, but he didn't. He could have allowed its inhabitants to worship him as Messiah, but he wouldn't. A great deliverance was procured that day. Alexander died shortly thereafter (334 B.C.) at age thirty-two in Babylon, and his kingdom was divided between his twelve generals, four of which are important as they correspond to the four horns in the prophecy of Daniel, despite the fact that only two of them figure in the historical setting of Daniel's Chapter 11. They are: Cassander, who ruled Macedonia; Lysimachus, who ruled Thrace and Asia Minor; Seleucus, who ruled Syria and lands east; and Ptolemy I, who ruled Egypt. Only Seleucus is important to the following discussion of Jerusalem's destruction by Antiochus Epiphanes.

II. DESTRUCTION BY ANTIOCHUS EPIPHANES

The destruction of the city of Jerusalem by Antiochus Epiphanes took place between the Old Testament and New Testament eras (450 B.C.-430 B.C.) Prophecies having to do with Antiochus and the atrocities committed by him against the city and the Jews are found in Chapters 8 and 11 of the book of Daniel.

Daniel has a prophetic outlook concerning most, if not all, of the Gentile enemies of the Jews. Serious study of the book of Daniel reveals that the times of the Gentile nations (enemies of Israel) began with King Nebuchadnezzar and will end with the destruction of the Antichrist (Dan. 12). Antiochus plays an important role within the times of the

Gentile nations; he is a type of the wicked one to come, and a study of his personage reveals a number of similarities to the Antichrist.

The eighth Chapter of Daniel describes the rise of the Grecian Empire under Alexander the Great and the division of that empire among his four generals following his death. Greece is typified as a goat with a single horn between its eyes; the horn subsequently is broken and four come up in its place (v8). One of those horns is Seleucus, Alexander's general who, following Alexander's death, ruled the lands of Syria and Asia Minor. Antiochus Epiphanes came forth from Syria (Dan. 8:9-12):

> And out of one of them [Seleucus] came forth a little horn [Antiochus Epiphanes], which waxed exceeding great, toward the south, and toward the east, and toward the glorious land. And it waxed great, even to the host of heaven; and some of the host and of the stars it cast down to the ground, and trampled upon them. Yea, it magnified itself, even to the prince of the host; and it took away from him the continual burnt offering, and the place of his sanctuary was cast down.
>
> And the host was given over to it together with the continual burnt offering through transgression; and it cast down truth to the ground, and it did its pleasure and prospered. (Dan. 8:9-12, ASB)

Dr. Harry Ironside did not question that Antiochus is the one to whom Daniel referred[3] and Dr. John Walvoord states that the most probable interpretation was Antiochus, the Syrian ruler.[4] Sir Robert Anderson the English chronologist agrees "[t]hat the career of Antiochus Epiphanes was in a special way within the scope and meaning of this prophecy [and] is unquestioned."[5]

The remaining prophecy concerning Antiochus is found in Daniel 11:21-35. It is a description of his persecution of the people of Israel and Jerusalem and refers to the "king of the north" and the "king of the south." Reading Chapter 11 with little knowledge of the history of the Intertestamental period could lead one to think that Daniel is prophesying of two individuals—the king of the north and the king of the south, however, one must think in terms of multiple kings of the north and multiple kings of the south; the wars about which Daniel prophecies cover a long period of time—300 B.C.-200 B.C. The kings of the north were the Seleucid kings. The kings of the south were the Ptolemaic kings.

The historical account of the revolt in I and II Maccabees of the Apocrypha compares with Daniel 8:9-14 and 11:21-35. The Apocrypha is a collection of fourteen partly historical and partly allegorical books and it generally is agreed that I Maccabees is more historically dependable than II Maccabees because I Maccabees presents eye witness accounts. Daniel's prediction and an extensive quotation from I Maccabees of the fulfillment of that prediction follow:

> And in his place shall stand up a contemptible person, to whom they had not given the honor of the kingdom: but he shall come in time of security, and shall obtain the kingdom by flatteries. And the overwhelming forces shall be ¬overwhelmed from before him, and shall be broken; yea, also the prince of the covenant. And after the league made with him he shall work deceitfully; for he shall come up, and shall become strong, with a small people. In time of security shall he come even upon the fattest places of the province; and he shall do that which his fathers have not done, nor his fathers' fathers; he shall scatter among them prey, and spoil, and substance: yea, he shall devise his devices against the strongholds, even for a time. And he shall stir up his power and his courage against the king of the south with a great army; and the king of the south shall war in battle with an exceeding great and mighty army; but he shall not stand; for they shall devise devices against him. Yea, they that eat of his dainties shall destroy him, and his army shall overflow; and many shall fall down slain. And as for both these kings, their hearts shall be to do mischief, and they shall speak lies at one table: but it shall not prosper; for yet the end time shall be

the time appointed. Then shall he return into his land with great substance; and his heart shall be against the holy covenant; and he shall do his pleasure, and return to his own land. At the time appointed he shall return, and come into the south; but it shall not be in the latter time as it was in the former. For ships of Kittim shall come against him; therefore he shall be grieved, and shall return, and have indignation against the holy covenant, and shall do his pleasure; he shall even return, and have regard unto them that forsake the holy covenant. And forces shall stand on his part, and they shall profane the sanctuary, even the fortress, and shall take away the continual burnt-offering, and they shall set up the abomination that maketh desolate. And such as do wickedly against the covenant shall he pervert by flatteries; but the people that know their God shall be strong, and do exploits. And they that are wise among the people shall instruct many; yet they shall fall by the sword and by flame, by captivity and by spoil, many days. Now when they shall fall, they shall be helped with a little help; but many shall join themselves unto them with flatteries. And some of them that are wise shall fall, to refine them, and to purify, and to make them white, even to the time of the end; because it is yet for the time appointed (Dan. 11:21-35).

And after that Antiochus had smitten Egypt, he returned again in the hundred forty and third year, and went up against Israel and Jerusalem with a great multitude, And entered proudly into the sanctuary, and took away the golden altar, and the candlestick of light, and all the vessels thereof. And when he had taken all away, he went into his own land, having made a great massacre, and spoken very proudly (I Maccabees 1:20-21, 24).

. . . .

And after two years fully expired the king sent his chief collector of tribute unto the cities of Juda, who came unto Jerusalem with a great multitude, and spake peaceable words unto them, but all was deceit; for when they had given him credence, he fell suddenly upon the city, and smote it very sore, and destroyed much people of Israel. And when he had taken the spoils of the city, he set it on fire, and pulled down the houses and walls thereof on every side. But the women and children took they captive, and possessed the cattle. Then builded they the city of David with a great and strong wall, and with mighty towers, and made it a strong hold for them. And they put there in a sinful nation, wicked men, and fortified themselves therein...For it was a place to lie in wait against the sanctuary, and an evil adversary to Israel. Thus they shed innocent blood on every side of the sanctuary and defiled it: Insomuch that the inhabitants of Jerusalem fled because of them (I Maccabees 1:29-34, 36-38a).

. . . .

For the king had sent letters by messengers unto Jerusalem and the cities of Juda, that they should follow the strange laws of the land. And forbid burnt offerings and sacrifice, and drink offerings, in the temple; and that they should profane the sabbaths and festival days: And pollute the sanctuary and holy people: Set up altars, and groves, and chapels of idols, and sacrifice swine's flesh, and unclean beasts: That they should also leave their children uncircumcised, and make their souls abominable with all manner of uncleanness and profanation: To the end they might forget the law, and change all the ordinances. And whosoever would not do according to the commandment of the king, he said, he should die (I Maccabees 1:44-50).

. . . .

And whosesoever was found with any the book of the testament, or if any consented to the law, the kings commandment was, that they should put him to death. Thus did they by their authority unto the Israelites every month, to as many as were found in the cities....And there was very great wrath upon Israel (I Maccabees 1:57-58, 64).[6]

Josephus' account of Antiochus' exploits parallels that of the Apocrypha.[7]

It may be safely said that the sufferings of the Jews at the hand of Antiochus can in no way be compared to their sufferings during the great Tribulation of the last days. Daniel 11:35 ends the account of Antiochus and his atrocities toward the city of Jerusalem. There is a gap of many centuries between verses 35 and 36, after which one will come who embodies the totality of the cruelty and hatred of Jerusalem's previous conquerors—the Antichrist.

Thus far we have seen that Jerusalem reached her height of glory during the Old and Intertestamental periods because God for the most part protected and delivered her. Chapter IV will trace her steps away from Jehovah and His guidance and protection.

CHAPTER IV

*Fulfilled Prophecies of the Deliverances
and Destructions of Jerusalem
During New Testament Times*

Many prophecies uttered in the Old Testament era (c. 2166 B.C., when reliable dating of events began, around the time of the call of Abraham) were not fulfilled until the New Testament era (and beyond), which began 6 B.C.-4 B.C. and ended with the death of the Apostle John (95 B.C.-100 A.D.). During this period Jerusalem experienced utter destruction by the Roman, Titus. It is debatable whether or not the level of this devastation was second to Nebuchadnezzar's. Indeed, Nebuchadnezzar carried the Jews captive to Babylon and forced them to remain there for a period of seventy years, but under the decree of Cyrus the Persian (445 B.C.) they were allowed to return to their home. The destruction of the city by Titus, however, led to the Jewish diaspora, which did not end until 1948. In my opinion, the result of the destruction of Jerusalem by Titus is the most tragic event the city experienced at the hands of her enemies, but it came only after she had fully rejected her Messiah.

I. DESTRUCTION OF JERUSALEM BY TITUS

A few facts concerning Titus' background are necessary at this point. Dr. Walvoord writes:

Long before Antiochus Epiphanes had fulfilled the prophecies of Daniel 8:23-25 and 11:21-35, the fourth empire of Daniel's prophecy was in the making in the rising power of Rome....The prophetic description of Rome as a monster with great iron teeth which trod under foot its opponents (Daniel 7:7) was fulfilled again and again. People seized in conquered countries were sold by the hundreds and thousands, and all menial tasks were performed by these slaves. Such was the power of Rome that Antiochus Epiphanes had previously been compelled to surrender Egypt to Rome, barely survived the threat of Roman domination until his death in 164 B.C., but thereafter Syria also became Roman. Roman conquest continued with the conquering of Palestine under the Roman general Pompeius who subdued Jerusalem in 63 B.C.[1]

When Pompeius came to Jerusalem, he took it by storm, completely demolishing the walls of the city and entering the temple "Holy of Holies." In 47 B.C. Antipater received permission from Rome to rebuild her walls. Seven years later the Parthians invaded and captured her. In 37 B.C., assisted by Sosius the Roman, Herod the Great, son of Antipater, recaptured the city. During the reign of Herod the Great, Jerusalem reached the height of her magnificence, surpassing all other ages. When he erected a golden eagle above the great gate of the temple, the Jews revolted and destroyed the eagle. Disturbances between Romans and Jews in Jerusalem continued from then until the campaign of Vespasian (68 A.D.-69 A.D.). When Vespasian was made governor of Judea he departed for Egypt to take control of the grain supply, leaving Titus in charge of the Judean campaign. Destruction of the city did not begin until 70 A.D.

Having been destroyed twice by Nebuchadnezzar and Antiochus, Jerusalem now faced her darkest hour. This time of trouble (70 A.D.) was first prophesied in Daniel 9:26. Verse 26 is set within what is known as 'the prophecy of the seventy weeks' (weeks of years). Each week is a period of seven years, or a total of 490 years. At this point it is necessary to digress from Titus' actions in order to demonstrate that the 490 years are definite and literal, not indefinite and symbolical. Arguments, supported by Scripture, are: the historical argument, the sabbatical argument, and the contextual argument.

Historical Argument. Prior to Daniel's prophecy there were three other 490-year periods (70x7 weeks of years) in Israel's history when God chose to deal with His people in definite literal years.

The first period was from Abraham to the Exodus (Gen. 12:4; 16:3; 21:5)—505 years from which must be subtracted the 15 years Isaac, the seed of promise, was delayed, leaving a total of 490 years.

The second period was from the Exodus to the foundation of the temple (Acts 13:18-21). Paul enumerates: 40 years in the wilderness (v18), 450 years for the taking of Canaan and dividing the land (v19), and 40 years for Saul's reign. He mentions David's reign but does not give the number of years of his reign, which was 40 (I Kgs. 2:10, 11), for a total of 570 years; to which must be added 3 of the first 4 years of Solomon's reign, when the foundation of the temple was laid (I Kgs. 6:37), for a total of 573 years; from which must be deducted 93 years for captivities during the time of the Judges (Jdgs. 3:8, 3:14; 4:3; 6:1; 13:1), for a total of 480 years; to which must be added 10 years for the construction of the temple from its foundation to its final completion, for a total of 490 years, 70x7 weeks of years (I Kgs. 6:38; 7:13-51).

The third period of 490 years was from the dedication of the temple to Nehemiah's return from Babylon. The return occurred during the 20th year of Artaxerxes (Neh. 2:1). This period, including the Babylonian captivity, totaled 560 years, from which must be deducted 70 years for the captivity, for a total of 490 years (70x7 weeks of years).

The fourth and last period of seventy times seven weeks of years appears in Daniel 9:27. Discussion of the preceding three periods of 490 years is necessary because they support the fourth and last period of seventy times seven weeks of years, yet they are literal, and not symbolical.[2]

Sabbatical argument. Turning to Leviticus 25:8 we find the same terminology, seven times seven years, used for the period of time between Jubilees; "And thou shalt number seven sabbaths of years unto thee, seven times seven years; and there shall be unto thee the days of seven sabbaths of years, even forty and nine years." In Daniel 9:24-27, we are told that the term "seven times seven years" is 49 years. If the 49 years are literal, so are the seventy weeks of seven years each—490 literal years in Daniel 9:24-27. God would not have us to believe otherwise.

The contextual argument. It consists of three facts that lend support to the term "sevens" as being literal years.

Fact one. Fact one is found in Chapter 4 of Daniel and relates to Nebuchadnezzar's psycho-pathological lycanthropic experience which lasted for a period of "seven times" (Dan. 4:16, 23, 32). Some scholars have interpreted the term "seven times" variously as two months, fourteen months, an indefinite period of time, or a definite seven years. Support for seven years can be found in the arguments immediately above, especially the sabbatical seven sevens of years (Lev. 25:8), and also within Daniel 4 itself.

Nebuchadnezzar had a dream which Daniel interpreted to mean that his kingdom would be taken from him and he would become like and live as a wild beast for a period of "seven times." In 4:28 Daniel tells us that everything mentioned in the dream actually happened twelve months later. Twelve months is one year and, based on Leviticus 25:8, it would equate to one of the years in the sabbatical sevens. If that is so, one of the seven times during which Nebuchadnezzar was in a deranged state of mind was one year; thus seven times would be seven years.

If Daniel used the term "twelve months" in 4:29, why would he use the term "seven times" instead of two months or fourteen months in verses 16, 23 and 32? Certainly he had no intention of using the term "seven times" to denote months and, therefore, we can deduce that the only reasonable length of time would be seven years. Furthermore, Dr. Bullinger states that Nebuchadnezzar's inscriptions show he did nothing for a period of several years (See the Companion Bible, Dan. 4:16). I understand Bullinger's statement to mean inscriptions that Nebuchadnezzar recorded during his reign. Archaeologists, too, have identified a seven-year gap in the history and documents of his reign.

If those years had been an indefinite period of time, Nebuchadnezzar would not have been convinced that God had spoken to him in the dream, much less recognized "that the Most High is ruler over the realm of mankind and bestows it on whomever He wishes" (Dan. 4:17, 25, 32,

35). But because the "seven times" was seven years, Nebuchadnezzar knew that, from the end of the twelve months when he began to boast; "' Is this not Babylon the great, which I myself have built as a royal residence by the might of my power and for the glory of my majesty?'" until the end of his madness, God had him on a definite time schedule of seven years. In other words, he knew that God kept His Word; he became insane at a definite time and returned to his original state of mind at a definite time.

Fact two. This fact is supportive of the contextual argument and is the angel Gabriel's explanation to Daniel of the prophetical "seventy weeks" (Dan. 9:24-27). In the historical argument above, three 490-year periods of time previous to this prophecy were presented to demonstrate that God had dealt with His people in seventy sevens of years. This, then (in Dan. 9), is the fourth and last seventy sevens of weeks in which God deals with His people. It extends from Daniel's time to the end of "the time of Jacob's trouble" (the great Tribulation).

Fact three. Gabriel's division of 483 years into two parts, bolsters the contextual argument (Dan. 9:25, 26) that the seventy sevens of weeks are weeks of years. He told Daniel that after seven weeks (7x7=49 years, during which time Jerusalem would be rebuilt following the Babylonian captivity), there would follow sixty-two more weeks (62x7=434 years). After the 49 years and the 434 years, a total of 483 years, Messiah (the anointed one) would be "cut off" (put to death). The same phrase is used in Isaiah 53:8; "for he was cut off out of the land of the living...." Following the return from Babylonian captivity, Jerusalem was rebuilt within 49 years and 434 years after that, Jesus, the Messiah, was crucified. (For a complete and accurate computation of Gabriel's figures, see Sir Robert Anderson's book, The Coming Prince.)

From these arguments (historical, sabbatical, and contextual) and the facts supporting them, it is clear that literal years are meant and any other interpretation skews one's view of the identity of "prince who is to come."

We now return to Titus and his destruction of Jerusalem in 70 A.D. To the logical question, "Who are the people and the prince in Daniel 9:26?" we find numerous answers and arguments. Young states, "'the people' are the Romans and 'the prince who is to come' is Titus

Vespasianus who invaded Palestine in A.D. 70 and destroyed the temple and the city."3 Unquestionably the people are the Romans, but Young is only half correct; "the prince who is to come" is not Titus. A.C. Gaebelein asked, "Who is 'the prince that shall come'?...It is the little horn predicted in Daniel 7 to rise out of the Roman Empire in the time of the end, when the Roman Empire is revived politically and has its ten horns."4

Closer examination of the context of Daniel 9:26-27 clearly shows that Titus is included with "the people" and is not "the prince that shall come." It is "the people," amongst them, Titus, who would cause the destruction of the temple and city, not "the prince who would come." Titus caused sacrifice to cease as a result of the destruction of the temple but nowhere in the historical record does he make and break a covenant with the Jews, causing sacrifice to cease. The time of the coming prince and the breaking of the covenant (the middle of the yet-to-come seventieth week) would not occur until long after 70 A.D.

From the time of the crucifixion until the present, the beginning of the seventieth week has been delayed and no one knows for sure how much longer the delay will continue. The event signaling the near commencement of the last week of the seventy is the Rapture of the true Church, but the event signaling the beginning of the seventieth week is the false covenant of peace that "the prince who shall come" makes with Israel, otherwise known as the covenant of Death and Hell (Isa. 28:18). It will be broken at the middle of the seventieth week.

More predictions of the city's destruction prophesied by Daniel are affirmed by Jesus Himself. Standing on the Mount of Olives overlooking the city He lamented, "O Jerusalem, Jerusalem, that killeth the prophets, and stoneth them that are sent unto her! how often would I have gathered thy children together, even as a hen gathereth her own brood under her wings, and ye would not! Behold, your house is left unto you desolate: and I say unto you, Ye shall not see me, until ye shall say, Blessed is he that cometh in the name of the Lord" (Lk. 13:34, 35).

The Lord predicted the desolation of the city and described the things that would be done to her by the Romans under the leadership of Titus. "And when he drew nigh, he saw the city and wept over it, saying, If thou hadst known in this day, even thou, the things which belong unto peace! but now they are hid from thine eyes. For the days shall come upon thee, when thine enemies shall cast up a bank about thee, and compass thee round, and keep thee in on every side, and shall dash thee to the ground, and thy children within thee; and they shall not leave in thee one stone upon another; because thou knewest not the time of thy visitation (Lk. 19:41-44, KJV). Parallel references to the statement "and they shall not leave in thee one stone upon another" are found in Matthew 24, Mark 13:2 and Luke 21:6, KJV.

At this point, it is important to expand on Dr. Chafer's comment concerning Matthew 24 and Luke 21. Mark 13 is relevant to Matthew and Luke and also needs to be addressed.

In each of the above passages the disciples asked Jesus the questions: "When shall these things be and what shall be the sign of your coming and the end of the age?" Notice that in Luke the disciples commented on the beauty of the temple and the size of the stones. Jesus told them: "As for what you see here, the time will come when not one stone will be left on another; every one of them will be thrown down." "Teacher," they asked, "when will these things happen? And what will be the sign that they are about to take place?" (Lk. 21:5-7). In verses 8-19 Jesus tells them certain things to look for before the temple-stones are leveled to the ground. Following that, He answers their first question: "When shall these things be [when will the stones be torn down]?" and tells them Jerusalem will be attacked and destroyed and trampled on by the Gentiles and will continue in that state until the times of the Gentiles shall be fulfilled (vv 20-24). The times of the Gentiles began with King Nebuchadnezzar in Daniel, Chapter 2, and will continue throughout the future 7-year period, ending with the return of Christ (Dan. 2:44). Jesus already had predicted the City's destruction in Luke 19:41. Luke 21:5-24 was fulfilled in A.D. 70 when the Romans destroyed Jerusalem and the Temple. Luke wrote before the destruction of Jerusalem and it was imperative that the answer be given as a warning that the destruction was impending.

It is important to note that "this generation shall not pass away until all these things be fulfilled" (Lk. 21:32) referred to those people who were living at the time Jesus warned of Jerusalem's destruction. "These things" (concerning the destruction of the temple and the city) would have had no meaning to any other generation. What Jesus said was important to them, not to the future generation at His coming. He was specific toward the close of Matthew 23:36 when He said: "I tell you the truth, all this will come upon this generation," and this is the reason Matthew and Mark did not record an answer to the first question: they wrote after the destruction of the city and there was no reason to warn of an event that already had transpired.

After Luke records the destruction of the city, the temple, and the worldwide dispersion of the Jews (Lk. 21:5-24), he jumps ahead to the future time when Christ will return (Lk. 21:25-35) and answers the second question (as did Matthew and Mark): "What shall be the sign of your coming and the end of the age?" For Jesus' answer to the second question, refer to Matthew 24:29-33 and Mark 13: 24-28. The second question and answer refer to the Tribulation, which will begin "When you shall see the abomination of desolation standing in the holy place..." (Matt. 24:15; Mk. 13:14). Also "this generation will certainly not pass away until all these things have happened" refers to those who will be alive at that time and see the signs in the heavens and the sign of the coming of the Son of Man in the sky (Matt. 24:34; Mk. 13:30). It does not refer to those of "this generation," during the time Jesus and the disciples lived. His return will immediately follow the Tribulation, at which time He will come to deliver His people at the battle of Armageddon. John records the battle in Revelation 19:11-21 and in v19 writes, "And I saw the beast, the kings of the earth, and their armies, gathered together to make war against Him who sat on the horse and against His army."

Christ then states that it would be a severe time for the city and its people when the Roman armies surrounded it. He warned them of difficulties they would have, should they be forced to flee during winter. "And they," says He, "shall fall by the edge of the sword, and shall be led captive into all the nations: and Jerusalem shall be trodden down of the Gentiles, until the times of the Gentiles be fulfilled" (Lk. 21:20-24). History has revealed that what the Lord predicted did happen, but it is important to note that Luke's account differs from Matthew's (24:18-20). Dr. Lewis Sperry Chafer offers an explanation:

> That all of this was accomplished by Titus in the year 70 A.D. is well known. There is need of warning, however,

lest some phraseology in Luke's account be confused with same phraseology in Matthew's account (cf. 24:18-20) and it be assumed on the basis of this similarity that the two accounts are parallel. In Luke's account Christ is describing conditions and giving directions to the Jews about the time when destruction of Jerusalem would be impending; Matthew's account records the conditions and timely instructions to the Jews that will be in order when the tribulation comes and the King is about to return. A careful comparison of these two Scriptures will vindicate this assertion.[5]

Dr. Wilbur Smith has combined the prophecies of Matthew, Mark and Luke which refer to the destruction of Jerusalem:

(1) The city will be destroyed, not by an earthquake, nor by fire from heaven, not by someone setting the city on fire, but by the attack of "thine enemies" (which turns out to be the Romans), i.e., by a military assault. (2) Around this city will be cast up a bank, literally, a palisade. (3) This circumvallation will be so complete and inescapable that the Jews will be forced to remain in the city. (4) The Jews and their children will be dashed to the ground or slain by the sword. (5) The destruction of the city will be so radical and complete that not one stone will be left upon another. (6) Many who do not meet death in this assault will be "led captive into all nations." (7) This city from now until the end of the age will "be trodden down of the Gentiles."[6]

The prophetic Word looks into the future and visualizes events; the moment those events transpire, they and the future become the present and pass into history. History once again has fulfilled and confirmed the reliability and trustworthiness of the Scriptures. Everything the Lord Jesus Christ spoke concerning the city's destruction came to pass, and within the short period of 35 years after Jerusalem's rejection and crucifixion of her Messiah she found herself face to face with Titus and the Roman army. Dr. George Adam Smith closes his monumental work, Jerusalem from The Earliest Times to A.D. 70, with the following words:

> Thus, then, did the city and the man confront each other: that great Fortress, with her rival and separately entrenched forces, for the moment confederate against Him; that Single Figure, sure of His sufficiency for all their needs, and, though His flesh might shrink from it, conscious that the death which they conspired for Him was His Father's will in the redemption of mankind. As for the embattled city herself, lifted above her ravines and apparently impregnable, she sat prepared only for the awful siege and destruction which He foresaw; while her spiritual promises, thronging from centuries of hope and prophecy, ran out from her shining into the West: a sunset to herself, but a dawn of a new day to the world beyond.[7]

Destruction was inevitable. Jerusalem's time of judgment had come and Jehovah now delivered her into the hands of the most powerful army in the world. The inhabitants could only wait and watch as the Roman eagles gathered. One has written that "The eagles seem, with wings dispersed, to watch their time for swooping! The towers are moving on; and lo! The engines, as though instinct with life, come heavily laboring upon their ponderous wheels; they nod destruction against our walls.[8]

The walls of the city seemed impregnable and yet, if the prophecy uttered by Jesus was to be fulfilled, one stone must not be left upon another. There were three walls surrounding Jerusalem: an outer wall, known as the third wall and two inner walls, the innermost of which surrounded the temple. Titus was amazed that he was able to accomplish such destruction and he attributed the fall of the city to God alone. "God indeed has been with us in this war. God it was who brought down the Jews from these strong-holds: for what power have human hands or engines against these towers?"[9]

Shortly before the Passover, many Jews came to Jerusalem to assist in its defense. As a result, one million, one hundred thousand people were crowded into the city. There was not a Jew present that should not have been there, for they loved the city with all their hearts and they were ready to defend her to the death. Titus appeared before the city and asked them to surrender, but the Jews refused and the siege worsened. Battering rams were employed and the Jews fought back, dropping massive stones and boiling oil upon the Romans.[10]

Day by day the situation grew worse for the people of Jerusalem. Josephus pled for them to surrender, reminding them of the faith of their fathers and of how their fathers depended upon God in the past. He told them that instead of trusting God, they not only were fighting against the Romans, but also against Him. But the Jews mocked him and some threw darts at him; they were entrenched and dead set on holding out against the Roman army and would have none of his advice.[11]

Titus set himself for a long siege against Jerusalem and as a result the horrors of famine and cannibalism were experienced throughout the city. Josephus gives an eyewitness account of the miserable situation in which the Jewish people found themselves:

> Now of those that perished by famine in the city, the number was prodigious, and the miseries they underwent were unspeakable; for if so much as the shadow of any kind of food did anywhere appear, a war was commenced presently; and the dearest friends fell a-fighting one with another about it, snatching from each other the most miserable supports of life. Nor would men believe that those who were dying had no food; but the robbers would search them when they were expiring, lest anyone should have concealed food in their bosoms, and counterfeited dying; nay, these robbers gaped for want, and ran about stumbling and staggering along like mad dogs and reeling against the doors of the houses like drunken men...Moreover, their hunger was so intolerable that it obliged such things as the most sordid animals would not touch, and endured to eat them...But why should I describe the shameless

impudence that the famine brought on men in the
eating inanimate things, while I am going to relate a
matter of fact, the like to which no history relates, either
among the Greeks or Barbarians! It is horrible to speak
of and incredible when heard.[12]

...Now there was a certain woman that dwelt beyond Jordan, her
name was Mary...She was eminent for her family and her wealth, and
had fled away to Jerusalem with the rest of the multitude and was with
them besieged therein at this time. The other effects of this woman had
been already seized upon...What she had treasured up besides, as also
what food she had contrived to save, had also been carried off by the
rapacious guards, who came every day running into her house for that
purpose...and if she found any food, she perceived her labors were for
others, and not for herself; and it was now become impossible for her any
way to find any more food, while the famine pierced through her very
bowels and marrow, when also her passion was fired to a degree beyond
the famine itself: nor did she consult with anything but with her passion
and the necessity she was in. She then attempted a most unnatural thing;
and snatching up her son, who was a child suckling at her breast, she
said, "O thou miserable infant! for whom shall I preserve thee in this
war, this famine and this sedition? As to the war with the Romans, if
they preserve our lives, we must be slaves! This famine also will destroy
us, even before that slavery comes upon us; yet are these seditious rogues
more terrible than both the other. Come on; be thou my food, and be
thou a fury to those seditious varlets and a byword to the world, which
is all that is now wanting to complete the calamities of us Jews." As
soon as she had said this, she slew her son; and then roasted him, and
ate the one half of him, and kept the other half by her concealed...so
that those thus distressed by the famine were very desirous to die; and
those already dead were esteemed happy, because they had not lived long
enough either to hear or see such miseries.[13]

Fifteen days into the siege battering rams were prepared
to breach the walls and Titus gave the Jews another
chance to surrender. Again, Josephus tried to persuade

them to do so, but they accused him of taking sides with the Romans, and refused. Titus eventually gained access to the city. He wanted the Temple left intact, but the Jews persisted in their fight and during the struggle a Roman soldier threw a torch and set the Temple ablaze. Titus ordered the fire to be put out, but no one listened to his command. The Temple was destroyed and not one stone remained on the other, just as Jesus had said. The Jews gave up the fight on September 8 and the walls of the city were leveled. The following are Josephus' final comments on the city's five captures, and the last of two desolations:

And from king David, who was the first of the Jews who reigned therein, to this destruction under Titus, were one thousand one hundred and seventy-nine years; but from its first building till this last destruction, were two thousand one hundred and seventy-seven years; yet not its great antiquity, nor its vast riches, nor the diffusion of its nation over all the inhabitable earth, nor the greatness of the veneration paid to it on a religious account, been sufficient to preserve it from being destroyed. And thus ended the siege of Jerusalem.[14]

That siege ended, and once again Jerusalem was in miserable condition. History had repeated itself; her saddened plight became as it was in the days of Jeremiah. Jeremiah's Lamentations were as applicable to her in A.D. 70 as they were in his day, "Mine eye runneth down with streams of water, for the destruction of the daughter of my people. Mine eye poureth down, and ceaseth not, without any intermission, Till Jehovah look down, and behold from heaven. Mine eye affecteth my soul, because of all the daughters of my city" (Lam. 3:48-51).

CHAPTER V

Fulfilled Prophecies of the Deliverances and Destructions of Jerusalem During the Present Age

The present age as it relates to the nation of Israel began when she rejected her Messiah (c. 35 A.D.-40 A.D.), but for the purpose of this study, the present age is reckoned from the destruction of Jerusalem (God's rejection of Jerusalem) in 70 A.D. to Israel's reception of the Messiah at His second advent.

The scope of the great prophecy uttered by Jesus in Luke 21:24b extends through the present age. He said, "...and Jerusalem shall be trodden down of the Gentiles, until the times of the Gentiles be fulfilled." Nebuchadnezzar dreamed of the same time period of which Jesus spoke and the dream was interpreted to him by Daniel the prophet (Daniel 2:1-45)—a visual aid of the times of the Gentiles. The times of the Gentiles began when Nebuchadnezzar (the head of gold) destroyed Jerusalem in 586 B.C. and took the Jews to Babylon. It will continue until the last great Gentile enemy, the beast, is defeated at the second coming of Messiah, Jesus. His coming kingdom is the great stone that smote Nebuchadnezzar's image on the feet, "the stone cut out without hands" (Dan. 2:34), destroying the Gentiles' (goyim) dominion over Israel. Only then will the times of the Gentiles be fulfilled; Jerusalem will be delivered for the last time, until the end of the Millennium and the close of the age of the ages (See chapter VIII). As Jesus predicted, Jerusalem continues to be "trodden down by the Gentiles." She has suffered more than enough destruction during the course of this age: (1) destruction by Hadrian, and (2) destructions not cited, but prophetic in general.

I. DESTRUCTION BY HADRIAN

Trajan and Hadrian were two major emperors who ruled Rome following the destruction of Jerusalem in A.D. 70. After Trajan's death on August 8, 117 A.D., his kinsman, Publius Aelius Hadrianus, came to the throne and would reign until 148 A.D. The incident that brought on the following destruction of Jerusalem resulted from Hadrian's visit to the city. Owen writes:

> After the destruction of the city by Titus, Jerusalem lay relatively quiet for approximately 60 years. The city was continually garrisoned, but had not been built. In 130 A.D. Hadrian visited the city and planned to found a Roman colony on the site of Jerusalem. The Jews were aroused to a final revolt because of this and fought for three years to win their freedom under the leadership of Bar-Cochba who declared himself to be the "Star" that was to come out of Jacob and "smite the corners of Moab, and destroy all the children of Seth" (Numbers 24:17). Not only did Rabbi Akiba accept Bar-Cochba as Messiah, he also declared that God was ready to smite the nations and usher in His Kingdom (Haggai 2:21, 22).[1]

Bar-Kokhba was not the "Star" who was to come out of Jacob, nor did he fulfill Haggai's prophecy (Haggai 2:21, 22). Julius Severus, commander of Hadrian's legions, put down the revolt. Bar-Kokhba was killed, the city of Jerusalem was devastated, and one-half million Jews perished or were taken captive. Jerusalem fell in 135 A.D. and Hadrian ordered the city to be plowed under, fulfilling the prophecy of Micah (Jeremiah 26:18, Micah 3:12): "Therefore shall Zion for your sake be plowed as a field, and Jerusalem shall become heaps, and the mountain of the house as the high places of a forest." Micah uttered his prophecy prior to the destruction of Jerusalem by Nebuchadnezzar. When Nebuchadnezzar came and destroyed the city, Micah 3:12 was fulfilled; however, that Micah's prophecy has application to the city's destruction by Hadrian is not questioned in the light of the following comments. Dr. A. C. Gaebelein says, "This prophecy was fulfilled when Babylon conquered Jerusalem, and when finally the returned remnant rejected the Lord of Glory, their King."[2] That rejection brought about Titus' humiliation and destruction of the city in 70 A.D. and would also cause a string of future disastrous times for Jerusalem; Hadrian's destruction, of course, would serve as a double fulfillment of Micah's prophecy. Wolfe states that "Micah had announced that Jerusalem would be plowed like a field and become a heap of rubble. This was literally fulfilled. Hadrian ran the plowshare over the hill of Zion."[3]

It is safe to conclude from the foregoing statements that Micah's prophecy covers the period from Nebuchadnezzar's destruction of the city (the beginning of the times of the Gentiles) "until the times of the Gentiles be fulfilled," spoken of by Jesus (Luke 21:24b).

II. DESTRUCTIONS OF JERUSALEM— NOT CITED BUT PROPHETIC IN GENERAL

The destructions of Jerusalem following that of Hadrian may be listed under the general prophecy uttered by Christ: "And Jerusalem shall be trodden down of the Gentiles until the time of the Gentiles be fulfilled" (Luke 21:24b). The following list of blockades, sieges, captures and destructions suffered by Jerusalem from 132 A.D.-1841 A.D. is taken from George Adam Smith:

1. Capture and plunder by Chosroes the Persian, 614
2. Recapture by Heraclius, 628
3. Occupation by Omar, 637
4. Capture by Moslem rebels, 842
5. Ruin of Christian buildings, 937
6. Occupation by the Fatimite Dynasty, 969
7. Some destruction by the Khalif Hakim, 1010
8. Occupation by the Seljuk Turks, 1075

9. Siege and capture by Afdhal, 1096
10. Siege, capture and massacre by Godfrey, 1099
11. Occupation by Saladin, 1187
12. Destruction of walls, 1219
13. Surrender to Fredrick II, 1229
14. Capture by the Emir of Kerak, 1239
15. Capture and sack by the Kharesmians, 1244
16. Plunder by Arabs, 1480
17. Occupation by Turks, 1547
18. Bombardment by Turks, 1825
19. Egyptian occupation, 1831
20. Re-occupation by Turks, 18414

Jerusalem passed from hand to hand for hundreds of years, the football of nations, kicked by one enemy and then another. She would experience two deliverances which would be significant to history and prophecy in the years following her occupation by the Turks: (1) deliverance by General Allenby, and (2) deliverance by Israel.

1. DELIVERANCE BY GENERAL ALLENBY

It was not until 1917 that Jerusalem saw her next great deliverance. General Edmund Allenby of the British Army was not unlearned in military science, especially that of the cavalry. He was well informed as to Jerusalem's historical significance and it is said that he often consulted the Bible, the Apocrypha, Josephus, and George Adam Smith's Historical Geography of the Holy Land to gain information on military successes and failures on the hills and plains of Judea. With this knowledge he advanced on Jerusalem with only three infantry and two mounted divisions. Before Allenby left England, the Prime Minister, Mr. David Lloyd-George, told him that he wanted Jerusalem for a Christmas present, giving Allenby six months to deliver Jerusalem from the shackles of Islam that had held the city for six centuries.

As the army began its advance into the hill country on November 18, 1917, the winter rains began and being in summer uniforms, the men were faced with much difficulty; however, despite opposition from the elements, they pressed toward their mark—Jerusalem. Much progress was made on the 21st; they took Neby Samwil that overlooked Jerusalem, where once Richard the Lion Hearted stood in 1192, refusing to look upon the city because he was unable to deliver it.

After rest and reorganization of his forces, on December 8, Allenby launched the main attack on Jerusalem. It is most significant that the city was taken without firing a shot, at least, not a shell fell on Jerusalem. As the sun set on Saturday evening, the Turks began leaving the city. Many Jews shouted for joy, "The Turks are running, the day of deliverance is come."[5] A reliable eyewitness gave the following comment:

> Toward midnight, the Governor, Izzet Bey, went personally to the telegraph office, discharged the staff and himself smashed the instruments with a hammer. At two o'clock on Sunday morning, tired Turks begin to tramp through the Jaffa gate from the west and south west, and anxious watchers, peering out through the windows of the Grand New Hotel to learn the meaning of the tramping, were cheered by the sullen remark of the officer, Gitmaya Mejboory, "we've got to go," and from two till seven o'clock that morning, the Turks streamed through and out of the city, which echoed for the last time their shuffling tramp.[6]

By seven o'clock Sunday morning, the last of the Turkish soldiers passed out through St. Stephens's Gate and made their way along the Jericho Road. The keys to the city were handed over to General Shea by the mayor of Jerusalem and on December 11 the deliverer, General Allenby, officially but humbly, walked through the Joffa Gate into Jerusalem. The Prime Minister received his Christmas present. Jerusalem was delivered once again and even though the deliverance came at the hand of a Gentile, the Holy City was handed over to the Christians.

Although Scripture does not specifically state that General Allenby would come and deliver Jerusalem, there is a prophecy that has been frequently applied to this event. The utterance was given by Isaiah and he describes how the Lord, Jehovah Himself would come and deliver the city which set on the hill of Zion. He would hover over Jerusalem as birds and protect her from the enemy. If Isaiah's words (Isa. 31:4, 5) are to be interpreted within the context, they must refer to Jehovah's protection and deliverance from the hands of the Assyrians, and yet, when it is remembered that Micah 3:12 and Luke 21:24b are prophecies having continual fulfillment, who is to say that Isaiah's prophecy cannot be applied to Allenby's deliverance of Jerusalem? Not a shot was fired during the deliverance, possibly due to Turkish fear of British planes flying overhead. It is possible that the "birds of Isaiah's prophecy were the planes of Allenby's air force. Whatever the case may be, God hovered over Jerusalem that day.

Even though Jerusalem was delivered into the hands of the Christians, she, nevertheless, was "trodden down of the Gentiles until the time of the Gentiles be fulfilled" (Lk. 21:24b). In 1917, Allenby's deliverance of Jerusalem was "to every Jew in the world the greatest event in history since the destruction of the city by the Roman, Titus, in the year 70 of our era."[7] However, the future was to bring the greatest, most heart-moving experience since the destruction of the city by Nebuchadnezzar in 586 B.C.

2. DELIVERANCE BY ISRAEL

Tiny, downtrodden, subjugated Israel deliver Jerusalem? Impossible—or so the world thought before June 5, 1967, when the Egyptian tank column began moving toward Israeli territory. That incident was the beginning of Jerusalem's deliverance from the hands of her enemies and sparked the third war between the Israelis and the Arabs in 19 years.

The roots of the war lay in the dispute over the land of Israel. Centuries ago, shortly after he was separated from his nephew, Lot, the land had been promised to Abraham for an "everlasting possession" (Gen. 13:14, 15), and God later would renew the promise of the land to Abraham when He made the covenant of circumcision with him (Gen. 17:8).

The Arabs accused Israel of illegal possession. After Allenby drove out the Turks, the Zionists pressured Britain to establish a "national home" for the Jews in Palestine under a mandate from the League of

Nations. Guerrilla warfare erupted between the Arabs and the Jews and, by 1947, because of the rise in population, Britain turned the Arab-Israeli problem over to the United Nations. A partition was effected between the Arabs and the Jews and when Israel became an independent state in 1948, the Arabs invaded Israel and were defeated. In 1949 a great number of Arabs were expelled from Palestine.[8]

Nasser came to power in Egypt in 1952, and by 1956, the Arabs were somewhat united and went to war with Israel over the Suez Canal. A cease-fire was put into effect, controlled and enforced by the United Nations troops, who also patrolled the "no man's land" along the partition line. The city of Jerusalem was divided and the Wailing Wall was included within the section under Arab control. The Jews were not allowed within this sector.

Nasser appealed to Russia for aid in 1956, receiving not only aid for humane purposes, but also financial assistance for war. Several times Nasser attacked the small section of Israel controlled by the Jews, and each time he was beaten back. Nasser vowed to destroy Israel and exterminate every Jew, echoing Psalm 83:4: "...Come, and let us wipe them out as a nation, That the name of Israel be remembered no more." In 1967, he set out to unite all Arabs to wage war on Israel. War was declared and on June 5, Nasser was in the process of deploying Arab forces against Israel, when Israel launched a surprise counter-attack, defeating the Arabs and breaking the blockade of the Gulf of Aqaba. It took the Jews just 60 hours to make Old Jerusalem theirs. The barriers dividing the city were broken down for the first time in 19 years and the ancient thoroughfares were crowded with celebration. Jerusalem was once again united (Psa. 126:2). "The Jews on their part flooded the Old City on the first Sabbath after reunification....A whole generation born since 1948, or too young then to remember the old surroundings, now enters the ancient heart of the city for the first time."[9]

The war of 1967 between Israel and the Arabs was a turning point in the history of the Jews. Prior to 1967, Jerusalem had not been under Jewish control for 1,897 years. Dr. Olson writes, "We have now witnessed some of the most remarkable events in all history—the rebirth of a nation and its return to the city after an absence of 2,500 years. Can the Jews hold the city?"[10]

Dr. Wilbur Smith made a most significant statement in 1950. Commenting on Luke 21:4, he said:

> I am not an alarmist, and I trust that through the years I have never attached to any world event a prophetic significance that was not justified; but it seems to me that almost any day or night this prophecy of our Lord could be fulfilled. Already there are more Jews living in Jerusalem than there were Jews living in the whole of Palestine at the dawn of this century. Furthermore, there is a government of a newborn nation in the modern city of Jerusalem—Israel. One hundred feet of no man's land, some barbed fences, and a few machine guns manned by a mere handful of Arabs—these are all that keep the Jews from fully occupying the city and setting up their government there.
>
> ....Why the Jews do not go in and take that city, I do not know; they certainly could do it. It may be that God will not permit this for some time. It may be that the Jews would enter into the city, capture it, attempt to set up their government, and bring down upon themselves the power and the wrath of the nations of the earth, and then this prophecy would not yet be fulfilled; for when it is fulfilled Jerusalem will never be trodden down of the Gentiles. I am only saying that, for the first time in two thousand years, we are amazingly near to the possibility of the fulfillment of this verse.[11]

According to other great prophecies, Israel has yet to undergo an unprecedented time of sorrow and suffering before Luke 21:24b is fulfilled (Jer. 30:5-11, Ezek. 37-38). The 1967 repossession of Jerusalem by the Jews is significantly relevant to prophecy that is in the process of being fulfilled. With the opening of the New Testament and the Messiah's entry into the city, the Jews were in possession of Jerusalem. Both Messiah and Jerusalem were lost to them because of their sin and blindness. The prophetic cycle shows the Jews in possession of the city again, but they still are blind and unbelieving; they are in the process of fulfilling the prophecies necessary for the second coming of their Messiah into Jerusalem.

Much has happened since the 1967 war. Jerusalem was delivered at that time, but the intervening 40 years reveal her still "trampled underfoot by the Gentiles until the times of the Gentiles are fulfilled" (Lk. 21:24b). Even though Jerusalem may not be specifically mentioned, her peace and security play a vital role in Middle East events.

The Knesset passed "the Jerusalem Law," in July, 1980, declaring the city united and the capital of Israel. This has further unified the Arabs in their hatred. They have vowed to destroy the nation of Israel and they will join with any enemy of Israel to do so, e.g., the leaders of Iran never cease to remind Israel of their burning desire to destroy her.

PART THREE

Unfulfilled Prophecies of the Deliverances and Destructions of Jerusalem During the Time Impinging the Tribulation Through the Ages of the Ages

INTRODUCTION

As stated in the Preface, Part Three, chapters VI through VIII follow and spotlight unfulfilled prophecies of the deliverances and destructions of the city. Chapter VI, Unfulfilled Prophecies of the Deliverances and Destructions of Jerusalem during the Time Impinging the Tribulation, presents a vivid description of the destruction of the Godless forces of Russia and her allies who attempt Jerusalem's destruction. Chapter VII, Unfulfilled Prophecies of the Deliverances and Destructions of Jerusalem during the Tribulation Period, brings to light the exploits of the Antichrist against the city and presents an excursus, comprising contextual and grammatical arguments that identify the Antichrist, and the Restrainer of the lawless one in II Thessalonians 2:1-12. Chapter VIII aims toward the very end of prophecy, at which point the Son of Man hands over the Kingdom into the hands of the Father, beyond which, as mentioned before, there is no revelation, except the revelation of the beginning of the ages of the ages that will never end.

CHAPTER VI

Unfulfilled Prophecies of the Deliverances and
Destructions of Jerusalem Impinging the Tribulation

As the present age approaches its close, Jerusalem will experience one of the most miraculous demonstrations of deliverance since her very beginning. She will be delivered from an alliance of nations attacking her from Israel's northern border, hence the term northern alliance. The 38th and 39th Chapters of Ezekiel's prophecy contain a vivid description, and though Jerusalem is not mentioned specifically, it is understood that whenever Israel is attacked it is always with the intent of ultimately taking Jerusalem. The nation capturing her will gain control of the nation of Israel and completely dominate the Middle East. If Jerusalem falls, Israel falls. The outcome of this invasion, however, will stun the entire world.

I. DELIVERANCE FROM THE NORTHERN ALLIANCE

As we have seen in prophecies already fulfilled, Israel's fiercest enemies, Babylon, Assyria, and Syria, have attacked her from the north. Ezekiel informs us that this new invasion originates from farther north than prior attacks. Various versions of the Bible have modified the word north to: the north parts; remote parts of the north; far north; far sides of the north; extreme north; north quarters; far recesses of the north; northernmost; distant north; all over the north; in the north; and the uttermost parts of the north. For purposes of this study, I am using north quarters, all over the north, and the uttermost parts of the north to best describe the area comprising the northern alliance. The following defining terms will identify those nations and reveal the time of the invasion: (1) terms applicable to the identity of the nations of the northern alliance, and (2) terms applicable to the attack-time of the nations of the northern alliance.

1. TERMS APPLICABLE TO THE IDENTITY OF THE NORTHERN ALLIANCE NATIONS

Each of the nations mentioned in Ezekiel Chapters 38 and 39 has a real place in history, and each will play a future role in the fulfillment of prophecy: Rosh, Persia, Ethiopia, Put, Gomer, and Beth-togarma. The best way to identify them is to follow what is known as the "law of first mention." Find the first place the name is mentioned in Scripture/ historical documents and use that as a starting point to work toward identification. For the most part, scholars have used this method to identify Rosh.

Rosh

Rosh in the original means "head" or "chief." The word has been problematic for biblical scholars throughout history. It has been transliterated into the English words "chief" and "Rosh," from which the name Russia is derived. Translators of popular versions of the Bible have favored both. A look at Ezekiel 38:1-3 in the following four versions reveals the difference: The Authorized Version (KJV), The New International Version (NIV), The New King James Version (NKJV), and The New American Standard Bible (NASB).

The KJV indicates that the word rosh is an adjective: "And the word of the LORD came unto me, saying, Son of man, set thy face against Gog, the land of Magog, the chief prince of Meshech and Tubal, and prophesy against him, And say, Thus saith the Lord GOD; Behold I am against thee, O Gog, the chief prince of Meshech and Tubal" (Ezek. 38:1-3). Here, in vv 2 and 3, the word rosh appears in English as the word chief; it is in the lower case, it is adjectival as to function, and it is meant to describe the word prince, who is Gog, the prince of Meshech and Tubal.

The NIV text reads: "The word of the LORD came to me: 'Son of man, set your face against Gog, of the land of Magog, the chief prince of Meshech and Tubal; prophecy against him and say: 'This is what the Sovereign LORD says: I am against you, O Gog, chief prince of Meshech and Tubal.'" The KJV and the NIV are almost identical and agree that transliteration of rosh is chief, however, the marginal reading of the NIV reads: v2 "Or the prince of Rosh" and v3 "Or Gog, prince of Rosh." It is obvious that the translators of the NIV preferred the adjectival translation chief to the word Rosh, otherwise Rosh would appear in the text rather than in the margin. While many agree with the textual translation of the NIV and the KJV, others prefer the textual translations of the NKJV and the NASB, which are exactly the same as the marginal reading of the NIV. Note the difference between the translations:

The NKJV reads, "Now the word of the Lord came to me, saying, "Son of man, set your face against Gog, of the land of Magog, the prince of Rosh, Meshech, and Tubal, and prophesy against him, and say, 'Thus says the Lord God: "Behold, I am against you, O Gog, the prince of Rosh, Meshech, and Tubal. Here, the word chief has been transliterated Rosh as meaning a place along with Meshech and Tubal, rather than a description of prince. In this version Gog is the prince of three places—Rosh, Meshech and Tubal—rather than chief prince of two places, Meshech and Tubal. Among the many documents that influenced the NKJV translators in their choice of Rosh over chief was the 1967/1977 Stuttgart edition of the Biblia Hebraica and The Septuagint (Greek) Version of The Old Testament.

The New American Standard Version's (NASV's) translation is almost identical to the NKJV: "And the word of the LORD came to me saying, Son of man, set your face toward Gog of the land of Magog, the prince of Rosh, Meshech and Tubal, and prophesy against him and say, 'Thus says the Lord God, "Behold, I am against you, O Gog, prince of Rosh, Meshech and Tubal." The NKJV (the updated translation of the KJV) and the

NASB transliterate the Hebrew word for chief into the English word rosh. According to these versions rosh is in the upper case—Rosh. It is a proper noun, refers to a place, and is a nation among the nations of the earth. It is interesting to note that long before the NKJV and the NASB, the seventy Jewish scholars who translated the Septuagint Version were unanimous in translating rosh as the Greek proper noun, Ros. Transliterated, Rosh becomes Ros. Considering the fact that the Septuagint was published 1,000 years before the name Russia was mentioned in modern literature, its influence weighs heavily toward the identity of Rosh as Russia.[1]

Smith gives an interesting discussion on the names mentioned in Ezekiel 38:1-3 concerning the word "Rosh" (Ros). His research demonstrates that the Byzantine writers mention a people dwelling in the country of Tarsus called 'ruz, that is "Rus," and these people later invaded the Byzantines. The people, Ros or Rus, were well known among the Byzantines. Byzantine authors later applied the appellation "Rucia" to the country, and it was affirmed in the Greek language. The word was written later "Rosiikii" and "Rosiya," and in the 17th century the word came to be written with two s's.[2] It is evident that Rosh (Ros, 'ruz, Rus, Rucia, Rosiikii, Rosiya) is identified as the nation of Russia. Price, in his excellent article, Rosh: An ancient Land Known to Ezekiel,[3] argues cogently against those who espouse the view that rosh is an adjective. His argument is detailed, technical, and fair.

The person addressed by God throughout Chapters 38 and 39 is Gog. Gog is mentioned in 38:2 as being "of the land of Magog." Since God addresses him throughout, it may be assumed that he is the ruler of Russia at the time of the invasion. Some feel this event is so near that as every new leader of Russia appears on the scene, the question arises: Is this the Gog to whom Ezekiel refers or do we look for another? The answer to that question remains a mystery and at this present time (2015an), no one knows. The tendency is to look for a dictator with a character like that of Joseph Stalin—cunning, calculating, violent, and cruel—but that is not how God presents him. The only insight we have into his personality is what God says to him: "On that day thoughts will come into your mind and you will devise an evil scheme" (Ezek. 38:10), which implies that the evil plan issues from an evil heart. Otherwise, little is said about him. He may not come off as an overt tyrant, but he could very easily be someone like Putin (or his successor), who on the surface appears somewhat different than Stalin—peaceful, promising a more democratic Russian government, ally of America and an enemy of Muslim terrorist organizations. And yet, by the time of Gog's planned invasion of Israel he will have become the leader of a Muslim coalition bent on taking Jerusalem and destroying the nation of Israel. Gog's ancestral line stretches back centuries to Japheth, from who descended Magog, Meshech, and Tubal. A look at each of these will support the fact that he is related directly to the peoples who settled what is now known as Russia. Interestingly, a straight line drawn from Jerusalem to the North Pole passes near the city of Moscow. Both cities are located near the same meridian: Jerusalem at 350 10' and Moscow at 370 40' east of Greenwich.

Magog

Magog is mentioned in Genesis 10:2—the second son of Japheth. Josephus identifies Magog as the Sythians who migrated from the immediate area in the north of Palestine to the Arctic Circle, spreading over the area encompassing today's Russia. "Japhet, the son of Noah, had seven sons: they inhabited so, that, beginning at the mountains Taurus and Amanus, they proceeded along Asia, as far as the river Tansis, and along Europe to Cadiz; and settling themselves on the lands which they light upon, which none had inhabited before, they called the nations by their own names.... Magog founded those that from him were named Magogites, but who are by the Greeks called Scythians."[4]

Meshech

Genesis 10:2 states that Meshech was the sixth son of Japheth, and other references reveal that he was the founder of a tribe (I Chron. 1:5; Ezek. 27:13; 38:2,3). Easton associates Meshech's descendants with those who

"... were in all probability the Moschi, a people inhabiting the Moschian Mountains, between the Black and the Caspian Seas. In Psalm 120:5 the name occurs as simply a synonym for foreigners or barbarians. During the ascendancy of the Babylonians and Persians in Western Asia, the Moschi were subdued; but it seems probable that a large number of them crossed the Caucasus range and spread over the northern steppes, mingling with the Scythians. There they became known as Muscovs, and gave that name to the Russian nation and its ancient capital by which they are still generally known throughout the East."[5] It is apparent that Meshech is the Moschi, and the word Moscow no doubt was derived from Moschi. A modern map of the area will reveal that the following named former Republics of the Soviet Union now occupy the southern part of Russia and the ancient land of the Scythians: Kazakhstan, Kyrgyzstan, Tajikistan, Turkmenistan, and, Uzbekistan.

Tubal

Tubal is the fifth son of Japheth (Gen. 10:2) and is synonymous with Tobolsk, a province of Russia. Josephus says: "Thobel founded the Thobelites, who are now called Iberes...."[6] By Iberes he probably is referring to the Tibareni. That the descendants of Tubal were the Tabereni is without question. They are mentioned as "... the Tubla of Assyrian inscriptions and the Tibareni or Tibarenoi of classical writers,"[7] and probably occupied areas within the former Soviet Republics mentioned above.

Each of the names identified is connected to one another by the same ancestral line and together will be part of one great military coalition which will, in the not-too-distant future, move from its location in the north. There are other haters of Israel who will answer the call of Gog and ally themselves with the clans who make up the nation of Russia. God says to Gog, leader of Russia: "Be prepared, and prepare yourself, you and all your companies that are assembled about you, and be a guard to them [italics mine]." The implication is that Russia will be powerful enough to protect the smaller nations allied to her from any challenge to the invasion (Ezek. 38:7). These smaller nations will be emboldened by Russia's influence and power, especially in the light of the fact that Israel is the greatest military might in the Middle East.

Having recognized Gog and identified Rosh, Meshech, and Tubal, we can identify those nations associated with Russia, when she makes her move southward. As mentioned before in the text of Ezekiel 38:5-6 they are: Persia, Ethiopia, Put, Gomer, and Beth-togarmah.

Persia

The original name for Persia is Parsa. The Septuagint has Persai, the exact translation of Persia from the Hebrew, leaving no doubt that Ezekiel referred to the Persia that was settled around 1500 B.C. and located in the land now known as Iran. Iran derives its name from the Aryan-speaking peoples; it means the land of the Aryans or the land of the Iranians. The name Iran was preferred over the name Persia and was officially changed by the Iranian Ministry of Foreign Affairs in 1935.[8] Iran, an ancient enemy of Israel, has vowed to eliminate her and presently is actively trying to acquire nuclear weapons; Iran will be ready when Gog gives the word to move toward the mountains of Israel.

Ethiopia

The Hebrew word for Ethiopia is Kush. The Septuagint renders the translation of Kush as Aithiopes. Ethiopia was the name for Kush when the Septuagint was translated from the Hebrew, so there is no question as to which country is meant. The Hebrew scholars who translated the Septuagint from the Hebrew to the Greek did so in Alexandria, Egypt, and they were familiar with the geography of the area. Ethiopia lies southeast of Egypt.

Put

There is some confusion as to the identity of the country of Put. The International Bible Encyclopedia (IBE) identifies Put as being composed of Yemen and Somalia.[9] Yemen is in Arabia and located toward the southwest tip of the Arabian Peninsula, east of the Red Sea and north of the Gulf of Aden. Somalia is in Africa and situated southeast of Egypt, across the Gulf of Aden from Yemen, east of Ethiopia. Because of their separation by the Gulf of Aden, it is difficult to imagine the two as the same nation state, and it is hard to agree with the IBE. The real identity of Put is found in the Septuagint version, which has the Greek word Libues, or Lybia, which lies west of Egypt. Again, the Septuagint translators were familiar with the geography around Alexandria when they translated the word Put in 202 B.C.

Gomer

It would be difficult to identify Gomer apart from Ashkenaz. During my days as a hospital chaplain I had the opportunity to work with many Jewish doctors and meet scores of Jewish patients. Many born and raised in Germany identified themselves as Ashkenazi Jews. Ashkenaz was the eldest son of Gomer and the grandson of Japheth (Gen. 10:1-3). Ashkenaz is the word for German and means a fire that spreads. Fire suggests destruction, but the term a fire that spreads can hardly be descriptive of the Jews. Israel does not deliberately attack other nations except in self-defense. In the not-to-distant future Ashkenaz will burn with rage against God's people like spreading flames in dry prairie grass. Gomer is, no doubt, Germany.

Beth-togarmah

Beth-togarmah (another son of Gomer) probably refers to southeastern Armenia. The Armenians consider themselves to be descendants of Gomer. They call themselves the House of Targum. Ezekiel 38:6 refers to Togarmah of the north quarters (see the Popular and Critical Bible Encyclopedia, Vol. 2, page 1671). The prefixed word Beth is Hebrew for house. A genealogical interpretation of house would include ancestors, descendants, and kindred. The descendants and kindred (military forces) of the House of Togarmah will fall upon the mountains of Israel.

Now that we know which nations comprise the Northern Alliance, we can attempt to determine when the invasion will take place.

2. TERMS APPLICABLE TO THE INVASION-TIME OF THE NORTHERN ALLIANCE NATIONS

In Ezekiel 38:7, God tells Gog to be prepared. Russia, even at the present moment, may be preparing for the event and, when the time is right according to God's prophetic plan, He will bring her down into the land of Israel: "And I will turn you about and put hooks into your jaws, and I will bring you forth, and all your army, horses and horsemen" (Ezek. 38:4). I believe this is the next important event on God's prophetic calendar, and Ezekiel gives an indication as to its timing. Chapter 38:8 uses the expression "latter years," and verse 16 uses "latter days." These terms no doubt refer to the future-time of Israel.

Latter Years

Dr. Dwight Pentecost writes:

> There are several similar expressions used which may need clarification at this point. The term last day is an expression that related to the resurrection and judgment program (John 6:39-40, 44, 54; 11:24; 12:48). The term last days is related to the time of Israel's glorification, salvation, and blessing in the kingdom age (Isa. 2:2-4; Micah 4:1-7). The term latter days or latter years is related to the time prior to the last days or the millennial age, which would be the Tribulation period. In Deuteronomy 4:27, Moses predicts a scattering because of unfaithfulness but promises restoration. In verse 30 he says: "When thou art in tribulation, and all these things are come upon thee, even in the latter days...." Here the latter days are linked with the Tribulation. In Daniel 2:28, the prophet reveals "what shall be in the latter days" and then carries the kingdom down to the final form of Gentile world power in the 70th week. Again in Daniel 8:19, 23, in discussing the "indignation" the prophet speaks of the "latter time" of their kingdom.

Again in Daniel 10:4 the term "latter days" is used in reference to the event preceding the millennial age.[10]

There are at least four differing views as to the time of this invasion: (1) at the beginning of the last week of the seventy-week prophecy of Daniel; (2) at the mid-point of the Tribulation (3-1/2 years); (3) at the conclusion of the Tribulation; and (4) at the close of the Millennium.

A detailed account of all views as to the time of this event are discussed by Dr. Pentecost in his book, *Things to Come*.[11] The last week has come to be understood as the over-all period of the Tribulation. According to Dr. Pentecost, the full period should be considered as the latter days or latter years of Israel's history, but I believe Israel's latter years began with the founding of the State of Israel on May 14, 1948.

The gist of Ezekiel 38 seems to be the following: God instructs Gog that He is going to bring him and his alliance against the land of Israel. He tells Gog to be prepared (vv 2-7). Then He tells him, "after many days," from the time He begins talking to him and the passing of many days, "you will be summoned ...." As I understand it, the "passing of many days" will not have passed until the beginning of "the latter years," but the "summons" itself is not given at that time. God seems to be putting Gog on notice that he will be summoned sometime during the latter years. That sometime will be "on that day when My people are living securely, will you not know it?" The expression "living securely" does not equate to a state of peace. The Hebrew word for securely is betach, not shalom. Betach is a military term and, unlike shalom, which is not in the context of the two Chapters, lends itself more to military competence and confidence. The question: "... will you not know it?" is God's way of saying that Gog will know when the time comes to move: "It will come about in the last days that I shall bring you against My land ...." (v16). The "last days" are the days that close the latter-year period.

Last Days

Other than the fact that Gog will move against Israel during a time when Israel feels secure, it is not revealed in the context when the "last

94

days" begin within the latter-year period. I assume the last days can begin any time within that time frame, sometime "On that day when My people Israel is living securely ...." (v14). Israel at the moment is living securely. She is militarily competent and confident that she can protect herself. According to verse 14, the invasion could take place at any time. Nothing has to happen in God's prophetic program prior to the invasion, which could occur before or simultaneous to the Rapture and the beginning of the Tribulation. The last days do not necessarily have to infringe upon the seven-year period of the Tribulation just because they are termed the last days.

The expression last days is used in different contexts throughout the Bible, e.g., when the Holy Spirit came at Pentecost, Peter quoted the prophecy from Joel and applied the term "last days" to that event: "'And it shall be in the last days,' God says, ' That I will pour forth of My Spirit upon all mankind ...'" (Acts 2:17). To Peter, the "last days" of Joel's prophecy were the last days of the old administration of God's works during Old Testament times that were being replaced by a new work God was in the process of initiating through the Spirit. But the prophecy had a double fulfillment. It would find completion farther into the future when changes would take place in the heavens; the same changes Jesus referred to when He spoke of His coming at the end of the Tribulation (Joel 2:28-32; Matt. 24:29-30; Mk. 13:24-26; Lk. 21:25-28; Acts 2:1-21). Paul expressed the same when he warned Timothy "... that in the last days difficult times will come" (II Tim. 3:1). No doubt he was referring to the last days of the Church before the Rapture, the scope of which would reach well into the Tribulation. Again, Peter used the phrase relative to the day of the Lord: "... in the last days mockers will come with their mocking ... (II Pet. 3:3).

According to Isaiah and Micah, "In the last days the mountain of the house of the Lord will be established" (Isa. 2:2; Mic. 4:1). Obviously, "the last days" referred to in those passages are after the Second Coming, falling within the Millennium, and well beyond the Tribulation period. "The last days" are not confined to any one time frame or period. Whenever the time frame of the Tribulation is mentioned, the phrases used are: the end time; the time of the end; the appointed time; that time; a time; times; a half time; and forty-two months (Dan. 8:19; 11:35,40; 12:1,4,7,9; Rev.

11:2; 13:5). Even these are set within what is known as the overall period of the Tribulation. The great Tribulation spoken of by Jesus refers only to the last 3-1/2 years of the overall 7-year period of the Tribulation as a whole. There is no Scriptural evidence that ascribes the last days to the Tribulation itself, especially to the last half. That is not to say, however, that the Tribulation does not fall within the last days of the latter-year period.

It is important to remember and understand that the Tribulation period begins when Israel signs the false covenant with the Antichrist, and not when the Church is raptured. It ends with Israel's deliverance upon Christ's return to earth. Since the Rapture is imminent and can occur at any moment, it would be unwise to use it to mark the beginning of Israel's severe time of trouble. There is no biblical evidence to support such a marker.

It appears that the invasion of the Northern Alliance is the marker, not the Rapture. The invasion will occur just prior to Israel's entering into the seven-year covenant with the Antichrist, and I believe his promise of protection from future aggression may be one of the reasons Israel signs.

The problem with placing the invasion at any time other than just prior to the signing of the covenant, or at the actual onset of the seven-year period of the Tribulation, is that it does not allow enough time (7 years) for the burning of the bodies of Gog, his allies, and their weapons (Ezek. 39:9-16). Since Israel presently meets the conditions required for the prophecy to be fulfilled, there is nothing to preclude it from happening 3-1/2 years before the beginning of the Tribulation.

If Russia attacks Israel today and 3-1/2 years from today the Tribulation begins, the 3-1/2 years added to the first 3-1/2 years of the Tribulation will total the exact number of 7 years required to burn the weapons mentioned above. Also, it is well to keep in mind that the first 3-1/2 years of the Tribulation is a time of peace, albeit a false peace, resulting from the covenant between Israel and the Antichrist, thus allowing Israel time needed before the last 3-1/2 years of persecution is initiated, spoken of by Jesus Himself (Mat. 24:21). Once the severe time of persecution begins, Israel will have little time for anything except survival. I am convinced that conditions are right for the Russian alliance to move at any time in the not-too-distant future.

Summarizing: Latter years is a time-line extending forward from May 14, 1948 to the Tribulation. The last days, according to the context of Ezekiel 38 and 39, can occur at any point on that line, beginning with the invasion of the Northern Allies: "It will come about in the last days that I shall bring you against My land ...." (v16).

II. DESTRUCTION OF THE NORTHERN ALLIANCE

The goal of the Northern Alliance will be to wipe the nation of Israel from the face of the earth. If left to herself, she would have no chance of survival, but destruction of the Alliance is determined and described by God.

1. THE DESTRUCTION DETERMINED

At the beginning of God's address to Gog He says, "'Behold, I am against you, O Gog .... (Ezek. 38:3)" That statement and the 38th and 39th Chapters of Ezekiel reveal God's determination to destroy him and his armies: "I will turn you about ... I will bring you out ... I shall bring you against My land ... I would bring you against them....'" God will bring them to the place of their destruction; they will not reach Jerusalem. Throughout Chapters 38 and 39 God describes the size of the invading forces as "all your army, horses and horsemen, a great company, all your companies, all your troops, many peoples, a great assembly, a mighty army, Gog's multitude, mighty men and men of war." (38:4, 7, 9, 15; 39:11, 20). Ezekiel gives no numbers, but the 2013 Central Intelligence Agency World Fact Book[12] provides approximate sizes of the armies of each of the countries belonging to the future Northern Alliance. The available military manpower of each is as follows:

Russia alone can boast of an army of 35,410,779.00, followed by the former Soviet Union Republics: Azerbaijan 2,354,249.00; Kyrgyzstan 1,470,317.00; Tajikistan 2,020,618.00; Turkmenistan 1,387,211.00; Uzbekistan 7,887,292.00; Persia (Iran) 23,619,215.00; Ethiopia 19,726,816.00; Put (Libya) 1,775.078.00; Gomer (Germany) 18,529,299.00; and Beth-Togarmah (Turkey) 21,079,077.00. The grand total of the opposing armies to Israel is the whopping figure of 135,259,940.00.

Israel's available manpower compared to the vast size of all the armies combined is a paltry 1,797,960.00; and is hardly a match for them. But Israel will not have to put one soldier in the field against them because God will make a quick end of those invading forces. God says to Gog and his forces, "You shall fall on the mountains of Israel, you and all your troops, and the peoples who are with you...." (Ezek. 38:4).

It is impossible to know the exact size of the armies listed but numbers will mean nothing. God has determined that the armies of the Northern Alliance will be destroyed upon the mountains of Israel.

The reason for the Russian invasion is given in Ezekiel 38:12: "To take a spoil and to take the prey; to turn thy hand against the waste places that are now inhabited, and against the people that are gathered out of the nations, that have gotten cattle and goods, that dwell in the middle of the earth." Russia will be attracted by the natural resources available in Palestine. Millions upon millions of tons of minerals have been deposited in the Dead Sea area throughout the centuries: magnesium chloride, potassium chloride, sodium chloride, calcium chloride; and in the ground lie vast quantities of oil. Physical control of Israel would ensure dominance over the entire Middle East, but God has determined that Israel will not be harmed and that the nations will know that He alone has accomplished it: "You shall fall upon the mountains of Israel, you and all your troops and the peoples who are with you; I will give you to birds of prey of every sort and to the beasts of the field to be devoured. You shall fall on the open field; for I have spoken," says the Lord God" (Ezek. 39:4-5). "It shall come about in the last days that I will bring you against My land [notice, He says that it is My land], so that the nations will know Me when I am sanctified through you before their eyes, O Gog.... I will magnify Myself, and make Myself known in the sight of many nations; and they will know that I am the LORD" (Ezek. 38:16, 23).

In Chapters 38 and 39, the word "LORD" is in the upper case. It is the Hebrew word Jehovah. Jehovah is the ever-existing one, the "I Am." He is, absolutely, the only God—there is no other. When the invasion and the destruction of the invading forces are accomplished, Jehovah wants the nations of the world to know that He and He alone will have brought it about. When he destroys the Islamic armies allied with Russia, He specifically will be telling the Islamic world that He, Jehovah, is God. There will be no challenge from Allah. "[A]nd all the nations will see My judgment which I have executed and My hand which I have laid on them" (Ezek. 39:21).

After leading the Israelites out of Egypt, Moses returned with them to Midian via an ancient trade route across the northern region of the Sinai Peninsula. They crossed the Red Sea (the Septuagint has, eruthran thalassan, Ex. 13:18) at the mouth of the Gulf of Aqaba and entered into the Arabian Peninsula and Midian. From there they went to Mt. Beder (Mt. Sinai in Arabia of which Paul wrote in Galatians 4:24-25) and shortly thereafter they were attacked by the Amalakites. They defeated the Amalakites and took the mountain (Sinai in Arabia) and the surrounding area from them. Moses' father-in-law, Jethro the Priest of Midian (a worshipper of Sin, the moon god, after whom Mt. Sinai was named) came to Moses and said, "Now I know that the Lord is greater than all other gods" (Ex. 18:11). Jethro realized that there was no God like unto Jehovah because God had delivered Moses and his people from the Amalakites, giving them Sinai, which was known as "the mountain of God," the mountain of the moon god, Sin. Muslims worship the moon god, Allah (masc. for fem., I'lalah), not Jehovah, the God of Israel. Their symbol is the crescent of the moon god of the Midianites. The shape of the crescent moon was chosen by the Midianites because it resembled the horns of a bull. Most ancient civilizations in the Middle East worshipped the moon. The moon God was probably the main God throughout Arabia. (See The Real Story of the Exodus, by Collin J. Humphreys, pp. 297-303.) Even though Mohammad did not begin his religion until 602 A.D., today's Muslims use the same ancient symbol, the crescent moon. When God defeats Gog, Russia, and the Islamic forces on the mountains of Israel, all nations, Islamic and otherwise, will say, as did Jethro, "Now I know that the Lord is greater than all other gods" (Ex. 18:11).

"Behold, it is coming and it shall be done, declares the Lord God. That is the day of which I have spoken" (Ezek. 39:8).

2. THE DESTRUCTION DESCRIBED

The meaning of Ezekiel 39:2 is not clear in the KJV. It has: "And I will turn thee back, and leave but the sixth part of thee ...." The marginal reading has: "Or, strike thee with six plagues; or, draw thee back with a hook of six teeth." The NKJV translates v2 in the following manner, " ... and I will turn you around and lead you on ...." The latter rendition is correct based on the root shasa (to lead) rather than shesh (six). In his excellent commentary on Ezekiel, Rabbi Dr. S. Fisch says that "The Hebrew verb is otherwise unknown."[13] I understand him to mean there is no other sense than shasa. There is no other indication in either the 38th or 39th Chapters that anyone will be left alive to return to their homeland, but assuming one sixth does survive and return home, what will they find? God Himself has given us a glimpse; He has looked upon it already and describes it.

God's Fury

God personally will be involved in the annihilation of Gog's forces. In Chapter 38:18 He says, "And it will come to pass at the same time, when Gog comes against the land of Israel," says the Lord God, "that My fury will show in My face. For in My jealousy and in the fire of My wrath I have spoken ...." God's anger will be the destructive force on that day. As I understand the context of Chapters 38 and 39, no other nation will come to Israel's aid or rescue.

Sword

"I will call for a sword against Gog throughout all My mountains," says the Lord God. "Every man's sword will be against his brother" (Ezek. 38:21). On other occasions in the Bible, Israel's enemies became confused and killed one another whenever unusual noises and events occurred. Gideon defeated the Midianites by blowing trumpets and breaking pitchers:

> So Gideon and the hundred men who were with him
> came to the outpost of the camp at the beginning of
> the middle watch, just as they had posted the watch;
> and they blew the trumpets and broke the pitchers that
> were in their hands. Then the three companies blew

the trumpets and broke the pitchers—they held the torches in their left hands and the trumpets in their right hands for blowing—and they cried, "The sword of the Lord and of Gideon!" And every man stood in his place all around the camp; and the whole army ran and cried out and fled. When the three hundred blew the trumpets, the Lord set every man's sword against his companion throughout the whole camp; and the army fled (Jdgs. 7:19-22).

Saul also would see his enemy the Philistines confused and killing each other with the sword, "Now it happened, while Saul talked to the priest, that the noise which was in the camp of the Philistines continued to increase; so Saul said to the priest, "Withdraw your hand." Then Saul and all the people who were with him assembled, and they went to the battle; and indeed every man's sword was against his neighbor, and there was very great confusion" (II Sam. 14:19-20). Rain, hailstones, fire, brimstone, and God's overwhelming presence and anger may cause mass casualties by what we term "friendly fire." In Chapter 38:4-6, God gives a general description of the dress and equipment of the troops and in 39:2-3 He says, "... and I will turn you around and lead you on, bringing you up from the far north, and bring you against the mountains of Israel. Then I will knock the bow out of your left hand, and cause the arrows to fall out of your right hand." In today's military terminology, the bow and arrows would be a missile platform and missiles.

Earthquakes

God will unleash the forces of nature with such rage that a great earthquake ensues, causing the land along with its inhabitants, both man and animals, to tremble. Such great shaking causes the mountains, walls and steep places to fall (Ezek. 38:18-20). God will intervene on behalf of His people and command the forces of nature to act. The elements of the earth and the heavens, "flooding rain, great hailstones, fire, and brimstone" (Ezek. 38:22), will be brought to bear upon Gog's millions. This is only a taste of what God will do in the not-too-distant future following Gog's shaking. Haggai writes: "For thus says the LORD of hosts, 'Once more in a little while, I am going to shake the heavens and the earth, the sea and also the dry land. I will shake all the nations...I will overthrow the thrones of kingdoms and destroy the power of the nations; and I will overthrow the chariots and the riders, and the horses and their riders will go down, everyone by the sword of another'" (Hag. 2:6, 21). John writes of another earthquake in Revelation: "...and there was a great earthquake, such as there had not been since man came to be upon the earth, so great an earthquake was it, and so mighty..." (Rev. 16:18).

Flooding Rain

He who said, "I thirst," made the rivers and the seas, and causes the rain to fall. He knows just how much to send to the earth, for whatever reason "He tips the water jars" (Job 38:37). He knew how much to send after telling Noah to build the ark. In this case God will send the rain on Gog and the hordes with him—"a torrential rain" (Ezek. 38:22). Flood and mud have halted armies throughout history, drowning men and halting the movement of equipment and supplies. Gog's armies will be caught in a quagmire from which they cannot escape.

Great Hailstones

The largest hailstone recorded in the US, was 17.5 inches in diameter and weighed 1.67 pounds; it fell in Coffeyville, Kansas, in 1970. In the year 2000, 8-pound monster hailstones hit Spain, although there was doubt as to whether they could be classed as real hailstones. The largest hailstones ever recorded weighed in at 2.2 pounds. They fell in Bangladesh, India, April 14, 1986, killing 90 people.14 When God tells Gog that He is going to rain great hailstones on him and his armies, he's not talking golf balls. The book of Revelation gives us the actual size of the hailstones that will fall during the Tribulation: "And great hail from heaven fell upon men, each hailstone about the weight of a talent [82-1/2 pounds]. Men blasphemed God because of the plague of the hail, since that plague was exceedingly great" (Rev. 16:21, NKJV). The stones that fall during the Tribulation will be enormous—megala (Nestle's Greek New Testament). John writes: "And greater hailstones, about 100 pounds each, came down from heaven upon men" (Rev. 6:21).

Fire

The fire of God mentioned in the Bible may refer to more than one type of fire.

Fire on the Mountains. The fire that falls with the rain upon Gog's horde may be lightening (Ezek. 38:22). Electricity in water kills, and God may very well cause mass electrocution

Fire on Magog. "And I will send fire on Magog and on those who live in security in the coastlands. Then they shall know that I am the LORD" (Ezek. 39:6). This could refer to a nuclear attack upon the homelands of the countries comprising the Northern Alliance at the same time the Alliance is destroyed on the mountains of Israel. God said that He would send fire; whether or not it means that He will send it from the heavens or by way of another nation is difficult to tell.

Brimstone

Brimstone is an "inflammable mineral substance found in quantities on the shores of the Dead Sea. The cities of the plain were destroyed by a rain of fire and brimstone (Gen. 19:24, 25). In Isaiah 34:9 allusion is made to the destruction of these cities. This word figuratively denotes destruction or punishment (Job 18:15; Isa. 30:33; 34:9; Psa. 11:6; Ezek. 38:22). It is used to express the idea of excruciating torment in Revelation 14:10; 19:20; 20:10."15 From Job 18:15; Isaiah 30:33; 34:9, and Psalm 11:6, one gets the sense that brimstone is liquid in form. The breath of God is likened to streams of brimstone. The substance is compared to rivers of pitch, like tar or bitumen. It was rained down upon Sodom and Gomorrah. In Genesis 14:10 we are told that "... the Valley of Siddim was full of asphalt pits ...." Brimstone may be akin to asphalt. Large deposits of asphalt are stored in the northern mountains, south of Syria where the Jordan rift begins. This area is the source of much of the asphalt that has accumulated in the Dead Sea. When God shakes the mountainous field of battle and cracks open the earth, a tremendous upheaval will occur and it is possible that brimstone/asphalt will act as God's napalm.

Feast

> Birds of prey of every sort will gather and dinner will
> be served:

> "Assemble yourselves and come;
> Gather together from all sides to My sacrificial meal
> Which I am sacrificing for you,
> A great sacrificial meal on the mountains of Israel,
> That you may eat flesh and drink blood.
> You shall eat the flesh of the mighty,
> Drink the blood of the princes of the earth,
> Of rams and lambs,
> Of goats and bulls,
> All of them fatlings of Bashan.
> You shall eat fat till you are full,
> And drink blood till you are drunk,
> At My sacrificial meal
> Which I am sacrificing for you.
> You shall be filled at My table
> With horses and riders,
> With mighty men
> And with all the men of war, says the LORD God"
> (Ezek. 39:17-20)

Funeral

The number of corpses strewn upon the mountains of Israel will be so numerous it will take seven months to bury the dead. God has selected a special place in a valley east of the Dead Sea for the burial ground, and He will appoint men throughout the land to bury the bodies. At the end of the seven months a special search will be conducted for bones that have been picked clean by the birds of prey, and when anyone sees a man's bone, he shall set up a marker by it, till the buriers have buried it in the Valley of Hamon Gog" (Ezek. 39:13-15). The land will be cleansed and a city will arise in the area where Gog is buried, the name of which will be Hamonah (Multitude).

One nation that was not mentioned as a member of the northern alliance is Iraq, and it remains to be seen what part, if any, that nation will play in the invasion. The presence of American forces there (2008) makes it difficult to speculate; however, if and when American forces are withdrawn, all bets will be off. Iraq is Israel's ancient northern enemy, Babylon.

God will bring Russia and her allies against the land of Israel to accomplish His four-fold purpose: (1) to destroy the northern alliance, (2) to make all nations know that the accomplishment was His and His alone, (3) to prove that there is absolutely no other God beside Him and, (4) to deliver Israel, strengthen her faith in Him, and cause her to glorify Him.

CHAPTER VII

Excursus of II Thessalonians 2:6-7: the Restrainer Recast

There will be a short interval of peace in the land of Israel following the Russian invasion. Not long thereafter, the archenemy of the nation will come and, unlike Russia, not only will enter and overrun the land with his forces, but he also will enter Jerusalem, bringing with him untold misery and destruction. It is absolutely essential at this point to fully establish the identity of the Antichrist and identify the restraining power that holds him in check until his release upon a Godless world. Therefore, it is necessary to make the following excursus—a full discussion of II Thessalonians 2 and related passages (Jn. 14-16), which heretofore, have been misinterpreted and misapplied by many to the II Thessalonians 2: 6-7 passage. The digression of this chapter will be well worth the time spent because of what the study reveals—a stark difference in the Person of the Holy Spirit and the Restrainer of the "lawless one," the Antichrist. The technicalities throughout will require a measure of patience.

I have embraced the pre-Tribulation view of the Rapture of the Church for approximately sixty-one years, but I must admit that as the years have passed I have felt a strong sense of frustration and uncertainty with what is considered to be an integral part of that view—that the Holy Spirit is considered to be the Restrainer, the one about whom the Apostle Paul writes in II Thessalonians 2: 6-7, "And now you know what is restraining, that he may be revealed in his own time. For the mystery of lawlessness is already at work; only He who now restrains will do so until He is taken out of the way." The pre-Tribulation Rapture view holds that the Holy Spirit is presently restraining the lawless one, the Antichrist, until He (the Holy Spirit), along with the Church, is removed just prior to the Tribulation.

None will deny that II Thessalonians 2: 6-7 has been a difficult-to-understand passage throughout the history of the Church and because of that, various and strange views have emerged. All sorts of works are replete with them and there is no need to cite them here, except to say that without question, the Holy Spirit-Restrainer view is considered to be the crux of Paul's teaching in II Thessalonians 2: 2-7. For many years I believed it was a necessary doctrine for maintaining the pre-Tribulation view. There are, no doubt, vital basic doctrines that are not optional, from which one should not deviate, but the teaching that the Holy Spirit is the Restrainer is not one of them. It should not be considered necessary for defending the pre-Tribulation view of the Rapture of the Church, if it can be shown to be unreliable by a logical presentation of evidence from Scripture. It is without question that the doctrine is contrary to Paul's thinking on the subject.

Therefore, with strong conviction that the Holy Spirit-Restrainer view is not that which Paul himself would have one adopt, and because it is not a vital basic doctrine, and since I am sure it will not prevent one's feet from leaving the ground at the Rapture, I have decided to abandon it based on the findings of this study. Hopefully, the evidence not only will arouse thoughtful reconsideration and reexamination, but also will bring about a recasting of the view. This was the desire of the great biblical scholar, Dr. Ethelbert W. Bullinger: "... it is clear that II Thessalonians 2:6-7 has suffered much at the hands of translators, and needs to be entirely recast."[1] Had Dr. Bullinger not made the statement above it is doubtful that my decision to initiate this section of the study would have been made. In defense of my position, the following arguments for recasting the Holy Spirit-Restrainer view are: (1) the co-contextual argument, (2) the grammatical-component argument, and (3) the natural-gender argument.

I. THE CO-CONTEXTUAL ARGUMENT

The co-contextual argument treats II Thessalonians 2 relative to three Chapters in John's Gospel: Chapters 4:7, 26; 5:26, and 6:3-4. For centuries they have been used to bolster the II Thessalonians 2: 6-7 passage, without which the view of the Holy Spirit as the Restrainer would have no support whatsoever. If the passages in John are proved not to be fitting proof texts for the II Thessalonians 2:6-7 passage, then the passages in John should be scrutinized with suspicion as to whether the doctrine of the Holy Spirit as Restrainer should continue to be advocated.

This argument takes issue with two negligent ways in which the context of II Thessalonians 2:6-7 and the relative passages in John have been treated: (1) the abuse of the II Thessalonians 2:6-7 context, and (2) the misuse of the John 4-6 context. It is my contention here that both contexts have been mistreated throughout the history of the Church and the gross abuse needs to be corrected according to the inherent makeup of each, and that neither context was meant to be infringed upon to mean anything other than what the authors, Paul and John, intended.

1. THE ABUSE OF THE II THESSALONIANS 2:6-7 CONTEXT

Keep in mind that two Greek terms, *to ketechon* and *ho ketechon* will be used in the following sections. *To* in the first term is pronounced *toe*, meaning *it*. *Ho* in the second term is pronounced hoe, meaning *he*; each will be bracketed to, hopefully, prevent confusion.

The abuse of the II Thessalonians 2:6-7 passage has come about by interpolation. Interpolation of a biblical text involves the act of corrupting a text by inserting new or foreign matter unintended by the author; e.g., if I wrote: "It held on with a strong grasp" and someone decided to change the statement to, "He held on with a firm grasp," the statement would be corrupted by the word "He" (second person pronoun, masculine gender) because the sense of the statement was intended to be an *it*, neuter gender, rather than a *he* holding on with a firm grasp. The error is that the Holy Spirit Restrainer view equates *to*[*toe*] *katechon*, the *it* holding fast, neut. gen., of v6 with the *he* [hoe] of v7, and corrupts what Paul actually meant. Obviously, when Paul wrote *ho* [hoe] *katechon* in v7, he did not mean for *to* [toe] *katechon* of v6 to be interpreted as the *he* of v7. The *it* of v6 is not the antecedent of the *he* in v7. As will be seen later, the *he* of v7, is not the Holy Spirit, but another person. That the name of the Holy Spirit is neither in v6 nor in v7 is indisputable. In fact, Paul makes only five references to the Holy Spirit in both of the Thessalonian letters. The list of each is as follows:

I Thessalonians
> 1: 5 pneumati agio (pneumati hago), Holy Spirit
> 1: 6 pneumatos agiou (pneumatos hagiou), of Holy Spirit
> 4: 8 pneuma autou to agion (pneuma autou to hagion),
>   the Holy Spirit of Him
> 5: 9 to pneuma (to pneuma), the Spirit

II Thessalonians
> 2: 13 agiasmo pneumatos (hagiasmo pneumatos),
>   holiness of Spirit

Dr. Bullinger makes a clear case in his excellent work, Word Studies on the Holy Spirit, that the references in I Thessalonians do not mention the Holy Spirit, but rather His holy power and gifts. He maintains that II Thessalonians 2:3 is absolutely the only one that definitely references the Holy Spirit (the Giver).[2] Given that each one of the four references in I Thessalonians referred to the actual Person of the Holy Spirit, there still would be no justification whatsoever for using them as antecedent to II Thessalonians 2:6-7; it is a different context altogether and was written for a different purpose, shortly following I Thessalonians, which was written in 50 A.D. And, as one can see, the only reference to the Holy Spirit throughout II Thessalonians is in 2:3; there Paul has no intention of connecting Him to verses 6 and 7, but writes: "But we should always give thanks to God for you, brethren beloved of the Lord, because God has chosen you from the beginning for salvation through sanctification *by the Spirit* [italics mine] and faith in the truth." There are no antecedents to the Holy Spirit anywhere in the context of II Thessalonians, Chapters 1-2. Since there is no reference to Him, it seems preposterous to cite *to* [toe] *katechon* as antecedent to Him, when in fact, He is not even mentioned in 2:7. Therefore, were it not for interpolation, the Holy Spirit would not be linked to the context of II Thessalonians 2.

The name of the Holy Spirit was not in the text from the very inception of Paul's letter, by virtue of the fact that Paul did not put it there when he wrote the epistle. Why should the name of the third Person of the Trinity have been associated with the II Thessalonians 2:6-7 passage in the first place? The only answer is that of an honest and sincere attempt to build a proof text for the pre-Tribulation doctrine of the Rapture of the Church. The only way to do that was to find texts that would supply the antecedents that were nonexistent in II Thessalonians 2:6-7 and apply them to verses 6 and 7. And where, of all places, was justification sought for that? --the Gospel of John!

2. THE MISUSE OF THE GOSPEL OF JOHN 14-16 CONTEXT

To reiterate: the originators of the view reverted to John, Chapters 14-16, as proof texts to bolster their argument. Their reasoning was this: since John uses the neut. gen. pronouns when referring to the Holy Spirit in John 14:17, 26 especially v17; 15:26; and 16:3-4, they too felt at liberty to do so. But they failed to see that John intentionally and rightly uses, with purpose, the neuter gender because his context is replete with the name of the Holy Spirit and relative appellations. Note the following: Holy Spirit, 1 time; Spirit of truth, 3 times; Helper, 4 times; He, 16 times; Him, 5 times; His, 2 times; and who, 1 time. No one doubts that John is writing about the same Person, not an *it* or a *thing*. See John 14:17 where pronouns, *which* and *it*, agree with the neuter gender of the antecedent, pneuma (Spirit), and are to be understood as *He*. It reads in the Greek like this: "The *spirit* of the truth, which the world cannot receive, because it beholds not *it* nor knows; you know *it*, because with you *he* remains and in you will be [italics are mine]. ---the Interlinear Greek-English New Testament, the Nestle Greek Text.

But a different situation exists in II Thessalonians 2:6-7; not one of the above names of the Holy Spirit precedes the neut. gen., *to* [toe] *katechon*, the *it* that holds fast, in v6 or the masc. gen., *ho* [hoe] *katechon*, *he* who holds fast, in verse 7. To say that the use of the masc. gen., *ho* (which), and the neut. gen., *auto* (it), in John 14:17 is justification for identifying *to*[toe] *katechon* in verse 6 and *ho* [hoe] *katechon* in verse 7 of 2Thessalonians 2 as the Holy Spirit is, without doubt, a serious misuse of John's context. In light of the above evidence, one can safely disregard the use of John's Gospel as an argument for the Holy Spirit-Restrainer view in II Thessalonians 2:6-7. The following text is supplied in order to show that there is not a shred of evidence for interjecting the name of the Holy Spirit into the II Thessalonians 2 context:

> 1 Now, brethren, concerning the coming of our Lord Jesus Christ and our gathering together to Him, we ask you, 2 not to be soon shaken in mind or troubled, either by spirit or by word or by letter, as if from us, as though the day of Christ had come. 3 Let no one deceive you by any means; for that Day will not come unless the falling away comes first, and the man of sin is revealed, the son of perdition, 4 who opposes and exalts himself above all that is called God or that is worshiped, so that he sits as God in the temple of God, showing himself that he is God. 5 Do you not remember that when I was still with you I told you these things? 6 And now you know what is restraining, that he may be revealed in his own time. 7 For the mystery of lawlessness is already at work; only He who now restrains will do so until He is taken out of the way. 8 And then the lawless one will be revealed, whom the Lord will consume with the breath of His mouth and destroy with the brightness of His coming. 9 The coming of the lawless one is according to the working of Satan, with all power, signs, and lying wonders, 10 and with all unrighteous deception among those who perish, because they did not receive the love of the truth, that they might be saved. 11 And for this reason God will send them strong delusion, that they should believe the lie, 12 that they all may be condemned who did not believe the truth but had

pleasure in unrighteousness. Stand Fast 13 But we are bound to give thanks to God always for you, brethren beloved by the Lord, because God from the beginning chose you for salvation through sanctification by the Spirit and belief in the truth, 14 to which He called you by our gospel, for the obtaining of the glory of our Lord Jesus Christ. 15 Therefore, brethren, stand fast and hold the traditions which you were taught, whether by word or our epistle. 16 Now may our Lord Jesus Christ Himself, and our God and Father, who has loved us and given us everlasting consolation and good hope by grace, 17 comfort your hearts and establish you in every good word and work. (II Thess. 2:1-17, NKJV).

That the name of the Holy Spirit is not in the above text, except in verse 13, is obvious. The only way to correctly ascertain the true identity of *to* [toe] *katechon* and *ho* [hoe] *katechon* is to examine their relationship with other integral parts within the context of II Thessalonians 2:6-7. Once this has been done, it will be clearly and unmistakably understood that the name of the Holy Spirit was never intended to be in the text.

II. THE GRAMMATICAL-COMPONENT ARGUMENT

This argument was formulated after a serious in-depth study of the following grammatical components, their relationship to one another and other constituent elements which makeup the context of II Thessalonians 2:6-7. The components are: (1) *to* [toe] *katechon*; and (2) *ho* [hoe] *katechon*. To say that *to* [toe] *katechon* and *ho* [hoe] *katechon* are one and the same is completely without grammatical justification; there is a marked difference between the two.

1. THE *TO* [TOE] *KATECHON* COMPONENT

To [toe] *Katechon: It* which holds fast—II Thessalonians 2:6
    As to its syntactic structure, *to* [toe] *katechon* is a present active participial verb. It is in the accusative case, singular as to number, and

neuter as to gender. The participle is crucial for understanding the true sense of the sentence in which it is used. Machen has the following important statement concerning the participle:

> The tense of the participle is relative to the time of the leading verb. The present participle, therefore, is used if the action denoted by the participle is represented as taking place at the same time as the action denoted by the leading verb, no matter whether the action denoted by the leading verb is past, present or future.[3]

The action of the leading verb in this instance is neither past nor present, but future. The leading verb is in verse 6; it is the infinitive, apokalupheesetai, (him to be revealed) and is 1st aorist passive. An interesting and crucial point is put forth by Dana and Manty: "'The participle is used when the real object of the governing verb is a person or thing whose act or state is described by the participle....'"[4] *To* [toe] *katechon* (the participle, the *it* holding fast) describes the state of a person, the "lawless one," who is the real object of apokalupheesetai (the infinitive and governing verb, him to be revealed). The revealing is future action that takes place in "his [the lawless one's] own time, not in Paul's and the Thessalonians time, even though Paul spoke the words in the then-present-time in which they were living. The lawless one was not being held fast at the time Paul spoke of him but he would be being held fast in the future.

As will be seen later, the to-be-revealed time of the lawless one will be at the mid-point of the seven-year Tribulation period. Now if that be true, and it surely is, a very real problem exists for the pre-Tribulation view of the Rapture of the Church: it would mean that the Holy Spirit and the Church still would be present on earth restraining the lawless one at the time of his revealing, if the Holy Spirit is *to* [toe] *katechon*. The adverb, "now" (nun), according to some versions, e.g., the NASB, would seem to indicate in verses 5 and 6 that the restraining action of *to* [toe] *katechon* was already in effect at the time Paul was speaking, "Do you not remember that while I was with you, I was telling you these things? And you know what restrains him now, so that in his time he will be revealed." This cannot be correct according to the tense of the leading verb; it would seem to indicate that he was already being held at the same time Paul was speaking. But how can that be, if what Machen says is correct? To reiterate: "The tense of the participle is relative to the time of the leading verb. The present participle, therefore, is used if the action denoted by the participle is represented as taking place at the same time as the action denoted by the leading verb, no matter whether the action denoted by the leading verb is past, present or future."

As stated above, the leading verb, the infinitive, apokalupheesetai, him to be revealed) is future and the holding action by the participle (*to* [toe] *katechon*) must also be future and not in the "now," at which time Paul was speaking. However, the NKJV renders Paul's statement correctly in keeping with the tense of the participle and the leading verb: "I told you. And now you know what holds fast," whereas, the rendering of the NASV, "And you know what restrains him now," does not. Obviously the verb, now (nun), does not refer to when *to* [toe] *katechon* was holding fast, but to when the Thessalonians had knowledge of what Paul had told them concerning *to* [toe] *katechon* and its holding relationship to the lawless one at the time of his revelation in the future.

2. THE *HO* [HOE] *KATECHON* COMPONENT

Ho [Hoe] *Katechon*, the One Holding Fast or He Who Holds Fast—II Thessalonians 2:7

On the one hand, by use of the term, *to* [toe] *katechon*, Paul has a thing in mind and, on the other hand, by use of the term, *ho* [hoe] *katechon*, he has a person in mind. Use of the 1st aorist active participle, masculine gender, 2nd person, is proof enough that Paul writes of an individual who can be spoken of as a *he*. One would be foolish to argue against that truth. Without a doubt, the Holy Spirit is a Person—the Third Person of the Trinity; no one who is a child of God and a true Bible-believer would deny that fact. To cite the many instances in Scripture which testify of Him as a Person would exhaust both time and space; that is not the purpose here, but the aim is to emphasize and prove the fact that the person about whom Paul writes in the passage under discussion is not the Holy Spirit, but another person who will be identified later.

Since Paul does not hesitate to mention the Spirit five times in both I and II Thessalonians, what logical reason would he have for not using His name in verses 6 and 7 if he meant the name of the Holy Spirit to be there? The logical answer is that *ho* [hoe] *katechon*, the one holding fast, of verse 7 is not the Restrainer of verse 6. The person in verse 3 who is being held fast by the restrainer (the subject) is the man of lawlessness, the son of destruction (the object). Together, verses 3 and 6 read thusly, "Let no one in any way deceive you, for it [the Day of the LORD] will not come unless the apostasy comes first, and the man of lawlessness be revealed, the son of destruction .... And now you know what restrains him, so that in his time he will be revealed." Paul chose to withhold the name of the lawless one in this second letter. The reason for doing so will be discussed later. The *he* who holds fast in verse 7 is not to be identified with the *it* of verse 6. Nor is it to be recognized as the Holy Spirit in John's Gospel. It is my contention that while *ho* [hoe] *katechon*, the one holding fast, is a person, masc. gen., he is not the Holy Spirit and, much more than that, Paul would have us understand that the individual spoken of here is not equivalent with *to* [toe] *katechon*. It is readily admitted that the presence of the Holy Spirit here on earth, His indwelling within the heart of every believer, and His abode in the universal body of the Church, has held down the influence of evil throughout the world. Considering the state of the world at present, it cannot be imagined what a hellish state the earth would be like without His blessed Presence. But even taking all that into consideration, one is not justified in identifying the Holy Spirit as the Restrainer. It would seem that if He were the Restrainer, restraint would be uniformly applied throughout humanity because of His attribute of omnipresence. Why? Because the nature of the Restrainer is to hold fast that which *it* holds without allowing any freedom whatsoever to that which it holds. The Presence of the Holy Spirit is most assuredly with us today, but He is not holding fast; evil is present, active and disproportionate.

III. THE NATURAL-GENDER ARGUMENT

This section will consider the following: (1) *to* [toe] *katechon*, *its* inanimate nature and present purpose, and (2) *ho* [hoe] *katechon*, *his* infernal identity and present position.

1. *TO* [TOE] *KATECHON*: ITS INANIMATE NATURE AND PRESENT PURPOSE

Its Inanimate Nature

An *It*. That Paul has a thing (an *it*) in mind is beyond question. He makes it very plain by the fact that he uses the neut. gen. An *it* is inanimate. This *it* has no life whatsoever. *It* is an entity that has substance, a spatial entity. *It* is relative to space and time and *it* is a unit whose measurements are known only to God, the Creator of that which is both animate and inanimate. *It* is *something*, a receptacle having sides, a top, and an unfathomed bottom.

A place. *It* is a place that exists in its own locale, somewhere in the depths of the earth. Some have suggested that the entrance to this place is in the vicinity of the Euphrates River (Rev. 9:2, 14-15). *It* is a holding place, a place—the strongest lockup in the universe—where any creature confined there will have no hope of ever being released, except at a designated time, when authority will be granted to the one who will open it. *It* is beyond the range of the human eye and outside the scope of any detection device. The only one who sees and knows what transpires in the *it* that holds fast is God.

A pit. *To* [toe] *katechon* is also a place and has a definitive name. In Revelation 9 John calls *it* the bottomless well or, pit (phreatos tas abussou). Chapters 11:7 and 17:8 of Revelation have only the bottomless (tas abussou). It is rather amusing here to think that the interpolators who misused John's Gospel to connect the Holy Spirit to II Thessalonians 2:6 used the right author but the wrong book. Had they searched John's other book, Revelation, they would have found that the pit is the connecting link to *to* [toe] *katechon* of II Thessalonians 2:6. The pit has a specific purpose relative to II Thessalonians.

Dr. Don V. Bailey

To [Toe] *Katechon*: *Its* **Present Purpose**

<u>To restrain</u>. The function of this entity is to do that for which God has designed it —to hold fast.

To [Toe] *Katechon* is from the word, *katecho*, which is made up of two words, *kata* (down), and *echo* (hold). It means to hold down with force or hold on with a strong firm grasp. While the holding action is for an interim period by *to* [toe] *katechon*, it is with fixed intent—to hold its object without releasing until expiration of the holding time. It is interesting to note that the Septuagint has *katecheen* (confine), in Genesis 39: 20: "So Joseph's master took him and put him in jail, the place where the king's prisoners were confined; and he was there in the jail." He was held there until the expiration of the holding time, the time when Potiphar decided to release him.

Paul uses the verb on another occasion when he writes to the Thessalonians. He says, "But examine everything carefully; hold fast [*katechete*, brackets mine] to that which is good." Other uses of the verb are found in Matt. 21:38; Lk. 4:42; 8:5; 14:9; Jn. 5:4; Acts 27:40; Rom. 1:18; II Cor. 6:10; Philem. 3; Heb. 3:6, 14 and 10:23. Even though Matthew uses a different verb *schomen* (we might have), it has the same sense as all the other occurrences.

While *to* [toe] *katechon* has been rendered by many scholars as the *it* which restrains, and rightly so, the word restrains is nevertheless questionable, in that the word would seem to apply less restrictive force than does *to* [toe] *katechon*. According to one definition in Webster's, the word means: "2: to moderate or limit the force, effect, development, or full exercise < ~ trade," Here, to restrain trade would imply that the practice could continue but with less freedom, whereas to katechon would allow no freedom to operate whatsoever; i.e., it would offer NO COMMERCE WHATSOEVER! Since restrain, by its very nature, does not, in every case, exert consistent and complete control, it seems a weak translation for *to* [toe] *katechon*. In any case, the word does not imply the same sense as does the holding grasp of *to* [toe] *katechon*, that which holds fast. *To* [Toe] Katechon is akin to solitary confinement of the penal system. The prisoner is segregated from other prisoners and put in "the hole" where he is totally isolated. He is in "the hole" and "held fast", with no freedom to move about whatsoever. The penal system has its prisoners, and *to* [toe] *katechon* has its prisoners, one of whom, at this moment, is being "held fast."

To restrain the lawless one. The Apostle is very specific in verses 3, 4, and 6 as to the object of the holding grasp of *to* [toe] *katechon*. The object is not a thing that is held, but a person. Remember Dana and Manty's statement from above: "The participle is used when the real object of the governing verb is a person or thing whose act or state is described by the participle...." In verse 3 Paul calls him "the man of lawlessness, the son of destruction [destruction being his destiny]." Then in verse 6 he specifically says that *to* [toe] *katechon* holds him (the object). Who is the "lawless one, the son of destruction," (the object) of verse 6?

Having established above that *to* [toe] *katechon* is the pit, one needs only to fast-forward to Revelation 11:7 to discover who the him of verse 6 is, "...the beast that comes up out of the abyss, *tas abussou*, and the bottom." In Revelation 17:1-7, John saw a woman seated on a scarlet-colored beast having seven heads and ten horns, v3, and in verse 7 the angel begins to reveal particulars concerning the beast, the seven heads, and the ten horns. The revealing angel tells John in verse 8: "The beast that you saw was, and is not, and is about to come up out of the abyss and goes to destruction." By the phrase "goes to destruction," the angel identifies the beast as being the same individual of whom Paul spoke, "the son of destruction." Further, the angel says, "And those who dwell on the earth ... will wonder when they see the beast, that he was and is not and will come."

Thus far, the angel has only revealed to John that the pit holds a person known as the beast, but as the angel continues, more comes to light concerning his identity. It is my contention that Paul had already revealed to the Thessalonians the precise identity of the beast. Remember, Paul had told them who the beast was. "I told you," says Paul, "and now you know...." (Full disclosure of the beast's identity will be presented later in this study.) The beast will come up out of the pit at the middle of the week, the beginning of the great Tribulation, the mid-point of the seven years. The Roman prince of Daniel's prophecy, who is the same as the rider on the white horse of Revelation 6:2 and the seventh one of Revelation 17:10, breaks the covenant and causes the

sacrifices to cease. Gabriel, the interpreting angel, told Daniel that "...
on the wing of abominations will one come who makes desolate, even
until a complete destruction, one that is decreed, is poured out on the
one who makes desolate" (Dan. 9: 27).

The one of whom Gabriel spoke, who comes on the wing of
abominations and makes desolate, is not the rider on the white horse,
the seventh one of Revelation 17:10, who breaks the covenant, but
rather an eighth king, about whom the interpreting angel also spoke in
Revelation 17:10. At this point, the mid-point of the Tribulation, the pit
will have ceased its restraint on the beast and he will have been revealed.
One must be careful and not equate the man of sin, the lawless one (the
beast) with the rider on the white horse, the seventh one who breaks
the covenant.

The man of sin, the lawless one who is the beast and the eighth,
cannot be recognized until his revealing time, the time he is released
from the pit. But how will this come about? How will the beast be
released from the pit? The answer lies in the true identity of *ho* [hoe]
katechon, the one who holds fast.

2. *'O* [HOE] *KATECHON*: HIS INFERNAL IDENTITY
AND HIS INTERSTELLAR POSITION

It was established above that *to* [toe] *katechon* (that which holds fast)
and *ho* [hoe] *katechon* (he who holds fast) are not one and the same.
The former is inanimate and the latter is animate; one is an *it* while the
other is a person; and neither is the Holy Spirit. Who is this person, *ho*
[hoe] *katechon*?

His Infernal Identity

His person will be immediately recognized by the two following
passages: Revelation 9: 1-11 and 12:7-9. The events in each transpire in
reverse order, i.e., the events in Chapter 12 take place before those in
Chapter 9. Chapter 9 depicts a star having fallen from heaven; Chapter
12 presents a moving picture as to why the star fell, how the star fell,
who the star that fell was, and reveals how the beast came to be already

on the earth in Chapter 11:7, just prior to his killing the two witnesses. "And there was war in heaven, Michael and his angels waging war with the dragon. The dragon and his angels waged war, and they were not strong enough, and there was no longer a place found for them in heaven. And the great dragon was thrown down, the serpent of old who is called the devil and Satan, who deceives the whole world; he was thrown down to the earth, and his angels were thrown down with him" (Rev. 12:7-9).

John, in the above passage is allowed to view a scene like no man has ever seen—angelic warfare. Great battles between these mighty beings have occurred at other times in ages past. The first one probably took place when "the covering cherub," Lucifer, mounted an attack against the throne of God (Isa. 14:12-14; Ezek. 28:11-19). Two words describe the outcome of that battle—Lucifer lost. Later, another battle involved at least three princes of the angels: Gabriel, Michael, and the Angelic Prince of Persia, a cohort of Satan (Dan. 10:1). Again, Satan lost. There are many chief princes among the angels, one being Michael. Michael, the guardian prince of Israel, holds a very special place relative to that nation, especially during the time of the great Tribulation. The interpreting angel, Gabriel, told Daniel: "Now at that time Michael, the great prince who stands guard over the sons of your people, will arise. And there will be a time of distress such as never occurred since there was a nation until that time; and at that time your people, everyone who is found written in the book will be rescued" (Dan. 12:1).

When Michael arises he is seen by John the Revelator as going forth (the Greek has *polemesai,* to make war). Satan does not start the war. Michael and his angels deliberately start the war against Satan and his angels for a specific purpose. John was "... in the Spirit on the Lord's day ..." (Rev. 1:10), not on Sunday, but on the great day of Judgment (the Day of the LORD). John, in visions, saw this awful battle as already having transpired, and his book of Revelation allows us to know the battle's outcome—Satan loses. John says: "...they were not strong enough" (v8). It is at this point that (*ho* [hoe] *katechon,* the one who holds fast, is identified. It is Satan. He took his stand and having done all to stand, he could not "hold fast."

His Interstellar Position

Restraint of that position. What was Satan so desperately trying to hold onto? Why would he put up such a struggle, especially against one of God's mightiest angelic princes, Michael, and his forces? *Ho* [Ho] *katechon*, a masculine participial verb, is transitive and requires an object in order to complete the idea of what is being held down. Example: If one says to me, "He who holds fast," I immediately want to know who he is and to what he is holding fast, otherwise, any sense of the incomplete statement remains a mystery. Since it has been shown above that *to* [toe] *katechon* is not the Holy Spirit, but rather the *it* that holds fast the lawless one, the question arises: what is Satan grasping so tightly? What is he "holding fast?" It can only be his sole possession of importance. The object that is being held fast is his place or position in the heavens, interstellar space. The word interstellar means among the stars, the literal stars. Since our solar system is among the stars it is rather difficult to know how far Satan's sphere of influence extends. Ever since that first rebellion he has been allowed to operate only with derived power. He is now known as, Satan, "...the prince of the power of the air...," and chief ruler of "...the spiritual forces of wickedness in the heavenly places." (Eph. 2:2; 6:12). He commands the high places. The "air" is probably that area of influence where he is allowed to affect the lives of men and nations (the children of disobedience). The "heavenly places" involve certain areas within an astronomical-sized region of stellar space wherein he commands and controls legions of angels who were cohorts when he led the first rebellion against God. No matter though, whether it is only within our solar system, throughout the galaxy or intergalactic, there is a region throughout where he is allowed to roam freely and exert his power.

 Removal from that position. Question: Can Satan cast out Satan? Answer: He cannot and he will not. But there is one who can, and will—Michael. He will remove Satan from his place in order to rid the heavens of his presence and power. Satan, "... he who now holds fast, will hold fast until he is taken out of the way" (II Thess. 2:7). The phrase, "out of the way" is literally "from the middle" or "from the midst" (*ek mesou,*). Michael will remove him from the "middle" or "the midst" of the heavens. Satan knows that once his sphere of influence is lost he no longer will be "the prince of the power (*exousias*) of the air." Paul says that he will hold fast to that position, the middle heavens, until he is removed: "... and there was no longer a place found for them in heaven ...." (Rev. 12:8). A speculative Scenario:

Warfare has broken out in the heavens. Legions upon legions of angels rush to battle; like enormous black and white clouds they intermesh. The battle is joined. They move with lightning speed. Michael and his angels attack. Satan and his angels fight back. Back and forth the two angelic bands make their moves. They move up and down among the heavenly spheres. In and out of one another's defenses they dart as with the velocity of arrows shot from a gigantic bow. They with light-year speed whirl, flip, dive, roll, and turn like giant Frisbees, spinning and plummeting throughout the heavenly heights. Onslaught after onslaught. Blitz after blitz. On the battle rages. White-cloud chariots rush! Weapons clash! If ever angel tongues are heard, it is now. If ever angels vent their anger, it is at this moment.

Then, above the sound of the fury and clamor, roars the earsplitting and fiendish voice of the Black Cherub, Satan: "Hold!" "Hold!" The fight continues with the ferocity that only angels know. Grunts and gasps are heard as they match one another's gargantuan-like strength. The struggle goes on. They thrash about. Chaos. Disorder. Confusion. Disarray. Bewilderment. Angels are in a frenzy. Then, black spirits begin to falter. Lines grow weary. They weaken. Weaker-still-weaker they grow. Ranks begin to break ... they break. Again, the foul voice of the Dragon is heard, only this time in greater desperation: "Hold! Hold! Hold Fast! Hold Fast!" He knows there is much at stake. He has too much to lose. He strains with one last effort...one last tumultuous cry ... "Hold Fast!" "I command you to hold fast!" But alas!--to no avail. John says: "... they were not strong enough ...." (v8). Those five words have caused the downfall of the greatest armies of the past --"they were not strong enough." Satan, HO [HOE] *KATECHON*, THE ONE WHO HOLDS FAST, took his stand and having done all to stand, he could not. Like Custer, Son of The Morning Star; Lucifer, Star of Morning, met his "Little Big Horn." He could not hold fast to his cherished position.

Having looked into the future with John, we know that Satan and his angels will have lost the battle with Michael and his angels. He and his angels are thrown down to the earth. Hurtling downward to earth, the tail of the great dragon drew a third of the stars (angels) with him (Rev. 12:4). Neither Satan nor his angels have a choice in the matter. Satan is forcibly removed, along with his angels; he drew them along with him. He drew (*surei*) means to drag along by force according to the inertia created by the weight of the object being pulled; the word *surei* may be used to put emphasis on the great number (1/3) of angels that his tail dragged along with him. We have no way of knowing the total number of angels making up the 1/3; it is an innumerable host, all of them.

Satan, having lost the exercise of his power in the heavens, descends to the earth with what seems to be greater power. The last 3-1/2 years of the Tribulation period is that time when both the wrath of God and the wrath of Satan will fall on the earth and, in particular, on the nation of Israel. It will be "the time of Jacob's trouble."

His Intended Purpose

The infinitive, "the to be revealed time," will involve the following twofold purpose of Satan after his expulsion from the heavenly places: release the beast from the pit, and to reveal the beast's identity.

Release of the beast from the pit. Satan will exert his derived power. " ... and the key of the bottomless pit was given to him." He will open the pit of the abyss. The pit will have restrained the lawless one until his "to be revealed time." That time is described in the following passage:

> 1 And the fifth angel sounded, and I saw a star from heaven fallen unto the earth: and there was given to him the key of the pit of the abyss. 2 And he opened the pit of the abyss; and there went up a smoke out of the pit, as the smoke of a great furnace; and the sun and the air were darkened by reason of the smoke of the pit. 3 And out of the smoke came forth locusts upon the earth; and power was given them, as the scorpions of the earth have power. 4 And it was said unto them that they should not hurt the grass of the earth, neither

any green thing, neither any tree, but only such men as have not the seal of God on their foreheads. 5 And it was given them that they should not kill them, but that they should be tormented five months: and their torment was as the torment of a scorpion, when it striketh a man. 6 And in those days men shall seek death, and shall in no wise find it; and they shall desire to die, and death fleeth from them. 7 And the shapes of the locusts were like unto horses prepared for war; and upon their heads as it were crowns like unto gold, and their faces were as men's faces. 8 And they had hair as the hair of women, and their teeth were as teeth of lions. 9 And they had breastplates, as it were breastplates of iron; and the sound of their wings was as the sound of chariots, of many horses rushing to war. 10 And they have tails like unto scorpions, and stings; and in their tails is their power to hurt men five months. 11 They have over them as king the angel of the abyss: his name in Hebrew is Abaddon, and in the Greek tongue he hath the name Apollyon. (Rev. 9:1-11)

While John does not mention in the above passage that the beast will come out of the pit, he does so elsewhere. In Revelation 17:8 he states that the beast " ... is about to come up out of the abyss ...." Then he says in Revelation. 11:7 that the beast that comes out of the pit will kill the two witnesses. That he will come out of the pit is a fact. The question is, when? Since the pit is "the it which holds fast" and will do so until the "to be revealed time" of the lawless one, and since this is the only passage in Scripture that mentions the opening of the pit, it is logical to assume that this is the time of his release. Then too, especially in light of the fact that the beast is allowed only 3-1/2 years to vent his anger on Israel and all who refuse to worship him, his release must take place at this time; the middle of the Tribulation, the time of Jacob's trouble (Jer. 30:7). "Then the fifth angel sounded, and I saw a star fall from heaven which had fallen to earth; and the key of the bottomless pit was given to him. He opened the bottomless pit ..." The action "having fallen" refers to

Satan's expulsion from his place by Michael in Revelation 12:7-9, not to the result of Lucifer's fall after the first rebellion in ages past. Remember that Chapter 12 transpires before the events in Chapter 9. After Michael removed Satan from his place in the heavens, John saw Satan as a star having fallen from heaven. Morris has an important comment on the above descriptive appellation of Satan as a star:

> There are, of course, stars without number and of almost infinite variety in the universe, any one of which might fittingly be described as a vast "lake of fire." Angels are occasionally called stars in Scripture (Job 38:7; Judges 5:20; Rev 9:1; 12:4); even Satan himself is the "day star," Lucifer (Isa 14:12). The ancients worshiped the stars, because they constituted the "host of heaven." The most plausible explanation for this apparent identification of the angelic hosts with the stars is that the latter constitute the residences of the former. But a great number have "kept not their first estate" and have "left their own habitation" (Jude 6), and are now clustered about the planet earth, the "powers of the air."

I agree with Dr. Morris that the many dwelling places among the stars are the residences of the former but those spoken of in Jude 6 are at the present time reserved in chains somewhere deep in the bowels of the earth until the time of their judgment. The remaining 1/3 are still clustered throughout the middle heavens far from our solar system. According to John, after having been cast out of their place in the heavens, the only place in which Satan and his cohorts can operate until their utter destruction will be the earth. The adversary will exercise every advantage to bring about utter chaos on those who dwell on the earth. "Woe for the earth and for the sea: because the devil is gone down unto you, having great wrath, knowing that he hath but a short time" (Rev. 12:12, KJV). He will waste no time. He will have been given the key (authority) to open the pit (the *it* which holds fast). The God of the universe is the only one who will allow him to unleash the powers that will execute His long-awaited judgment on the planet. And from it will ascend in chariots a multiplicity of hellish creatures unlike any mankind has imagined.

The Theological Word Book Of The Old Testament lists the following derivatives of the word chariot: chariot (rekeb = chariot; chariotry, rikba = act of riding; rakkab = driver, charioteer; rekub = chariot; merkab = chariot; merkaba = chariot); and indicates that the chariot is a vehicle used for transportation with two wheels, pulled by horses, ridden and commanded by a charioteer (driver).[6]

When the word chariot is associated with God and His holy angels it retains its original meaning as that of a vehicle having an operator, and is a mode of transportation. Beyond that, the word takes on a far different significance—strange flying craft with space-flight characteristics. A study of relative passages in the Old and New Testaments reveals that those who came in contact with God's chariots were faced with objects unlike any they had ever experienced.

The Old Testament passages relative to flying craft are: "The chariots of God are twenty thousand, even thousands upon thousands; the Lord is among them as at Sinai, in holiness." (Psa. 68:17). "He bowed the heavens also, and came down; And thick darkness was under His feet. And he rode upon a cherub, and did fly; Yea, he was seen upon the wings of the wind. And he made darkness pavilions round about him, Gathering of waters, thick clouds of the skies. At the brightness before him Coals of fire were kindled..." (II Sam. 22:10-13). "And it came to pass, when they were gone over, that Elijah said unto Elisha, Ask what I shall do for thee, before I be taken away from thee. And Elisha said, I pray thee, let a double portion of thy spirit be upon me. 10 And he said, Thou hast asked a hard thing: nevertheless, if thou see me when I am taken from thee, it shall be so unto thee; but if not, it shall not be so. And it came to pass, as they still went on, and talked, that, behold, there appeared a chariot of fire, and horses of fire, and parted them both asunder; and Elijah went up by a whirlwind into heaven. And Elisha saw it, and he cried, My father, my father, the chariot of Israel, and the horsemen thereof. And he saw him no more..." (II Kings 2: 9-12). "Now Elisha was fallen sick of his sickness whereof he died. And Joash the king of Israel came down unto him, and wept over his face, and said, O my father, my father, the chariot of Israel, and the horsemen thereof" (II

Kgs. 13:14). "For, behold, Jehovah will come with fire, and His chariots shall be like the whirlwind; to render His anger with fierceness, and His rebuke with flames of fire. For by fire will Jehovah execute judgment, and by His sword, upon all flesh; and the slain of Jehovah shall be many (Isa. 66: 15,16).

New Testament passages relating to flying craft are: "For the Lord Himself shall descend from heaven, with a shout, with the voice of the archangel, and with the trump of God: and the dead in Christ shall rise first; then we that are alive, that are left, shall together with them be caught up in the clouds, to meet the Lord in the air: and so shall we ever be with the Lord" (I Thess. 4:16, 17). "I saw in the night-visions, and, behold, there came with the clouds of heaven one like unto a son of man, and He came even to the ancient of days, and they brought Him near before Him. And there was given Him dominion, and glory, and a kingdom, that all the peoples, nations, and languages should serve Him: His dominion is an everlasting dominion, which shall not pass away, and His kingdom that which shall not be destroyed" (Dan. 7:13-14). "... and then shall appear the sign of the Son of man in heaven: and then shall all the tribes of the earth mourn, and they shall see the Son of man coming on the clouds of heaven with power and great glory. And He shall send forth His angels with a great sound of a trumpet, and they shall gather together His elect from the four winds, from one end of heaven to the other" (Matt. 24:30, 31). "Jesus said unto him, Thou hast said: nevertheless I say unto you, Henceforth ye shall see the Son of man sitting at the right hand of Power, and coming on the clouds of heaven" (Matt. 26:64). "Behold, he cometh with the clouds; and every eye shall see Him, and they that pierced Him; and all the tribes of the earth shall mourn over Him. Even so, Amen" (Rev. 1:7).

While the verses cited by no means exhaust the subject, the following references found in the Old and New Testaments characterize and describe the chariots and their movements: (Gen. 17:22; 28:12; Ex. 19:18,19; 24:15; 40:34-38; Num. 9:15-22; 10: 11,12, 34; 16:12; II Sam. 22:10; II Kgs. 2:11; 6:17; Psa. 18:10; 30:34; 68:17; 104:3; 30:34; Isa. 66:5; Jer. 4:3; Ezek. 1; 10:4-19; 8:3; 9:3; Dan. 7:13-14; Zech. 6:1; Matt. 2:9; 17:5; Mk. 9:7; 16:19; Lk. 24:51; Jn. 1:51 [See Gen. 28:12,13]; Jn. 3:13; 6:62; Acts 1:2, 9, 12; II Cor. 12:4; I Thess. 4:16; Rev. 1:7; 11:11,12).

A close study of the above will reveal the following: They are described as cloud-like vehicles; they are disc-shaped (the word chariot, rekeb, is used of the circular shaped upper millstone used during biblical times); they spin like a whirlwind and fly at lightning-like velocity; their gigantic size ("the chariot of Israel") is observed as being escorted by smaller craft ("the horsemen thereof"); they descend and ascend, and also hover; they guide, defend, and scout out camping grounds for God's people; they fly between mountains and are seen at other times landing on their summits with great noise and commotion. Enoch, Elijah, Elisha, and Jesus were caught up by them, and so shall the saints of this age; and they will be instrumental in the destruction of the beast at the second coming of the Lord Jesus with His great and mighty army of angels and chariots (Rev. 19:11-21).

It is obvious from the foregoing that there is definite correspondence between each and that the chariots and horsemen of the Almighty are, in no way, to be understood as being of the same nature as those used during the times of the prophets and kings. They could only describe them in accordance with the means of transportation at the then present time, and while their means of expression may seem poetic and visionary, the strange craft they observed were genuine.

Satan, the black cherub, has his chariots and charioteers. There is an allusion to them in Gen. 6:1-4. They were known as the Nephilim (fallen ones) and had descended to the planet in chariots. They were instrumental in corrupting the earth, which eventually resulted in God's judgment by flood. Later, "then after that," [after the flood], there was another descent. The Book of Enoch, written prior to 165 B.C., alludes to them. Enoch is told to tell them (Watchers) what would be the consequences of their having lain with the women of the earth. The result of the union would be that children born to them would become evil spirits and in the end time would "rise up," causing destruction until the end of "the consummation."[7] Although one cannot be sure, I interpret the term, "rise up" as referring to their release from the pit. Both Jude and Peter allude to them as being shut up in pits of darkness until their release for judgment on the great day (II Pet. 2:4; Jude 6). Whether these will be released along with those mentioned in Revelation 9 is difficult to know, but for a fact those in Revelation 9 will ascend from the pit, the

Dr. Don V. Bailey

it which holds fast at the "to-be-revealed time" of the lawless one (the beast), "...that is, the one whose coming is in accord with the activity of Satan..." (II Thess. 2:9). His activity begins on the earth when he opens the pit, and he will continue in one accord with the beast and the false prophet "...with all power and signs of false wonders..." and will be active throughout the latter half of the Tribulation.

"And the Beast that you saw was, and is not, and is about to come up out of the abyss and go to destruction" (Rev. 17:8). How and by what means does he ascend from the pit? In his book, The Antichrist, the learned and well-known conservative author, Arthur W. Pink, describes what might take place:

> ... the setting up of this "image" to the Antichrist will, most probably, be attended with supernatural phenomenon. We gather this from Daniel 9:27, where we read, "And he shall cause the sacrifice and the oblation to cease, and for the overspreading of abominations he shall make it desolate." Now the word here translated "overspreading" is never so rendered elsewhere. Seventy times is this word translated "wing" or "wings." It is the word used of the wings of the cherubim in Exodus 25:20 and Ezekiel 10:5, etc. And in Psalm 18:10 we read of Jehovah that "He rode upon a cherub, and did fly: yea, He did fly upon the wings of the wind."
>
> One profound Hebrew scholar has rendered the last clause of Daniel 9:27 as follows, "And upon the wing of abominations he shall come desolating." Remembering that "abomination" has reference to an idol or false god, the force would then be "upon the wing of a false god shall he come desolating." Now in view of Psalm 18:10 it is highly probable that Daniel 9:27 refers to a satanic imitation of the Chariot of the Cherubim. This is strengthened by 1 Corinthians 10:20—"The things which the Gentiles sacrifice, they sacrifice to demons, and not to God"—which shows the demoniacal nature of the "idols" or "abominations" worshiped. If this view be

correct, then the Antichrist will be supernaturally borne aloft (in invisible demons), and apparently descending from on high (in blasphemous mimicry of Malachi 3:1) will finally persuade the world to worship him as God. The ¬apostate Jews will, no doubt, believe that their eyes at last behold the long-awaited sign from heaven, and the return of the Glory to the Temple. For it is thither the false Christ will be borne, and there his image set up. We believe that the words of II Thessalonians 2:4, "He as God sitteth in the temple of God, showing himself that HE IS GOD" may, most likely, have reference to this same event.[8]

The spirit of the beast will be borne aloft on (in) one of the black cherub-chariots, ("the wing of abominations"). "Wing" is singular, and Daniel's use of it may be as it is in Genesis 7:14, where it has "birds of every sort" (sort, kanaph, wing). It may refer to many craft, just as it is used in the military terminology of today, e.g., during the Iraqi War: the 32nd Air Wing Expeditionary Force (many aircraft) was launched from the aircraft carrier Abraham Lincoln against the enemy. From the pit the beast will go to Jerusalem where the body of the seventh one lies in state; there he will enter and indwell the body of the seventh. Scott Peck interprets Satan in the neuter gender as it, and asks and answers an interesting question: "Why do demonic spirits have such an attachment to bodies? ... Satan has no power except in a human body. Satan cannot do evil except in a human body.... Although 'a murderer from the beginning,' it does not have the power to kill or even harm by itself. It must use human beings to do its deviltry."[9] (Of course there have been occasions when Satan has been allowed to use nature for murder and mayhem, but that seems to have been for special reasons (Job 1:2). Satan knows he has but a short time in which to accomplish his purpose, so he chooses to do it through the only instrument whereby he will be able to be the most effective—a human body.

The spirit of the beast will ascend from the pit "on the wings of abomination" (Dan. 9:27) to the vicinity of the rebuilt temple; it will be a mimicry of the Shekinah (the glory of God) having descended to dwell above the mercy seat in the most holy place in the temple. When the beast indwells the dead body of the seventh one, he will come alive and those on the earth will see the deadly wound as having been healed, and from all appearances to those who dwell on earth, the same individual, the seventh, will have been resurrected. What better way to prove that he is God? The seventh, in fact, will become the beast, a composite character—the body of the seventh and the spirit of the beast will be one—the most dreadful counterfeit miracle since the beginning of the universe. "I saw one of its heads as if it had been slain, and his fatal wound was healed. And the whole earth was amazed and followed after the beast; they worshiped the dragon because he gave his authority to the beast; and they worshiped the beast, saying, 'Who is like the beast, and who is able to wage war with him?'" (Rev. 13: 3-5).

Amazed by the fact that he returned from the dead, and further persuaded and convinced by the false prophet and his miracles, they choose to believe the lie rather than the truth—that he really is God (Rev. 13:11-15; II Thess. 2:8-12). He will descend "...on the wing of abominations" (Dan. 9:27) to the rebuilt-temple (a mimicry of God having descended to His place in the past), set himself, probably on the Mercy Seat between the Cherubim, and proclaim himself God! The Mercy Seat is God's seat. It was atop the Ark of the Covenant, between the two two-winged cherubim where His radiant presence dwelt in the Tabernacle and Temple (Ex. 25:22; Lev. 16:2; II Sam. 6:2; II Kgs. 19:14,15; Psa. 80:1; Isa. 37:16; Ezek. 9:3; 10:18; Heb. 9:5). He had descended there where he communed with His people through the priests. In order for the beast to show utter contempt for God and opposition to Him, he seats himself in that position of worship, to be worshiped—the worship for which God alone is worthy. Paul says of this wicked one "... that he takes his seat in the temple of God, displaying himself as being God" (II Thess. 2:4). The word "displaying" (apodeiknunta) means that he not only will proclaim deity, but will at the same time make a great exhibition of it, as though to say: "Look at me, world. You are beholding God, in the flesh!" Satan's man, in the flesh! The beast will have been reincarnated, both spiritually and literally.

He, by the power and authority of Satan, will instigate the Tribulation, the great one, of which the prophet Jeremiah spoke, "'Alas! for that day is great, There is none like it; And it is the time of Jacob's distress, But he will be saved from it" (Jer. 30:7). The Lord Jesus also spoke of it, "Therefore when you see the Abomination of Desolation which was spoken by Daniel the prophet, standing in the holy place (let the reader understand), For then there will be a great tribulation, such has not occurred since the beginning of the world until now, nor ever will'" (Matt. 24; Mk. 13; Lk. 2). The Abomination Of Desolation will be the image made like unto the beast, which will be set up in the Temple by the false prophet (Rev. 13: 14,15). Jesus said that it would stand in the "holy place." It is imperative that we take the Savior's word as to where the Abomination of Desolation will be set up. He specifically says, "The holy place." There are two words for "holy place" which must be differentiated; otherwise one is in danger of getting caught in a maze of endless and needless interpretations. Strong's Enhanced Lexicon explains the difference between the two. The first word, *hieron* is used in the following ways:

2411 [hiepov]
1) a sacred place, temple 1a) used of the temple of Artemis at Ephesus 1b) used of the temple at Jerusalem

HB-1964 [keykal]
The temple of Jerusalem consisted of the whole of the sacred enclosure, embracing the entire aggregate of buildings, balconies, porticoes, courts (that is that of the men of Israel, that of the women, and that of the priests), belonging to the temple; the latter designates the sacred edifice properly so called, consisting of two parts, the "sanctuary" or "Holy Place" (which no one except the priests was allowed to enter), and the "Holy of Holies" or "the most holy place" (which was entered only on the great day of atonement by the high priest alone). Also there were the courts where Jesus or the apostles taught or encountered adversaries, and the like, "in the temple"; also the courts of the temple, of the Gentiles, out of which Jesus drove the buyers and sellers and the money changers, court of the women.[10]

The second word for "holy place" is naon, (naov) and is used as follows:

> 3485 naos {nah-os'}
> from a primary naio (to dwell);
>
> GK - 3724 {naov"}
> 1) used of the temple at Jerusalem, but only of the sacred edifice (or sanctuary) itself, consisting of the Holy place and the Holy of Holies (in classical Greek it is used of the sanctuary or cell of the temple, where the image of gold was placed which is distinguished from the whole enclosure)[11]

The key to understanding what Jesus meant by "holy place" is found in the meaning of naos. To repeat: Naos was the sacred edifice; the edifice consisted of two parts, the Holy Place and the Holy of Holies. Which of the two words did Jesus use? Neither. The words Jesus used were *topo hagios*, place holy or holy place). The solution is still left open to question unless the answer is to be found elsewhere. The only place for the correct answer, relative to the Abomination of Desolation being set up in the holy place, is to be found in the words of the Apostle, Paul: "... he takes his seat in the temple of God..." (II Thess. 2:4). For "temple" Paul uses the word, *naon*. Here the Apostle uses the same word as in I Cor. 3:16, 17: "Do you not know that you are a temple (*naon*) of God and that the Spirit of God dwells within you?" I understand Paul to mean that the Holy Spirit, who is God, the very presence of God, dwells in the innermost recess (the inner sanctum, the holy of holies) of the believer. The dwelling of the Holy Spirit in the heart of the believer is analogous to God's radiant presence dwelling atop the Ark of the Covenant on the Mercy Seat between the cherubim in the Holy of Holies of the Tabernacle and the Temple. Therefore, the only correct explanation of Jesus' words "the holy place" is that the Abomination of Desolation will be set up in the first part (the holy place) of the sacred edifice, where in classical Greek the golden images were set; and the "lawless one" will seat himself on the Mercy Seat in the Holy of Holies. Thus, the whole of the sanctuary will have become corrupted, an abomination to God because of the detestable thing, the likeness of the despicable person, the beast.

The statue of the beast probably will be in the likeness of the seventh one since it will be his body that has been resurrected. But who is the beast, (the eighth), the one who comes out of the pit and indwells the body of the seventh? It must be kept in mind that Paul chose not to reveal the identity the beast in his second letter. Paul knew who the beast was and so did the Thessalonians. He had told them already, so it was not necessary for him to identify the beast publicly. While future readers may be puzzled as to the identity of the lawless one, the Thessalonians were not. The following scenario should simplify the matter: Two friends meet in a supermarket and Mr. Smith says to Mrs. Jones, "I found this letter in the parking lot and it doesn't make any sense whatsoever; I can make neither heads nor tails of it." He hands the letter to Mrs. Jones. After reading it she smiles warmly and says, "Oh, I am sure this letter belongs to our Pastor. I saw him in the parking lot not more than five minutes ago; he evidently dropped it as he was getting out of his car. It is signed by the man who spoke at our church on Sunday morning. I happened to be present and fully understand what the letter is all about. It is no big secret. If you had been there, the letter would make perfect sense to you. He explained everything when he was with us. Sorry you were not there. Have a nice day." Mr. Smith walks away, scratching his head, still puzzled as to the meaning of the letter.

We read Paul's second letter today and are just as mystified as Mr. Smith as to what the letter means because we were not present when Paul said, "I have told you and now you know" the beast's identity. We have scratched our heads trying to understand what he meant. Paul, on the one hand, had no need to explain the beast's identity to the Thessalonians. But, on the other hand, he may intentionally not have revealed it to anyone other than the Thessalonians, leaving a mystery for others to figure out, because the beast (the fifth one of the five who had fallen in Rev. 17:10) was alive and had not yet died and been confined to the pit. Paul may not have wanted to endanger himself or other believers.

Reveal the beast's identity. John says that the following three characteristic features can positively identify the beast: the number of the beast; the nationality of the beast; and the nature of the beast.

The number of the beast. The number is threefold: succession, possession, and composition. The order of succession is presented in Revelation 17:8-13. In the first part of the Chapter, one of the seven angels directs John's attention to a woman riding a scarlet beast; the beast has seven heads and ten horns (v3). The vision is a mystery to John (vv 4-6) and the angel explains the mystery to him (v7). In verse 8 the angel tells John "The beast that you saw was, and is not, and is about to come up out of the abyss and go to destruction." The world will wonder when this event occurs because it will be so unusual as to appear miraculous. The angel explains further, saying, "Here is the mind which has wisdom. The seven heads are seven mountains on which the woman sits, and they are seven kings..." (vv9, 10). Then the angel gives John the beast's number of succession, "...five have fallen, one is, the other has not yet come; and when he comes, he must remain a little while. The beast which was and is not, is himself also an eighth and is one of the seven, and he goes to destruction" (vv 10,11). The most simple and sensible of all comments written on the succession of the Roman emperors are those of Smith:

The seven heads of the beast signify seven kings, and since a beast has only one head at a given time it is clear that the seven kings rule successively, not simultaneously. This much is implied also from the fact that Rome was an imperial power and that universal dominion was vested in one imperial head, namely, the emperor ruling at a given time. The seven heads therefore refer to seven particular emperors of Rome. These points become increasingly plain.

Five are fallen. The word fallen implies that these died an unnatural death as by violence. Cf. Judges 3:25; II Samuel 1: 19, 25; 3:38. The thought then is that when John wrote five of the kings or emperors had died a violent death. It is true that of the twelve Caesars, all but one—Domitian, the one then reigning—had died when John wrote. However, three of these—Galba, Otho, and Vitellius—met violent deaths within the years 68 and 69, and Augustus, Vespasian, and Titus died natural deaths. For those reasons the six mentioned do not enter into the prophetic picture. Additional reasons might also disqualify them from consideration; for example, these kings did not blaspheme (13:1) nor deify themselves as did the rest. While some of his subjects apparently worshiped Augustus, Tertullian expressly states that Augustus refused the title "Lord."[12]

The following figure is a sketch of the beast with seven heads and ten horns (Rev. 17:8-13), a depiction of John's order of succession. I have "blocked" the verses, encircled each head, and depicted the ten horns, up from which the "little horn" will arise.

THE BEAST WITH SEVEN HEADS AND TEN HORNS

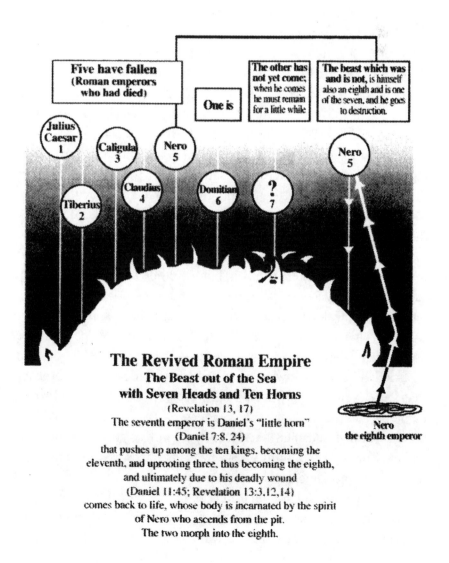

Five have fallen
(Roman emperors
who had died)

One is

The other has
not yet come;
when he comes
he must remain
for a little while

The beast which was
and is not, is himself
also an eighth and is one
of the seven, and he goes
to destruction.

Julius Caesar 1

Caligula 3

Nero 5

Nero 5

Tiberius 2

Claudius 4

Domitian 6

? 7

The Revived Roman Empire
The Beast out of the Sea
with Seven Heads and Ten Horns
(Revelation 13, 17)
The seventh emperor is Daniel's "little horn"
(Daniel 7:8, 24)
that pushes up among the ten kings, becoming the
eleventh, and uprooting three, thus becoming the eighth,
and ultimately due to his deadly wound
(Daniel 11:45; Revelation 13:3,12,14)
comes back to life, whose body is incarnated by the spirit
of Nero who ascends from the pit.
The two morph into the eighth.

Nero
the eighth emperor

According to Revelation, chapters 13 and 17, the beast out of the sea with seven heads and ten horns is the revived Roman Empire. The seventh emperor is Daniel's "little horn," (Dan. 7: 8, 24), that pushes up among the ten horns (kings), becoming the eleventh. During the process, he uproots three, becoming the eighth, and ultimately due to his deadly wound (Dan. 11:45; Rev. 13:3, 12, 14) comes back to life. His body is incarnated by the spirit of Nero that ascends from the pit and morphs into the eighth. Thus, Nero becomes the eighth emperor.

As stated by Smith, emperors Galba, Otho, Vitellius, Augustus and Vespasian are not to be considered as part of the prophecy. The five kings who had fallen (met violent deaths) and been deified were: (1) Julius Caesar, (2) Tiberius, (3) Gaius Caligula, (4) Claudius, and (5) Nero. Nero, the fifth and eighth king, is presently in the abyss (the it that holds fast) awaiting his time to be revealed (II Thess. 2: 6, 8). Again, recall what Machen said above concerning the participle, to katechon: "The tense of the participle is relative to the time of the leading verb. The present participle, therefore, is used if the action denoted by the participle is represented as taking place at the same time as the action denoted by the leading verb, no matter whether the action denoted by the leading verb is past, present or future." Also remember that the leading verb is the infinitive, to be revealed, which is future.

Nero was not dead at the time Paul wrote to the Thessalonians and, therefore, had not entered the pit, but would do so upon his death by suicide. His body would go to the grave, but his spirit would go to the pit, there to await his revealing at which time he would become "an eighth." It is not known for sure why Paul did not divulge his name, but chose to describe him as "...the man of lawlessness," "the son of destruction," and "the lawless one." As I mentioned before, it is probable that since Nero was still alive Paul purposely avoided revealing his name because he knew that the madness of the emperor would have been unleashed, causing great difficulty for himself, the Thessalonians, and the Christian community as a whole. Peter may have used the same method of concealment in I Peter 5:13.

If IPeter was written by the Apostle Peter prior to his death under Nero, as the traditional view states, there may be a very specific analogy implied by the use of the terms "Babylon" and "Diaspora." Tacitus seems to imply that the Neronian persecution, unlike those that followed, was directed only against Christians in Rome. If this is true, certainly as many Christians as possible would have fled the city, as the Quo Vadis story states. Peter shows evidence of having been written to just such a group of Christians. Peter refers twice to the readers as "sojourners," or as other translations say, "refugees," "pilgrims," or "exiles" (I Pet. 1:1, 2:11). In addition, Peter uses a similar word when he refers to the time of the readers' "sojourning" (I Pet. 1:17). Although these words are usually considered metaphorical, some writers, e.g. Salmon, interpret them literally.

> This may explain Peter's use of the name "Babylon" in referring to Rome. Babylon was the great world power which made war against God's nation, Judah, and dispersed its people throughout the world. Similarly, Rome had dispersed God's nation, the Christians. In this analogy, then, the Christians would correspond to the Diaspora, and Rome to Babylon.
>
> . . . .
>
> If I Peter was written to refugees from Rome, this may also explain the need for Peter to use figurative names for the origin and destination of the epistle. Obviously, Peter could not have said, "I am writing this from Rome to those who have fled to Asia Minor to avoid prosecution as criminals." And yet this is the message he would have needed to convey to the readers, without conveying it to the Romans. What better way could there be to do this than through the analogy of Babylon and the Dispersion?[13]

Nero eventually would have Paul and Peter put to death toward the end of the Neronic Persecution, A.D. 64-68. Later, when John wrote Revelation he would use the figurative term, "the beast" (*to therion*), rather than the name, Nero, to conceal the fact that he was referring to the wicked emperor, even though Nero already was dead. He knew that if he named either of the emperors as "the beast" there would be serious repercussions. His intent was the same as that of Paul and Peter—to protect not only himself, but also Christians in general.

Like Paul and Peter, John knew the identity of the beast, as his use of the definite article, *to* (the), with the word, *therion* (beast) would indicate. John's use of the article with the noun sets "the beast" apart from any other. The beast of which John writes is not a beast, but *the beast*, a definite one—one that was identifiable to him. As with Paul and Peter, John's knowledge of Old Testament prophecy and what had been revealed to them in their present day concerning beasts would most certainly give him enough wisdom and insight to recognize the one of whom Daniel prophesied (Dan. 7:2-25; 9:27; 11:35-45). The interpreting angel of Revelation 11:7; 13; and 17 was, no doubt, the angel, Gabriel, who interpreted the beasts to Daniel. Obviously, Daniel and John were given the same information, but John was given more detail and, therefore, was able to identify the exact person of whom Daniel had prophesied, but who had not as yet appeared on the scene during Daniels time. The beast was not alive at the time John was given the information by the angel, but the beast had lived and John knew who he was; "The beast that you saw," says the angel, "was and is not, and is about to come up out of the abyss .... The beast which was and is not, is himself also an eighth and is one of the seven ..." (Rev. 17:8, 11).

Based on all the prophecies and explanations of those prophecies by Paul, Peter, and John having to do with "the beast," his death and resurrection, it is fully understandable how those early Christians believed that Nero would return from the dead with beast-like cruelty. Some may criticize this writer for holding to the same view as the early Christians—that Nero would return from the dead—but others will agree. Those who disagree are to be classed among those who have been neglectful of the beast passages in Daniel and Revelation, especially Revelation 13:18, where it is Nero's name John means to be calculated. John was simply too aware of the succession of the emperors (as were Paul and Peter) not to know which of the seven was the beast. If all the notorious figures of history were taken to court and all the evidence presented as to which one is the beast, Nero would be convicted. While one may speculate and try to guess as to who the seventh one will be, there is no sure way of knowing until he appears on the scene; but as to identification of the eighth, the convicting evidence points its finger at the villain, Nero, and says, "You are the prisoner from the pit; you are the eighth, and you are the beast!" Those who would challenge John's order of succession by attempting to interpret the beast's identity apart from the fact that the seven heads of the beast from the sea and the "an eighth" from the pit are other than Roman emperors (the succession is on Roman ground only), are unwise in doing so.

The number of possession. It will be seen that Nero is the only one of the five whose name and number exactly solves John's riddle, ".... Let him who has understanding calculate the number of the beast, for the number is that of a man and his number is six hundred and sixty-six." Those who seek to interpret Revelation 13:18 apart from Revelation 17: 8-11 will find themselves entangled in a mass of wild speculation and fantasy, so it behooves one to apply John's "his number is six hundred and sixty-six" to one of the "five who have fallen" in 17:10, 11, otherwise identity becomes impossible.

That John may have been thinking of the Hebrew form for the name of Nero is explained by Smith, "The name Nero Caesar does not occur in Revelation; in fact, nowhere in the New Testament except in the postscript to II Timothy in the Authorized Version, where it occurs in the Hebrew form Kaisar Neron. Had John used the name, he doubtless would have written it with the Hebrew endings as he does the other names, viz., Abaddon, Apollyon, and Armageddon, in which the second to last letter is a long o."[14, 15] The early Hebrews used each letter of the Hebrew alphabet to represent a number, e.g., Aleph = 1, Beth = 2, etc. Since John was Jewish and familiar with the numerical value of each letter and already knew the name of the beast, he simply directed his readers to use the same system to reckon the number and name of the beast. No mystery was attached to the process; it required only the wisdom to know the numerical equivalent of each Hebrew letter and how to apply the value of each letter to whatever name was being considered. One could assign a number to any biblical word. Take the Hebrew word, pregnancy (*herayon*), for instance. If John had wanted his readers to figure out the exact number of days of a woman's pregnancy, he might have said something like, "Let him who understands calculate the number of months of a woman's pregnancy for the number of pregnancy is 270." Two hundred seventy is the equivalent to 9 months, and 270 divided by 9 = 30, which is the number of days for a biblical month. It isn't rocket science.

Smith has his own explanation above, but the author's table below is meant to simplify Revelation 13:18, "Let him who has wisdom reckon the number of the beast, for it is the number of a man and his number is 666."Compare with Revelation 17:7-13. Following are four columns, each reading vertically. Column (1) lists the Hebrew consonants . The name is one word in the Hebrew, but if divided, as at the top of the chart, the English equivalent under it, reading from right to left, would read NORN RSK. The English in reverse would read KSR NRON. If read from left to right according to the English consonants with vowels supplied, it would read, KaeSaR NeRON. The vowels, with the exception of the "O" are not supplied in the Hebrew. Column (2) lists in English the name of each Hebrew consonant. Column (3) lists the letters of the English alphabet equivalent to each Hebrew consonant, and Column (4) lists the numerical equivalent of each consonant, ending with the total, 666.

קסר נרונ

NORN RSK

ק	Koph	K	100
ס	Samek	S	60
ר	Resh	R	200
נ	Nun	N	50
ר	Resh	R	200
ו	O	Waw	6
נ	Nun	N	<u>50</u>
		Total	666

Again, Revelation 13:18 reads, "Here is wisdom. Let him who has understanding calculate the number of the beast, for the number is that of a man; and his number is six hundred and sixty-six." The transliterated reading in the Greek text for six hundred and sixty-six is *hexakosioi hexekonta hex*, which are the following three Greek letters: *hexakosioi* is Chi = 600; *hexekonta* is Xi = 60; and *hex* is Sigma = 6. It is important to note that one should not apply the above calculation to the seventh one, since he appears on the scene at the beginning of the seven years and makes the covenant with Israel. That would be unwise because the above formula has to do only with the calculation of the number of the name of the beast, the fifth and the eighth.

The number of composition. It is a union. of the spirit of the fifth, "the beast which was and is not" who "is himself also an eighth" who "is one of the seven," with the body of the seventh, "the other," who "has not yet come." To re-emphasize: the spirit of the fifth and the eighth are one and the same, Nero, and are not relative to the seventh until he (Nero) ascends from the pit, where he is at present, and becomes incarnate in the dead body of the seventh.

The nationality of the beast. This is another important factor in determining his identity. The following relationship with the seventh one in particular reveals that he must be a Roman in order to fulfill those prophecies that predict his national origin.

The Roman "little horn" rises from the midst of ten kings who make up the revived Roman Empire, thus becoming the eleventh. But after subduing three of those ten kings he becomes the eighth (Dan. 7: 8-11, 24, 25). The "little horn," who becomes the eighth king of Daniel 7 is prophetic of the composite character of the seventh and "an eighth" in Revelation 17: 10-11. In order to fulfill Daniel's prophecy the beast must be a Roman.

The "little horn" of Daniel 7, with whom the eighth morphs in Revelation 17:10-11, is also a Roman prince, "the prince who shall come." "The people of the prince..." in Daniel 9:26b and Titus were the Romans who destroyed Jerusalem in 70 A. D. "...the prince who shall come" was not Titus, but another prince, the rider on the white horse, the seventh one, who appears on the scene in Revelation 6:2; 17:10, who makes and breaks the covenant with Israel, the covenant of Hell and Death (Isa. 28: 14-18; Dan. 9: 27a, b).

The "prince who shall come" is a Roman emperor, the seventh emperor, "the seventh who has not yet come" (Rev. 17:10), and follows Domitian in the line of succession. He is a different emperor than the other six: Julius Caesar, Tiberius, Gaius Caligula, Claudius, Nero, and Domitian—but still a Roman. He is not the same individual as Nero, the "one who shall come on the wings of abomination" (Dan. 26c), but his body will be indwelt by the spirit of Nero. He will be assassinated and receive the deadly wound at the close of the 3-1/2 years of the seventieth week, thus ending his "little while" (Dan. 11:40-45; Rev. 13:3; 17; 10). He will be resurrected when the spirit of the fifth (Nero, an eighth) comes out of the abyss and enters his body. The two shall become one, his deadly wound will be healed and the beast from the abyss will take on the semblance of the seventh. The world will believe "the lie" (II Thess. 2:10-12) that the seventh has returned from the dead and can be no less than God, as proclaimed by the false prophet. The whole world will wonder at the beast. When the spirit of Nero enters the body of the seventh, the personality of the seventh will not be the same as it was before he received the deadly wound. His nature will have changed from a man of peace (Rev. 6:2), albeit a false peace, to that of the Roman emperor, Nero.

His nature is described by figures of speech. His nature is that of a beast. John uses two words for beast. Rev. 4:6 has *zoa*, which means "living creatures," but John uses a different word for beast when referring to the beast from the abyss; the word is, *therion*, and indicates a wild ferocious beast (Rev. 11:7; 13:1-18; 14:9-11; 15:2; 16:2; 17:3-17; 19:19-20; 20:4,10). This ferocity will be unleashed during the last half of the Tribulation. His nature will be that of evil personified: lawlessness, destruction, blasphemy, lies, deception, wickedness, and falsehood, all of which brings one back to the passage identifying "the thing that holds fast" (the pit or the abyss) and its object, the lawless one, Nero (2Thess. 2:1-12). Historically, Nero was one of the worst persecutors of God's people, Jew and Christian alike.

Not only will his nature be that of a beast and evil personified, he will exhibit the nature of a warrior. The warrior nature of the seventh one, who rode forth in peace, but "to conquer and to conquer" (Dan. 11:36-45; Rev. 6:2) will become the expertise of the eighth, thus constituting him a warrior par-excellence. The prominence of his military genius is revealed in Revelation 13:3-10; 16:13-16; 17:14; 19:19. Satan's power over him indicates that his reason for existence is only for the purpose of waging war against God's people. His nature will reveal him as being all of history's wicked dictators rolled into one. He will dictate his policies to ten underling dictators who will in turn see that those policies are implemented. It is important that the seven emperors are not confused with the ten dictator kings. The emperors (seven heads) are set forth by John to identify the beast (an eighth) and show his relationship to the seventh emperor, both of which are of Roman origin and are to come out of the revived Roman Empire. As for the ten kings, John states their purpose:

> "The ten horns which you saw are ten kings who have not yet received a kingdom, but they receive authority as kings with the beast for one hour. These have one purpose, and they give their power and authority to the beast. These will wage war against the Lamb, and the Lamb will overcome them, because He is Lord of lords and King of kings, and those who are with Him are the called and chosen and faithful." And he *said to me, "The waters which you saw where the harlot sits, are peoples and multitudes and nations and tongues. And the ten horns which you saw, and the beast, these will hate the harlot and will make her desolate and naked, and will eat her flesh and will burn her up with fire. For God has put it in their hearts to execute His purpose by having a common purpose, and by giving their kingdom to the beast, until the words of God will be fulfilled. The woman whom you saw is the great city, which reigns over the kings of the earth." (Rev. 17:12-18)

The woman, the great city, is Rome, who reigns over the cities of the earth. Rome reigned supreme during John's day and will do so in the future. Her authority will extend over ten regions of the earth. It is difficult to tell at this point how the regions will be divided, but the process already has started. The common market nations probably will comprise one region that may, in fact, be the model for the other nine. Some believe that at this very moment there are plans to erase the borders of America, Canada, and Mexico, creating one region having one common continental border, all under the guise of providing security for the three North American countries. Each country eventually will lose its sovereignty and the three will become North America—no more America, Canada or Mexico—and it is possible that this is the reason why no action has been taken to close the borders of the United States. (All of the candidates seeking to be elected in 2016 promise that they will close the borders; but will that happen?) Many members of Congress are in agreement with the plan to merge the three nations under one great North American system of government, and it behooves all who are interested in our national sovereignty to read The Late Great USA: The Coming Merger with Mexico and Canada by Jerome R. Corsi.[16] If what Mr. Corsi writes is true, we could be seeing the beginning of the process that eventually will bring the North American continent under the authority of one of the ten kings whose authority will be delegated by the beast.

In conclusion, the reason for having presented the arguments above has been to fully identify the Antichrist (the one who appears on the scene in Revelation 6:2), with the beast who will rise from the abyss. Before his identity could be established, it was imperative to set forth evidential proof that the Holy Spirit is not the Restrainer of II Thessalonians 2. The following evidence was presented: (1) neither *to* [toe] *katechon* nor *ho* [hoe] *katechon* is the same. *To* [toe] *katechon* is inanimate while *ho* [hoe] *katechon* is animate; (2) neither *to* [toe] *katechon* nor *ho* [hoe] *katechon* is the Holy Spirit; (3) *to* [toe] *katechon* is the Restrainer (the abyss, the pit) which presently is "holding fast" the beast, Nero, who will be released in his own "to be revealed time," at the mid-point of the Tribulation; and (4) *ho* [hoe] *katechon* is Satan who presently is "holding fast" to his position in the mid-heavens and will be cast down to earth by Michael the archangel at the middle of the Tribulation (Rev. 12:7-9), at which time he will release the beast from the pit that holds him fast (Rev. 9).

God's wrath will be allowed to do its work through the power allowed Satan who will, in turn, delegate his power to the beast. The "to be revealed time" of the beast will transpire when Satan is removed from his place and cast down to earth, the result of the angelic combat described above (Rev. 9:1-11).

A word to the unwise: The United States is well beyond Barak Obama's first term as President. Because of his evil ambitions, the lack of wisdom on the part of many, and their ignorance of prophecy, especially as to the identification of the Antichrist, Barak Obama has been readily identified as the Antichrist. While Obama has manifest many characteristics of the liar, the man of sin, and the lawless one who is to come, he is definitely not the Antichrist. Based on the evidence presented above the Antichrist will come out of the revived Roman Empire.

Having taken the above circuitous route to identify the Antichrist, chapter VIII will continue with events that relate to him and his diabolical attack against Jerusalem in the not-too-distant future.

CHAPTER VIII

Unfulfilled Prophecies of the Deliverances and Destructions of Jerusalem During the Tribulation

Thus far, I have presented all fulfilled prophecies having to do with Jerusalem's deliverances and destructions, and I also have identified the Antichrist and his Restrainer. It is of paramount importance to present a fair treatment of the *unfulfilled* prophecies having to do with the Antichrist, his conflicts with the nations around him, his relationship to Israel and the city of Jerusalem, and her future destruction and deliverance during the Tribulation.

I. DELIVERANCE OF JERUSALEM FROM THE KING OF THE NORTH AND THE KING OF THE SOUTH

This event precedes the rise of the beast from the pit. The players involved are: (1) the willful king, (2) the king of the south, and (3) the king of the north.

1. THE WILLFUL KING

Chapters 2 and 7- 9 of Daniel are important in tracing and establishing the identity of the willful king in Daniel 11:36-45. A look at those Chapters reveals the following specifics concerning him: (1) the willful king has a kingdom of origin, (2) the willful king is the little horn, (3) the willful King is the king of fierce countenance, (4) the willful king is the prince of the people who shall come, (5) the willful king is not Antiochus Epiphanes, and (6) the willful king is not the king of the north.

The Willful King has a Kingdom of Origin (Daniel 2:39, 40).

The Lord reveals to King Nebuchadnezzar a series of three Gentile kingdoms that will be crushed by a fourth kingdom. "After you, another kingdom will rise, inferior to yours. Next, a third kingdom, one of bronze, will rule over the whole earth. Finally, there will be a fourth kingdom, strong as iron—for iron breaks and smashes everything—and as iron breaks things to pieces, so it will crush and break all the others" (Dan. 2:39,40). There is no doubt that this fourth kingdom is that of the Roman Empire, both in its historical and eschatological form. Historically it immediately followed the kingdom of Greece, described by Daniel as the belly and thighs of bronze, the third kingdom of bronze, a leopard, and a male goat—explicitly identified by Gabriel as "the kingdom of Greece" (Dan. 2:32, 39; 7:6; 8:5,21).

The fourth kingdom will have given birth to the individual who will have come to prominence through a succession of six emperors of the Roman Empire. Domitian ("one is," Rev. 17:10) was the last of the six. The seventh ("the other," who, "has not yet come") will be the self-willed person who will be the seventh emperor of the revived Roman Empire. It is indisputable that the interpreting angel was referring to the Roman Empire: "The seven heads are seven hills on which the woman sits" (Rev. 17:9). Rome sat on seven hills in John's day, and still does today: Palatine Hill, Capitoline Hill, Quirinal Hill, Viminal Hill, Esquiline Hill, Caelian Hill, and Aventine Hill.

The Willful King is the Little Horn (Daniel 7:1-28)

Chapter 7 of Daniel is devoted to the same fourth kingdom discussed above, but is more precise as to the makeup of the kingdom, its ruler, and that ruler's ultimate end. There is every indication that the willful king is the same person Daniel describes earlier as "the little horn." Daniel relates his dream-vision in the first 14 verses and receives an interpretation in verses 15-28. The beast Daniel saw had ten horns on its head that were interpreted by the angel to mean ten kings. An eleventh horn (a little horn, king) pushes up through the ten and subdues three. The subjugation of the three probably corresponds to the phrase in Revelation 6:2, "to conquer and to conquer," which probably means that he would conquer the aforementioned three. The rider on the white horse is seen with an empty bow in his hand, indicating that at his first appearance he comes in peace, but his ultimate purpose is conquest by war. In Revelation 6:2 he is seen as the white-horse rider and in 17:10 as "the other," and "the seventh one who has not yet come" (Rev. 17:10). The subjugation of the three kings is part of the conquering process that eventually positions him (his body) as the eighth. Again, simple math: 10 kings + 1 king = 11 kings - 3 kings = 8 kings.

Gabriel explains virtually the same vision to John:

> "I will explain to you the mystery of the woman and of the beast she rides, which has the seven heads and ten horns. The beast, which you saw, once was, now is not, and will come up out of the Abyss and go to his destruction. The inhabitants of the earth whose names have not been written in the book of life from the creation of the world will be astonished when they see the beast, because he once was, now is not, and yet will come. "This calls for a mind with wisdom. The seven heads are seven hills on which the woman sits. They are also seven kings. Five have fallen, one is, the other has not yet come; but when he does come, he must remain for a little while. The beast who once was, and now is not, is an eighth king. He belongs to the seven and is going to his destruction (Rev. 17:7, 8, NIV).

There is little doubt that Daniel and John saw separately, but primarily the same visions that dovetail with each other. The time factor is the only major difference; Daniel's vision awaited explanation in greater detail by John. Five of the ten horns (emperors/kings) had died already ("five have fallen") while "one is," (Domitian), who was alive as John wrote. After Domitian died, an unknown period of time—a parenthesis—would elapse from Domitian's rule to the appearance of the Willful King. That duration of time so far has lasted approximately 2,000 years, and eventually will end with his appearance. His initial appearance will reveal him to be the rider on the white horse (Rev. 6:2) who will "remain for a little while" (Rev. 17:10). That "little while" will end at the mid-point of his reign, as will be seen in the later discussion of Daniel 11:40-45.

The Willful King is the King of Fierce Countenance (Daniel 8:23-25).

Gabriel tells Daniel that the king of fierce countenance will arise at the latter part of the reign of the kings represented by the four horns in 8:22. Two of those horns were Ptolemy of Egypt and Seleucus of Syria, representing a series of kings known as kings of the south and the kings of the north. Gabriel also tells Daniel that the king of fierce countenance would not be one of these kings, but would arise at the end of their reign in the far distant future (v26).

In Chapter 11:40-45 Daniel provides a clearer picture of what will transpire between the king of fierce countenance and the last in the series of the kings of the south and the kings of the north:

> "At the end time the king of the South will collide with him, and the king of the North will storm against him with chariots, with horsemen and with many ships; and he will enter countries, overflow them and pass through." One also finds in the two Chapters mentioned above that the king of fierce countenance and the willful king are one and the same in that they come to their end at the end time. It is my opinion that the king in 11:45 is the seventh one. He receives his deadly wound following his return to the Beautiful land, having put down the kings of the south and north (11:40). By the time he opposes the Prince of princes (8:25), his deadly wound will have healed, he will have become the eighth—Nero the beast, and he will be destroyed by the Prince of

princes Himself: "Then that lawless one will be revealed whom the Lord will slay with the breath of His mouth and bring to an end by the appearance of His coming..." (II Thess. 2:8).

The Willful King is the Prince of the People who shall come (Daniel 9:25-27).

This passage is a direct link to the "fourth kingdom" (the revived Roman Empire) of Daniel 2, the "little horn" in Daniel 7, and "the king of fierce countenance" in Daniel 8. They are antecedent and equivalent to the one who is here brought into view, "the prince who will come." "The people of the prince who will come will destroy the city and the sanctuary..." History shows that "the people of the prince" were the Romans who destroyed Jerusalem in 70 A.D., and any other conclusion would be ludicrous. "The prince who shall come," of whom Daniel writes, is a future Roman ruler who will rise from the revived Roman Empire. He will come on the scene sometime following the parenthesis between the 69th and 70th weeks of the prophecy. The parenthesis is the same as that which occurs between the death of Domitian ("one who is") and the seventh, "the other who has not yet come" (Rev. 17:10). This "prince who will come" will ride forth as the rider on the white horse (Rev. 6:2) and, as Daniel's interpreting angel says, "Then he shall confirm a covenant with many for one week; But in the middle of the week he shall bring an end to sacrifice and offering" (Dan. 9:27). The covenant is a treaty of peace (promised security) the prince will make with Israel for one week (a week of years = 7 yrs.), and during the first half (3-1/2 years) of that treaty, Israel will be allowed to rebuild the Temple.

The Willful King is Not Antiochus Epiphanes.

The identification of this individual is not difficult since we are told that he will arise at the time of the end, long after the period of history that deals with Antiochus Epiphanes (Dan. 8:9-14; 11:21-35). Antiochus may have been a type of this one—attacking Jerusalem, persecuting the Jews, and desecrating the temple by offering a pig on the altar—but the Willful King, the anti-type, appears at a later time and must not be confused with Epiphanes, the earlier enemy of God and His people. Many years would elapse from Daniel 11:35 to "the time of the end," the time when the wicked king would appear on the scene (vv 36-45). This wicked king already had been mentioned in Daniel 8:23-25, following the account of Antiochus in verses 9-14.

2. THE KING OF THE SOUTH AND THE KING OF THE NORTH

Following the death of Alexander the Great, his kingdom was divided between four of his generals, the two most prominent being Ptolemy and Seleucus. Ptolemy became ruler of Egypt (the South) and Seleucus ruled Syria (the North), thus the terms "king of the South" and "king of the North." These kings engaged in constant intrigue and warfare. Daniel 11:2-45 presents a brief historical account of those wars. The two Kings of vv 40-45 of Daniel are the last in the series and they will become active at "the time of the end" when the Willful King begins to exert himself (Dan. 11:36-39).

The King of the South

"At the time of the end the king of the South shall attack him; and the king of the North shall come against him like a whirlwind, with chariots, horsemen, and with many ships..." (Dan. 11:40). Verse 40 seems to be an introductory statement as to what will transpire from verses 41-45. We are told this event takes place "at the time of the end." The time of the end is the last half (3-1/2 years) of Daniel's seventieth week of seven years. The two kings will engage the Willful King in battle, but the text does not say that they will attack him at the same time. The king of the South will do battle with him and shortly thereafter the king of the North will attack him.

It is difficult to determine the event sparking the battle between Egypt (the king of the South) and the Willful King. I believe that battle will begin sometime after Russia and her allies are destroyed (Ezek.

38-39). The Willful King already will have made the 7-year covenant with Israel under the guise of protecting her from any future enemy attempting to invade her as did Russia. At the mid-point of the 7-year-covenant period (approximately 3-1/2 years later) Egypt will threaten Israel and the Willful King because of his covenant with her. Then the Willful King will move from his place in Europe, enter the Beautiful Land" (Palestine) and begin his drive south where "many countries" fall to him. He will skirt Edom, Moab, and Jordan (Dan. 11:41) because of the urgency of the situation with Egypt. It should be remembered that Edom, Moab, and Jordan will be spared because the Jewish remnant must have a place to which it can escape the awful impending persecution by the beast (Rev. 12:13-17).

Petra, the great rock-city fortress to which that remnant will flee, is located in Edom. Egypt will be moved to attack him because his actions will pose a serious threat. Consequently, the king of the South will collide with him somewhere in the vicinity north of the Sinai Peninsula. The word "collide" in the Hebrew is *nagach*, and means to move in a linear motion to pierce through by goring. The picture here is similar to that in Daniel 8:4 where the male goat was seen rushing over the ground to gore the ram (Dan. 8:3-8). Egypt's intent will be to defeat and destroy the Willful King, however; the latter will defeat the Egyptian army and her Arab allies and move into Egypt (Dan. 11:42-43). "But, while he is in Egypt rumors from the East and from the North will disturb him, and he will go forth with great wrath to destroy and annihilate many" (Dan. 11:44). The word "rumors," (*shemuw'ah*), can mean both good and bad news. Since what he hears is disturbing, it is bad news from the East and the North.

The news from the east is probably a reference to the armies of the kings of the "sun rising" mentioned in Revelation 16:12: "The angel poured out his bowl on the great river, Euphrates; and its water was dried up, so that the way would be prepared for the kings from the east." John says, "The number of the armies of the horsemen was 200 million; I heard the number of them" (Rev. 9:16). The multitudinous oriental army will have been held in abeyance by four angels until the battle of Armageddon (Rev. 9:15; 16:16). To date it is difficult to imagine any other oriental nation than China leading such a horde. She is a prime candidate because of her location and standing army, however, Korea should not be ruled out. The Willful King will be pressured by the marshaled forces of the eastern army to bestir himself, return to the Beautiful Land, and position himself to protect his interest when the onslaught begins. He will think, as will they, that their intention is to attack him, but the truth of the matter is that the spirits of demons will be working behind the scenes to gather them for the great battle of Armageddon (Rev. 16:13-16). Thus, "He will pitch the tents of his royal pavilion between the seas and the beautiful Holy Mountain; yet he will come to his end, and no one will help him" (Dan. 11:46). Again, I believe that the words "yet he will come to his end" do not refer to the destruction of the beast at the coming of Christ (cf. Dan. 7:11b; II Thess. 2:8; Rev. 16:13-16; 19: 20). The one who comes to his end in this incident is the "little horn" whom Gabriel interpreted in Daniel 7:24-25 and whom John saw as a rider on the white horse in Revelation 6:2. "...he will come to his end" means that at this point in his career, he receives the "deadly wound" of Revelation 13:3a. This is the only place in the Bible where there may be a hint as to when and how he receives "the deadly wound" from which he will be healed, thus becoming the eighth—the beast.

The evidence presented above leaves no doubt that the Willful King arises out of the Roman Empire and is the same individual as the little horn, the king of fierce countenance, the prince of the people who is to come; and he is neither Antiochus Epiphanes nor the king of the north.

The King of the North

Since the kings of the South and the North have been identified as those kings which made up the Ptolemaic (Egyptian) and Seluecide (Syrian) empires, and since each of them retained the same identification throughout the verses leading up to Daniel 11:40-45, there is no justification for believing them to be otherwise. The king of the South has been identified as Egypt (Dan. 11:8). The king of the North is not identified as Syria, but it is well known that Alexander's general, Seleucus, took control of the Syrian empire following Alexander's death, and the appellation *north* encompasses all of the ancient lands (including Syria) making up the Assyrian empire, an ancient enemy of Israel from the north. Syria could very well be the leader of those nations now occupying that area of the ancient Assyrian empire who will move "like a whirlwind" against the Willful King following his defeat of Egypt, the king of the South.

Scholarly opinion differs as to whether the king of the North is Russia (and it is not my intention to rehash them here), but it is difficult to fit Russia into the boundaries of the ancient Assyrian empire and the context of Daniel 11. Russia's aim is to attack Israel, not the Willful King; and besides, it is understood that the 7-year covenant between the Willful King and Israel will not be in place before Russia's move from the far north. Consequently, there would be no reason for him to become involved with Russia. She will have attacked from "the uttermost parts of the north" and been destroyed by the time the events of Daniel 11:40-45 occur. The King of the North (Syria and her allies—possibly Iraq and Iran) will attack the Willful King from the northern borders of Israel. "The king of the North will storm against him with chariots, with horsemen and with many ships," just as Israel's northern enemies did in the past (Isa. 5:28; Jer. 4:13). This will be a land attack and Keil has provided an explanation of the curious term "with many ships": "The words, 'with chariots, and with horsemen, and with many ships,' are an oratorical exemplification of the powerful war-host which the king of the north displayed; for the further statement, 'he presses into the countries, overflows and passes over' does not agree with the idea of a fleet, but refers to land forces."[1] However, since Keil commented, Iraq and Iran have the ability to employ ships for warfare. One cannot rule out the use of ships against the Willful King.

The Willful King will prosper (be successful) "until the indignation is finished." The phrase, "until the indignation is finished" in Daniel 11:36b coupled with "and he shall come to his end" in Daniel 11:45 seems to blend the career of "the little horn" during the first 3-1/2 years with that of "the eighth" in Daniel 7. To repeat: "The little horn" comes to his end in Daniel 11:45, but he sees them as one and the same throughout the seven-year period of the Tribulation. The "little horn," (the Willful King) will not survive, but "he will come to his end" at the end of the first 3-1/2 years; he will be killed, "receive the deadly wound" of Revelation 13:3a. His death clears the stage for the beast (the eighth).

II. DESTRUCTION AND DELIVERANCE OF JERUSALEM FROM THE ARMIES OF THE BEAST AND THE ARMIES OF THE EAST

The body of the Willful King will lie in state for 3 days and nights, an exact counterfeit of the 3 days and nights the body of the Lord Jesus was in tomb, proving to the world that he is dead. The beast (the spirit of Nero) will be released from the pit ("the *it* that holds fast," I Thess. 2:6; Rev. 9:1ff; 11: 7; 13: 1ff; 17:7-13) and enter the body of the Willful King, bringing the body to life and healing the deadly wound (Rev. 13:3b, 12). The beast (the eighth of Rev. 17: 9-12) will be on earth once more, in the body of the Willful King (the rider on the white horse of Rev. 6:2, the seventh who had not come, but at his coming was to remain for a little while). Everyone marvels at this event; the false prophet proclaims the Willful King to be God, and the world believes, until his true nature is revealed and he sets out to destroy the city of Jerusalem.

One point should be made here relative to the archangel Michael and the destruction of Jerusalem by the beast at the time of the end. Gabriel told Daniel, "Now at that time Michael the prince who stands guard over the sons of thy people will arise." Michael was standing guard over Israel at the time Gabriel was speaking and in his role as guardian of Israel he had assisted Gabriel in his battle against the Prince of Persia. But what of the end time, the time of wrath when the beast is released from the pit (Dan. 12:1)? One can hardly deduce from Michael's actions when he casts Satan to the earth that he does it for Israel's protection: "Woe to the earth and the sea, for the devil has come down to you, having great wrath" (Rev. 12:12). "And there will be a time of distress such as never occurred since there was a nation until that time..." (Dan. 12:1b). If Michael casts Satan to the earth and Satan's man, the beast, is allowed to persecute Israel for the whole of 3-1/2 years, at what point will Michael defend Daniel's people? Certainly not at the beginning of the time of trouble; Gabriel expressly states that the time of trouble must transpire. Israel will not be delivered until after the time of trouble so how can it be said that Michael will stand up and deliver Israel before the time of trouble begins? The answer, of course, depends upon the meaning of the word "arise." It makes no sense for Gabriel to tell Daniel that Michael will arise to defend his people and then allow them to suffer persecution. There are various shades of meaning of the word "arise" (*amad*). Strong's Concordance has the following:

5975—Amad

1a1) to stand, take one's stand, be in a standing attitude, stand forth, take a stand, present oneself, attend upon, be or become servant of

1a2) *to stand still, stop (moving or doing), cease* [italics mine]

1a3) to tarry, delay, remain, continue, abide, endure, persist, be steadfast

1a4) to make a stand, hold one's ground

1a5) to stand upright, remain standing, stand up, rise, be erect, be upright

1a6) to arise, appear, come on the scene, stand forth, appear, rise up or against

1a7) to stand with, take one's stand, be appointed, grow flat, grow insipid[2]

The italics (1a2) in the above list are mine, emphasizing what Gabriel no doubt meant when he said that Michael would "arise," *amad*. With this in mind, the following paraphrase of Daniel 12:1 is offered: "Now at the time of the end, Michael, the great prince who normally stands guard over Israel, will stand aside, stop (moving or doing), cease on Israel's behalf in order to allow for a time of trouble such as had never taken place since there was a nation until the time of the end; and at that time every one of your people, who are found written in the book, shall be rescued." The above meaning also is found in Job 32:16, where Job speaks about his friends, "Shall I wait, because they do not speak, because they stop and no longer answer?" The word "stop" is *amad* (stand). Job's friends were standing and at the same time had ceased speaking. Michael will remain standing, but inactive, during the time of the following trouble. There will be no intervention on Israel's behalf by Michael until the coming of Christ, when the Lord breaks through the heavens with His mighty army of holy angels, led by Michael, to deliver Israel from the beast (Matt. 24: 29-31; II Thess. 2:8).

1. DESTRUCTION OF JERUSALEM BY THE BEAST

The appellation, beast, is to be applied to both the rider (the seventh one) on the white horse of Revelation 2:6 and the (an eighth) from the pit because the composite character of the two demands it, especially since the controlling force of the body of the seventh one is that of the spirit of Nero. The only time John refers to the coming enemy of God and His people as Antichrist is in I John 2:18-22, but in the book of Revelation he uses the term, the beast, no less than 31 times. The release of the beast, an eighth, and his embodiment of the body of the seventh, who has not as yet appeared on the scene, clears up much confusion relative to the name Antichrist. From his birth, his riding forth in Revelation 6:2, his making the false covenant with Israel in Daniel 9:27, and his death in Daniel 11: 40-45, the seventh one is the Antichrist. One may recall Paul's words to the Galatians: "But when the fullness of the time came, God sent forth His Son, born of a woman..." (Gal. 4: 4). When the time was right, God brought His Son, Jesus Christ, into the world and so it will be with the Antichrist. When the time is right, Satan will bring forth his man, who will be born of a woman. No one knows when that birth will occur—it may already have happened. Just as there was a body prepared for the Word (Heb. 10:5) who was spirit in the form of God as to His form before He became incarnate, so there will be a body prepared for the beast (the spirit of Nero), maybe a body resembling that of Nero when Nero was previously on the earth.

When the spirit of the beast Nero ascends from the pit and indwells his body, the "risen" seventh takes on the nature of the beast. Release from the pit and fusion of the spirit of the beast with the body of the seventh will unleash the worst enemy Israel has ever known. There is no way of knowing for sure what the physical aspect of the seventh will be, but when the fusion occurs, the result will be Nero's spirit in the flesh. After His death and resurrection, Jesus ascended back to Heaven and as He went the angel told His disciples that the "same Jesus" would return (Acts 1: 9-11); When He returns Israel will recognize Him as the same person (Zech. 12:10; Rev. 1: 7). Nero may also be recognized as the same in the body of the seventh. Once again Israel will be face-to-face with her old enemy, Nero. Like Jesus who said, "I am the Alpha and the

Omega ... who is and who was and who is to come, the Almighty" (Rev. 1:8), Nero "was and is to come." He will set himself in the temple of God and proclaim himself God, the Almighty (II Thess. 2:4; Rev. 17:8, 11). The second coming of Nero will be Satan's counterfeit of the Second Coming of Christ, the difference being that Nero will return to destroy Jerusalem and her people, whereas Jesus will return to deliver them; and so "... shall all Israel be saved" (Rom. 11:25-27; Rev. 19:11-21).

Before her Deliverer returns to Zion, Jerusalem will be faced with the most horrific period of her history. When the great opponent of God and His people goes forth to destroy Jerusalem, the time of which the Prophet Jeremiah prophesied will be upon her: "'Alas! for that day is great, There is none like it; And it is the time of Jacob's distress, But he will be saved from it.'" (Jer 30:7). Jesus spoke of it in Matthew 24:21-22: "For then shall be great tribulation, such as hath not been from the beginning of the world until now, no, nor ever shall be. And except those days had been shortened, no flesh would have been saved: but for the elect's sake, those days shall be shortened."

Three acts of the beast result in the destruction of Jerusalem: (1) desecration of the Temple of Jerusalem, (2) death of the two witnesses in Jerusalem and (3) dispossession of the city of Jerusalem.

Desecration of the Temple of Jerusalem

The beast's first act of wickedness will be to install himself in the temple of God. This cannot be said of the "little horn," the Willful King in Daniel 11:36. Paul said that he "opposes and exalts himself above every so-called god or object of worship, so that he takes his seat in the temple of God, displaying himself as being God" (II Thess. 2:4). This act of desecration takes place after the beast ascends from the pit (Rev. 17:8; 9:1ff; Dan. 9:27b) and incarnates himself in the body of the one who makes the covenant (Dan. 9:27a), who is the white-horse Rider of Revelation 6:2 (the seventh king of Revelation 17:9 who comes "for a little while," "the Willful King" of Daniel 11:36-45). As previously mentioned, "his seat" probably will be the mercy seat in the Holy of Holies, the seat of God Himself. Then the false prophet proclaims him God, but because the people reject the truth, the true God "will send upon them a deluding influence so that they will believe what is false, the lie" (II Thess. 2:10, 11). The false prophet directs the people of the earth to erect an image of the beast and to fall down and worship it. Undoubtedly, many images of the wicked and lawless one will be setup throughout the world and anyone who refuses to worship him will be put to death. We see them later: "Then I saw thrones, and they sat on them, and judgment was given to them. And I saw the souls of those who had been beheaded because of their testimony of Jesus and because of the word of God, and those who had not worshiped the beast or his image, and had not received the mark on their forehead and on their hand; and they came to life and reigned with Christ for a thousand years" (Revelation 20:4). As stated in Revelation 13:11ff, those who do not receive the mark of the beast will not be able to buy or sell; they must conform or die. (Even now [2015], the world is experiencing the gruesome practice of beheadings by ISIS, which is nothing compared to the slaughter that will ensue under the rule of the beast.)

Death of the Two Witnesses to Jerusalem

The second act of the man of sin will be the instigation of the time of Jacob's trouble, the Tribulation, the great one predicted by Jesus in the above passage of Matthew 24:21: "For then there will be a great tribulation, such as has not occurred since the beginning of the world until now, nor ever will." He begins the last great holocaust of God's people by putting to death the two witnesses who preach the gospel of the kingdom during the first half of the 7 years, a peaceful time following the making of the covenant during the time the seventh emperor (the rider on the white horse of Revelation 6:2). John's account of the witnesses' ministry follows:

> "And I will grant authority to My two witnesses, and
> they will prophesy for twelve hundred and sixty days,
> clothed in sackcloth." These are the two olive trees and
> the two lamp stands that stand before the Lord of the
> earth. And if anyone wants to harm them, fire flows out
> of their mouth and devours their enemies; so if anyone

wants to harm them, he must be killed in this way. These have the power to shut up the sky, so that rain will not fall during days of their prophesying; and they have power over the waters to turn them into blood, and to strike the earth with every plague, as often as they undesired they have finished their testimony, the beast that comes up out of the abyss will make war with them, and overcome them and kill them. And their dead bodies will lie in the street of the great city which mystically is called Sodom and Egypt, where also their Lord was crucified. Those from the peoples and tribes and tongues and nations will look at their dead bodies for three and a half days, and will not permit their dead bodies to be laid in a tomb. And those who dwell on the earth will rejoice over them and celebrate; and they will send gifts to one another, because these two prophets tormented those who dwell on the earth. But after the three and a half days, the breath of life from God came into them, and they stood on their feet; and great fear fell upon those who were watching them. And they heard a loud voice from heaven saying to them, "Come up here." Then they went up into heaven in the cloud, and their enemies watched them. (Rev. 11:3-12)

Since the two witnesses are not named, their identity is uncertain, however it is my opinion that they are Moses and Elijah. But until they appear, we must be satisfied knowing that they will be two special individuals anointed by God. We can follow the progression of the beast from the pit to his encounter with the witnesses. In Revelation 17:8 the angel says, "The beast that you saw was, and is not, and is about to come up out of the abyss and go to destruction." Previously, in Revelation 9:1-2, John said: "Then the fifth angel sounded, and I saw a star [Satan] from heaven which had fallen to the earth; and the key of the bottomless pit was given to him. He opened the bottomless pit, and smoke went up out of the pit, like the smoke of a great furnace; and the sun and the air were darkened by the smoke of the pit." The beast, one of the occupants (the most prominent) ascends from the pit when it is opened, proceeds to the temple and desecrates it (Dan. 9:27b). Shortly thereafter, the progression ends with the account of the two witnesses, Revelation 11:7: "When they have finished their testimony, the beast that comes up out of the abyss will make war with them, and overcome them and kill them." They will have prophesied 1,260 days (42 months = 3-1/2 years). Under no condition will the beast allow the witnesses to continue preaching their message about the true God, since he will have proclaimed himself to be God. He will have them put to death and great rejoicing will result from the death of the witnesses. People throughout the earth will send gifts to each other in celebration.

After 3-1/2 days and nights, the witnesses will be caught up to God before the people's very eyes. They will be transported by the same process as were Enoch, Elijah, Jesus, and, as will have been the Church at the Rapture. Following their removal the beast will begin his assault on Jerusalem herself.

Dispossession of the City of Jerusalem

Satan has known since Michael the Archangel expelled him from the middle heavens that he has but a short time to destroy God's people (Rev. 12:12, 13). He also knows it will be his last opportunity to do his worst through the wicked man, to whom he promised the kingdoms of the world (Lk. 4: 6, 7). The devil is not omniscient, but he does have access to the Word of God and he knows the outcome of all prophecies that pertain to his destruction. And yet he, the great deceiver, has deceived himself into believing that he can actually win his battle against God and rule the kingdoms of this world through his man, the beast. God has promised that His people will not be completely destroyed. Paul recalls the words of the prophet Isaiah concerning Israel: "Though the number of the sons of Israel be like the sand of the sea, it is the remnant that will be saved; for the Lord will execute His word on the earth, thoroughly and quickly."(Isa. 10:22, 23) Just as Isaiah foretold, "Unless the Lord of Sabaoth had left to us a posterity, we would have become like Sodom, and would have resembled Gomorrah" (Isa. 1:9; Rom. 9:27-29).

Sodom and Gomorrah were destroyed and but for the remnant, Israel would be destroyed. God in His great mercy and love will intervene on their behalf. He has prepared a way for their escape from the beast and his armies. Jesus warned the future remnant to escape if it is to survive the onslaught from the beast: "Therefore when you see the abomination of desolation which was spoken of through Daniel the prophet, standing in the holy place (let the reader understand), then those who are in Judea must flee to the mountains. " "Whoever is in the field must not turn back to get his cloak. " But woe to those who are pregnant and to those who are nursing babies in those days! "But pray that your flight will not be in the winter, or on a Sabbath. " For then there will be a great tribulation, such as has not occurred since the beginning of the world until now, nor ever will" (Matt. 24:15-21).

The remnant part will consist of 1/3 of the whole population that will be dispossessed of the land of Judea. Zechariah prophesied, "It will come about in all the land," Declares the Lord, "That two parts in it will be cut off and perish; But the third will be left in it." And I will bring the third part through the fire, Refine them as silver is refined, And test them as gold is tested. They will call on My name, And I will answer them; I will say, 'They are My people,' And they will say, 'The Lord is my God' " (Zech. 13:8-9). God is very specific in His Word as to how He intends to protect the remnant. The prophet Micah said, "I will surely assemble all of you, Jacob, I will surely gather the remnant of Israel. I will put them together like sheep in the fold; Like a flock in the midst of its pasture they will be noisy with men" (Mic. 2:12). How will God get them to the sheepfold of which he speaks? Zechariah prophesies a great earthquake will split the Mount of Olives in two; one half of the mountain will move toward the north and the other half will move toward the south, creating a valley extending east to west through which the remnant shall escape from Judea (Zech. 14: 4-5).

> "Then the woman fled into the wilderness where she had a place prepared by God, so that there she would be nourished for one thousand two hundred and sixty days" (Rev. 12:6).

"And when the dragon saw that he was thrown down to the earth, he persecuted the woman who gave birth to the male child. But the two wings of the great eagle were given to the woman, so that she could fly into the wilderness to her place, where she was nourished for a time and times and half a time, from the presence of the serpent. And the serpent poured water like a river out of his mouth after the woman, so that he might cause her to be swept away with the flood. But the earth helped the woman, and the earth opened its mouth and drank up the river which the dragon poured out of his mouth" (Rev. 12:13-16).

The sheepfold of which Micah prophesied is none other than Bozrah in the region of Petra. Petra in the Greek is a feminine noun, and is the same word for "rock" that Jesus used in Matthew 16:18 when he referred to the building of His Church. Petra is located in Edom, and Edom is to be rescued from the hands of the Willful King (Dan. 11:41) for the express purpose of preserving a place to which the remnant can escape. Petra is an ancient impregnable fortress city carved from rock from which the beast will be unable to dislodge God's people. They will remain within the shelter of the "sheepfold" until the Jesus delivers them at the end of the "one thousand two hundred and sixty days."

After the remnant escapes, the beast will turn his attention to the Jews left in Israel. John says, "So the dragon was enraged with the woman, and went off to make war with the rest of her children, who keep the commandments of God, and hold to the testimony of Jesus" (Rev. 12:17). "The rest of her children" are the 2/3 of which Zechariah spoke as being "two parts" who would not only be dispossessed of the land, but would also perish (Zech. 13:8). It is impossible to estimate the number of Jews that will be slain during the time of the Tribulation. According to Wikipedia, there are approximately 15 million in the world today (2015), but there is no way of knowing how many will have returned to Israel before the beginning of the time of Jacob's trouble.

One study predicted that in the next 80 years America's Jewish population would decline by one-third to 3.8 million if current fertility rates and migration patterns continue. In the same period, according to the study, the number of Jews in Israel would likely double, swelling to 10 million. The study also anticipated a severe decline in the number of Jews in the former Soviet Union. By 2080, the data suggested, the Jewish community there would be virtually non-existent.

Among the study's conclusions was that Israel would be home to the world's largest Jewish community as early as 2020, and the majority of the world's Jews by 2050. Between the years 2030 to 2040 the majority of Jews will be living in Israel rather than the Diaspora, where communities are aging.[3]

One thing is sure; over seven million people will die at the hand of the beast and his armies, at least one million more than the six million who perished during the German Holocaust, and among them will be many who choose to believe the lie of the false prophet—that the beast is God (II Thess. 2: 11, 12; Rev. 13:11-18). It is important to emphasize that the loss of life at the mid-point of the Tribulation brings into serious question the view that the Russian invasion takes place at that time. There is no evidence that Russia will be allied with the armies of the beast and the armies of the Kings of the Sun rising (the east) when those armies come face to face with the Lord in the valley of Meggido, and Ezekiel, in Chapters 38 and 39, does not record any loss of life in the city of Jerusalem or in Israel during the Russian invasion. Russia is destroyed in the mountainous regions of the northern borders of Israel before the time of Jacob's trouble.

Destruction of the Destroyer and Deliverance of Jerusalem

The event for which the hearts of the saints have been longing and praying will arrive when the beast and the kings of the earth face the other white-horse rider, the King of Kings and the LORD of LORDS (Rev. 19:11-19). This confrontation will not occur until after the Tribulation. Jesus said, "But immediately after the tribulation of those days the sun will be darkened, and the moon will not give its light, and the stars will fall from the sky, and the powers of the heavens will be shaken. " And then the sign of the Son of Man will appear in the sky, and then all the tribes of the earth will mourn, and they will see the Son of Man coming on the clouds of the sky with power and great glory" (Matt. 24:29-30). Matthew informs us that the Lord does not come until "immediately after the tribulation of those days." Many scholars believe He descends to the Mount of Olives and the touch of His feet causes the Mount to split apart. According to Keil and Delitzsch, "He appears upon the Mount of Olives, and as His feet touch the mountain it splits in half, so that a large valley is formed. The splitting of the mountain is the effect of the earthquake under the footsteps of Jehovah, before whom the earth trembles when He touches it . . . ."[4] However, if the Lord does not come until after the Tribulation, and if the Mount of Olives is split in order to provide a way for the remnant to escape the beast at the middle of the Tribulation, how is it possible for the feet of the Lord to have been the cause of the split?

The Mount of Olives will split (the Hebrew verb for 'split' is reflexive and means that the mount splits apart by itself) as the result of the earthquake and provide a way for the Remnant to flee to Petra. The context of Zechariah 14 shows that His coming does not precede the earthquake, even though v4 seems to indicate that it does: "In that day His feet will stand on the Mount of Olives, which is in front of Jerusalem on the east; and the Mount of Olives will be split in its middle from east to west by a very large valley, so that half of the mountain will move toward the north and the other half toward the south." The geological structure of the Mount of Olives allows for such an event. Tatford explains:

> There was an earthquake on July 11, 1927, which shook Palestine from the Sea of Galilee to the border of Egypt and, after the tremors, geologists discovered a fault in Olivet, running from east to west. Prof. Bailey Willis, of Stanford University, said that the land could expect to suffer from seismological disturbances and that the area around Jerusalem was a region of potential danger, a fault line, along which slippage might occur, passing directly under the Mount of Olives. It is evident, therefore, that what Zechariah described is precisely what geologists would expect to occur.[5]

A close look at verse 5 reveals that He does not come until after the earthquake and the flight through the valley: "Then the LORD, my God, will come, and all the holy ones with Him!" Verse 3 states that "He will go forth and fight against those nations . . .," that had dispossessed the remnant (the 1/3) of Jerusalem and slain the 2/3 (vv1-2), but this fight against the nations will not happen until He comes. Then, most likely 3-1/2 years after the split, His feet will touch down somewhere near Petra, for we know from Isaiah's prophecy that He comes from Bozrah with the remnant:

> Who is this who comes from Edom,With garments of glowing colors from Bozrah, This One who is majestic in His apparel, Marching in the greatness of His strength? "It is I who speak in righteousness, mighty to save." Why is Your apparel red, And Your garments like the one who treads in the wine press? "I have trodden the wine trough alone, And from the peoples there was no man with Me. I also trod them in My anger And trampled them in My wrath; And their lifeblood is sprinkled on My garments, And I stained all My raiment. "For the day of vengeance was in My heart, And My year of redemption has come. " I looked, and there was no one to help, And I was astonished and there was no one to uphold; So My own arm brought salvation to Me, And My wrath upheld Me. "I trod down the peoples in My anger And made them drunk in My wrath, And I poured out their lifeblood on the earth." (Isa. 63:1-6)

The Remnant will accompany Him in His fight against the beast and the armies of the nations (Zech. 12:1-9; 14:12-15; Rev. 17:14; 19:11-19). The book of Joel is a description of the great and terrible Day of the Lord, when He brings the nations down into the Valley of Jehoshaphat and there enters into judgment with them (Joel 3:1-17; Zech. 12:11). The beast, who clothed himself in the body of the one who rode forth on the white horse in Revelation 6:2, will confront the other rider on a white horse "who was made in the likeness of men and being found in appearance as a man . . .," who rides forth in Revelation 19:11-19 to destroy Satan's man and the false prophet. "And I saw the beast and the kings of the earth and their armies assembled to make war against Him who sat on the horse and against His army. And the beast was seized, and with him the false prophet who performed the signs in his presence, by which he deceived those who had received the mark of the beast and those who worshiped his image; these two were thrown alive into the lake of fire which burns with brimstone" (Rev. 19:19-20). The prophet Daniel looked into the future and saw in detail what John saw in Revelation 19. He saw the Ancient of Days and the court set for judgment, and the opening of the books. He watched until he saw the beast slain, and its body destroyed and given to the burning fire (Dan. 7:9-11). Following the Millennium, Satan will be "thrown into the lake of fire and brimstone, where the beast and the false prophet are also; and they will be tormented day and night forever and ever" (Rev. 20:10).

Those who receive the mark of the beast and choose to worship him during his short reign on the earth will be judged at the Great White Throne and cast into the lake of fire (Rev. 20:11-14)—their reward for following the beast.

This chapter has presented those prophecies, yet to be fulfilled, having to do with the destructive forces brought to bear upon Jerusalem during the Tribulation period: the king of the South and the king of the North, and their relationship to the white-horse rider of Revelation 6:2 and his end in Daniel 11:40-45; the beast's origin, identification, nature, and activities against Jerusalem along with the Kings of the East; and his confrontation with, and destruction by "the King of Kings and LORD of LORDS."

CHAPTER IX

Unfulfilled Prophecies of the Deliverances and Destructions of Jerusalem During the Millennial Age and the Age of Ages

This chapter deals with the remainder of prophecies from the close of the Tribulation period to the end of all prophecy, beyond which the human mind has no record. That which God has revealed to us belongs to us and our children (Deut. 29:29); beyond that one can only speculate. Further deliverances and destructions of Jerusalem will be discussed in the following three sections: (1) the destruction and deliverance of Jerusalem during the millennial age, (2) the deliverance and destruction of Jerusalem prior to the age of ages and, (3) the deliverance of Jerusalem's citizenry during the age of ages.

The chart below is the author's conception of the plan of the ages.

Plan of the Ages
By Dr. Don Bailey

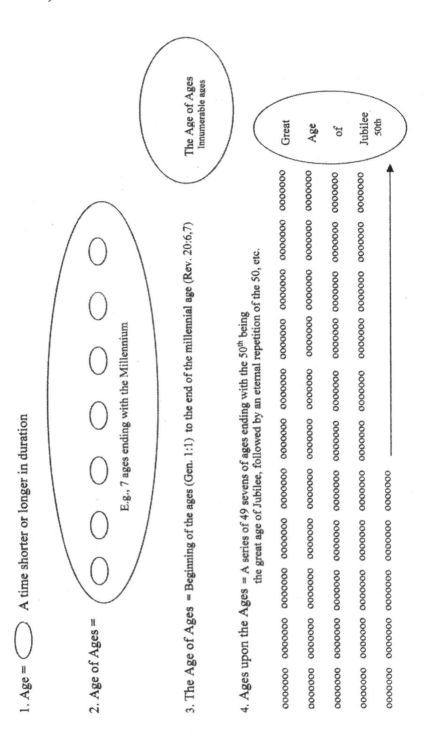

1. Age = ⬭ A time shorter or longer in duration

2. Age of Ages =

E.g., 7 ages ending with the Millennium

3. The Age of Ages = Beginning of the ages (Gen. 1:1) to the end of the millennial age (Rev. 20:6,7)

The Age of Ages
Innumerable ages

4. Ages upon the Ages = A series of 49 sevens of ages ending with the 50th being the great age of Jubilee, followed by an eternal repetition of the 50, etc.

Great
Age
of
Jubilee
50th

I. THE DESTRUCTIONS AND DELIVERANCES OF JERUSALEM DURING THE MILLENNIAL AGE

We now have reached that time in the future when the Ancient of days will have turned over to His Son the kingdom that was promised and prophesied: "And to Him was given dominion, Glory and a kingdom, That all the peoples, nations and men of every language Might serve Him. His dominion is an everlasting dominion which will not pass away; And His kingdom is one Which will not be destroyed" (Dan. 7:14). But before the actual kingdom is inaugurated, the full and complete destruction of Israel's enemies must be accomplished. Daniel provides some insight into the closing events of the Tribulation and the beginning of the kingdom age: "From the time that the regular sacrifice is abolished and the abomination of desolation is set up, there will be 1,290 days. " How blessed is he who keeps waiting and attains to the 1,335 days!" (Dan. 12:11-12). The 1,290 days exceed the Tribulation by one month (the Tribulation being 1,260 days). The extra 30 days is to bring the destruction of all enemies to an end. Forty-five days are added to the 1,290 that make up the 1,335 days before the full blessing of Israel begins. Daniel is told to rest until the end of those days, at which time he will be resurrected and partake of Israel's kingdom blessings. (The Church-age saints already will have been resurrected at the Rapture prior to the Tribulation.)

Following 1,335 days, the kingdom of the Son of God will be set up and will extend 1,000 years into the future—the Millennium. The word millennium means 1,000 years, but it is not used in the Bible. However, the word, chiliad, the Greek word for 1,000, is used six times by John in Revelation 20:1-6. Different forms of the word chiliad are used throughout the Bible, when reference is made to plurals of 1,000, e.g., I Kings 19:18; Romans 11:4; Numbers 31:4-5; Revelation 7:5-8; and Revelation 21:16. Obviously, the number is literal and not symbolical. The 1,000 years will be as literal as the city of Jerusalem is now, with some marked differences. Jerusalem will be the capitol city of Israel and the world, and its position and location will have changed geologically (Isa. 2:2; Zech. 14:8-10).

The unfulfilled prophecies relative to Jerusalem's deliverances and apparent destruction during the Millennium will be discussed under three headings: (1) Deliverance of Jerusalem Determined by the Son of Man during the Millennium, (2) Destruction of Jerusalem Dared by Satan during the Close of the Millennium, and (3) Deliverance of Jerusalem Dramatized by God during the Close of the Millennium.

1. DELIVERANCE OF JERUSALEM DETERMINED BY THE SON OF MAN DURING THE MILLENNIUM

With the return of Jesus to earth and the destruction of the beast and his armies, the city of Jerusalem will begin to experience complete deliverance from those nations of the earth that have sought her utter destruction since David delivered her from the Jebusites. Deliverance of the city from the beast and his armies at the end of the Tribulation period will overlap with and continue throughout the Millennium. While the deliverance of Jerusalem from the beast is real and complete as relates to him (he will have been removed from off the scene and cast into the lake of fire along with the false prophet.), the Millennium will not be a perfect reign. Deliverance will be ongoing and must be maintained throughout the age, even though Satan will be bound (Rev. 20:1-3). Until the terminus of the Millennium, at which time Satan will be released, the Son of Man will determine to assert deliverance. The intended significance of the title, Son of Man, and the inherent sovereignty of the Son of Man are two important facts to consider relative to an asserted deliverance of the city of Jerusalem. When Jerusalem is delivered the whole world will experience benefit from that deliverance.

The Intended Significance of the Title, Son of Man

Jesus as to His essence is fully God and fully Man; He is God-Man. His meaningfulness as God is that He is the Second Person of the three Persons of the Godhead, the Son of God, the other two being: God the Father, and God the Holy Spirit. He is uniquely the Son of God. His uniqueness as the Son is expressed by the Hebrew word, yachad (pronounced, yakh' ad), meaning one. It does not mean one, as in 1, 2, 3, but it means, absolute one; the Triune God is absolutely the only One existing; there is no other, none before Him, presently with Him, or after

Him. His oneness is unique in that He is the only One. Two examples of the word yachad: (1) Isaac was Abraham's son in a very unique way because there was no other son like him. Ishmael also was Abraham's son, but not like Isaac, the son of promise, through whom the Seed, Christ, would come. Isaac was absolutely his only (yachad) son in that respect (Gen. 22:2, 12, 16), and (2) Jesus is God's Son in a very unique way. He is absolutely God the Father's only (yachad) Son (Jn. 3:16; I Jn. 4:9). The fact that each was an only one (a yachad) gives profound meaning to the willingness of Isaac's father, Abraham, to offer him as a sacrifice (Heb. 11: 17), and the actual offering by God the Father of His Son, Jesus. The only (yachad) God Who has ever been, is, and Who will ever be, offered His only (yachad) Son, for us. Jesus, the only Son who has ever been, is, and who will ever be, offered Himself for us.

But Jesus is not only the Son of God, absolutely; He is also the Son of Man, absolutely. While the fullness of Deity (Jn. 1:1; Col. 1:19) is expressed in His Person as the Son of God, the fullness of His humanity is expressed in His Person as the Son of Man; both fullness's are the God-Man, "For in Him all the fullness of Deity dwells in bodily form (Col. 2:9). He is God as to His essence and at the same instance Man as to His essence. He is God to the core and Man to the core. He is the Son of Man and will remain so until He delivers over His kingdom to God the Father (I Cor. 15: 24-28). There was not, is not, and never will be another man like Him; that truth is revealed in the following references: Daniel 7:13; 8:17; Matthew 9:6; 10:23; 11:19; 12:8, 32, 40; 13:37, 41; 16:13, 27, 28; 17:9, 12, 22; 19:28; 20:18, 28; 24:27, 30, 30, 37, 39, 44; 25:31; 26:2, 24, 45, 64; John 1:51; 3:13, 14; 5:27; 6:27, 53, 62; 8:28; 9:35; 12:23, 34; 13:31; Acts 7:56; Hebrews 2:6; Revelation 1:13; 14:14. Cumulatively, they reveal the answer to the questions: "Who do men say the Son of man is?" (Matt. 16:13) and "Who is this Son of Man?" (Jn. 12:34). Each gives some insight into His Person as the Son of Man. One outstanding characteristic of His Person revealed relative to the Millennium is that of His inherent sovereignty.

The Inherent Sovereignty of the Son of Man

Following the Rapture and once He has rewarded the saints at the Judgment Seat of Christ (in the meantime the Tribulation will have occurred.), the Father will indicate to Him that it is time to return to the earth (Matt. 24:31; Mk. 13:32; Acts 1:7). When Christ descends to earth the second time, He will come as Sovereign. His sovereignty is inherent because He is God the Son who, along with the Father and the Holy Spirit, created all things, maintains all things, and directs all historical events toward His desired end. The desired end as far as the kingdoms of the world are concerned is that "In the days of those kings the God of heaven will set up a kingdom which will never be destroyed, and that kingdom will not be left for another people; it will crush and put an end to all these kingdoms, but it will itself endure forever" (Dan. 2:44). He will demonstrate to the world that He and He alone can rule the nations as no other potentate. He is the Seeker, Servant, Savior and Sovereign of all men.

The Millennium will be a literal reign over the earth by the Lord Jesus Christ; a time of peace enforced by the rod of righteousness (Psa. 2:1-12) because the Prince of Peace will have come (Isa. 9:6-7). Enforced righteousness will be necessary because children born to righteous parents who enter the kingdom will be born in sin, with evil hearts bent toward wickedness which must be kept in check. Man will continue to sin and die. The prophet Isaiah reminds us that a man being one hundred years old will be considered as a little child, and the man that does not reach one hundred will be considered cursed (the curse, probably death, will result from a particular sin committed.) Those who adhere to a life of obedience most likely will live the full length of 1,000 years. A man will live so long as to outlast the things he makes with his hands. There will be harmony within the animal kingdom, and little children will play with them without fear of being harmed (Isa. 65:20-25).

During the kingdom age, nations will not be allowed to make war because the Prince of Peace will judge all differences between them; all weapons of warfare will have been destroyed and never again will they learn war (Isa. 2:4). Following the Millennium, Satan will gather the nations for the last war that will end all wars (discussed later in this chapter).

The millennial reign of Christ will reveal to the universe that He is the Son of God and the Son of Man, and that He alone is absolute Sovereign. Nebuchadnezzar, who began the times of the Gentile kingdoms, after having been subjugated to the status of a wild animal for a period of seven years, acknowledged His sovereignty to all the nations:

> Nebuchadnezzar the king to all the peoples, nations, and men of every language that live in all the earth: "May your peace abound! " It has seemed good to me to declare the signs and wonders which the Most High God has done for me. "How great are His signs And how mighty are His wonders! His kingdom is an everlasting kingdom And His dominion is from generation to generation (Dan. 4:1-3). But at the end of that period, I, Nebuchadnezzar, raised my eyes toward heaven and my reason returned to me, and I blessed the Most High and praised and honored Him who lives forever; For His dominion is an everlasting dominion, And His kingdom endures from generation to generation. "All the inhabitants of the earth are accounted as nothing, But He does according to His will in the host of heaven And among the inhabitants of earth; And no one can ward off His hand Or say to Him, 'What have You done?' "At that time my reason returned to me. And my majesty and splendor were restored to me for the glory of my kingdom, and my counselors and my nobles began seeking me out; so I was reestablished in my sovereignty, and surpassing greatness was added to me. "Now I, Nebuchadnezzar, praise, exalt and honor the King of heaven, for all His works are true and His ways just, and He is able to humble those who walk in pride (Dan. 4: 34-37).

Prior to his humiliation, Nebuchadnezzar dreamed of an enormous statue having a head of gold (Nebuchadnezzar—Babylon), chest of arms and silver (Medo-Persia), belly and thighs of bronze (Greece), legs of iron (Rome), and feet partly iron and partly clay (Revived Roman Empire). Daniel informed Nebuchadnezzar that he was the head of gold and that all the kingdoms making up the other parts of the statue would be destroyed by a great stone which would strike the feet and bring to an end the times of the Gentiles. The dream, itself prophecy, has been fulfilled to the letter, except the smiting of the feet of the image. The stone is the kingdom of Messiah, Jesus, the Son of God, the Son of Man (Dan. 2:31-44).

The fall of the Revived Roman Empire is simultaneous with the destruction of the beast, its head (Dan. 7:7-27). Verse 27 reads, "Then the sovereignty, the dominion and the greatness of all the kingdoms under the whole heaven will be given to the people of the saints of the Highest One; His kingdom will be an everlasting kingdom, and all the dominions will serve and obey Him." Servitude of all the nations to the Sovereign of the Universe, Israel, and Jerusalem, will characterize the Millennium. Jerusalem will experience complete deliverance from the nations of the world for a period of 1,000 years, but when those 1,000 years expire, those nations will be led in the last rebellion in the history of man against the city.

2. DESTRUCTION OF JERUSALEM ATTEMPTED BY SATAN AND THE NATIONS AT THE END OF THE MILLENNIUM

The time of Jacob's trouble (the middle of the Tribulation) begins when Michael and his angels go to war with Satan and his angels (Rev. 12:7-17). Satan will be cast down to earth and persecute Israel for 3-1/2 years, during which time Michael will stand aside (Dan. 12:1a). When those 3-1/2 years have run their course, Michael will come with the Lord Jesus to the aid of Israel and deliver her (Dan. 12:1b). Matthew gives a more detailed account: "But immediately after the tribulation of those days the sun will be darkened, and the moon will not give its light, and the stars will fall from the sky, and the powers of the heavens will be shaken. And then the sign of the Son of Man will appear in the sky, and then all the tribes of the earth will mourn, and they will see the Son of Man coming on the clouds of the sky with power and great glory. And He will send forth His angels with a great trumpet and they will gather together His elect from the four winds, from one end of the sky to the other." (Matt. 24:29-31).

According to Daniel 12:1, Michael is the angel described by John, and up to this point Michael will have stood aside long enough. "Then I saw an angel coming down from heaven, holding the key of the abyss and a great chain in his hand. And he laid hold of the dragon, the serpent of old, who is the devil and Satan, and bound him for a thousand years; and he threw him into the abyss, and shut it and sealed it over him, so that he would not deceive the nations any longer, until the thousand years were completed; after these things he must be released for a short time" (Rev. 20:1-3). Upon Satan's release from the pit, he really believes that he can destroy Jerusalem.

Destruction Attempted through Self-Deception

Since his first rebellion and his fall from Heaven in eons past, Satan has allowed himself to imagine that he can dethrone the God of the universe. In Eden, he deceived himself into believing he could thwart God's purpose of salvation for man by leading the first man and woman in rebellion against their Creator. The trail of his history throughout the Bible is a commentary on his self-deception when, at the Cross of Calvary, he led the people, priests, princes, and kings of the earth in rebellion against the Son of God. That crucifixion brought about the very means of man's salvation. Satan was defeated by his own self-deception. He fulfilled completely the eternal purpose of God.

Once again Satan's wishful thinking will deceive him into believing that through his man, the beast, the lawless one, he can defeat the KING OF KINGS and LORD OF LORDS (Rev. 19:11-21). The beast will gather the nations of the earth and come face to face with Jesus Christ in the valley of Megiddo and there be destroyed by the brightness of His coming (II Thess. 2:8; Dan. 7:11).

The above record of self-deceptive defeatism is so dismal and pathetic that one would think the most intelligent and beautiful of all God's creatures would have enough wisdom to know when to end his ages-long rebellion (Ezek. 28:12-19), but he will not stop and his stance against the God who created him will persist until his last defeat.

Destruction Attempted through National Deception

Satan's 1,000 years of confinement in the pit will have given him plenty of time to develop a strategy to convince the nations of the earth to attack Jerusalem and, upon his release he will waste no time in putting his plan into action. "When the thousand years are completed, Satan will be released from his prison, and will come out to deceive the nations which are in the four corners of the earth, Gog and Magog, to gather them together for the war; the number of them is like the sand of the seashore. And they came up on the broad plain of the earth and surrounded the camp of the saints and the beloved city, and fire came down from heaven and devoured them" (Rev. 20:7-9). The national deception involves two aggregates: (1) the nations in the far corners of the earth, and (2) Gog and Magog.

The Nations in the Far Corners of the Earth. Who are the nations of whom John writes? The nations of the earth are the descendants of the righteous nations that entered the millennial age when Christ set up His Kingdom. The unrighteous nations will already have been judged and consigned to eternal fire:

> But when the Son of Man comes in His glory, and all the angels with Him, then He will sit on His glorious throne. "All the nations will be gathered before Him; and He will separate them from one another, as the shepherd separates the sheep from the goats; and He will put the sheep on His right, and the goats on the left. "Then the King will say to those on His right, 'Come, you who are blessed of My Father, inherit the kingdom prepared for you from the foundation of the world. 'For I was hungry, and you gave Me something to eat; I was thirsty, and you gave Me something to drink; I was a stranger, and you invited Me in; naked, and you clothed Me; I was sick, and you visited Me; I was in prison, and you came to Me.' "Then the righteous will answer Him, 'Lord, when did we see You hungry, and feed You, or thirsty, and give You something to drink? 'And when

did we see You a stranger, and invite You in, or naked, and clothe You? 'When did we see You sick, or in prison, and come to You?' "The King will answer and say to them, 'Truly I say to you, to the extent that you did it to one of these brothers of Mine, even the least of them, you did it to Me.' "Then He will also say to those on His left, 'Depart from Me, accursed ones, into the eternal fire which has been prepared for the devil and his angels; for I was hungry, and you gave Me nothing to eat; I was thirsty, and you gave Me nothing to drink; I was a stranger, and you did not invite Me in; naked, and you did not clothe Me; sick, and in prison, and you did not visit Me.' "Then they themselves also will answer, 'Lord, when did we see You hungry, or thirsty, or a stranger, or naked, or sick, or in prison, and did not take care of You?' "Then He will answer them, 'Truly I say to you, to the extent that you did not do it to one of the least of these, you did not do it to Me.' "These will go away into eternal punishment, but the righteous into eternal life [italics mine]." (Matt. 25:31-46).

Their ancestors (those on the right) will have been judged righteous at the beginning of the Kingdom, but they themselves who will have been born in sin during the Kingdom will not have committed themselves to the Lord based on the message of the Kingdom preached by God's messengers during the Kingdom age. They will have allowed their evil hearts to become hardened against the Lord and His righteous rule and kept themselves aloof from any influence of righteousness on their rebellious spirits. They will have removed themselves to the far corners of the earth because of their hatred of the KING OF KINGS, the saints, and Jerusalem. Their hatred will be the result of their having been ruled for 1,000 years with a "rod of iron," (enforced righteousness), and not having been allowed to express the evil inclinations of their hearts. Zechariah describes how some nations will react to God's directives during the Millennium:

> Then it will come about that any who are left of all the
> nations that went against Jerusalem will go up from year
> to year to worship the King, the Lord of hosts, and to
> celebrate the Feast of Booths. And it will be that whichever
> of the families of the earth does not go up to Jerusalem to
> worship the King, the Lord of hosts, there will be no rain
> on them. If the family of Egypt does not go up or enter,
> then no rain will fall on them; it will be the plague with
> which the Lord smites the nations who do not go up to
> celebrate the Feast of Booths. This will be the punishment
> of Egypt, and the punishment of all the nations who do
> not go up to celebrate the Feast of Booths (Zech. 14:16-19).

Just how Satan will deceive the nations into believing that they can destroy Jerusalem is not revealed in Scripture, however; one need only study his deceptive ways from Genesis to Revelation to conclude what tactics he might use. In the past he worked in and through men to accomplish his purposes, but when he makes his last attempt to overthrow the city of God he may appear upon the earth just as he is—in his own person, and the rebellious nations will actually see their Commander-In-Chief.

The world will be as vulnerable at the close of the Millennium as it was when the Antichrist, the seventh one, seduced it when he first appeared at the signing of the 7-year covenant with Israel. This time, however, the great enemy of man will not have the Antichrist at his behest, and will of necessity personally appear on the scene. He will not only deceive the nations of the four corners of the earth but also a previous enemy who, once again, will have become prominent on the world stage.

Gog and Magog. Gog and Magog have been discussed in a previous section, but this particular incident occurs under different circumstances and approximately 1,007 years later. Gog and Magog were identified as Russia, dwelling in the uttermost regions of the far North, and had been the leader of the great horde of Muslim nations who had come down upon the mountains of Israel to destroy her. God dealt with those invading forces and gave their carcasses to the vultures (Ezek. 38-39).

Since that time, and over a period of 1,000 years, the Russian people and the Russian army will have reproduced to untold millions and will join Satan in one final assault on Jerusalem. This time the invasion forces will reach the city and surround her. John does not reveal how long God allows the encirclement to last; but once it has taken place, God will act in the heat of His wrath to deliver His beloved city.

3. DELIVERANCE OF JERUSALEM DRAMATIZED BY GOD DURING THE TERMINUS OF THE MILLENNIUM

The age of the Millennium and the history of the nations are terminating at this point and events move precisely and quickly. God's patience has finally run out. No battle ensues; God responds in fiery wrath.

Deliverance by Fiery Destruction from the Nations, Gog, and Magog

The last great alliance of nations having unquestionable devotion to the great Adversary of God will embark upon their last performance on the world stage. Just before the curtain falls, fire will come down from heaven and devour them. John does not go into detail as to how the fire is delivered; he says only that it "comes down from heaven." It may be that God's chariots will deliver the fire. Since Michael is the guardian angel of Israel, God may allow him to command an angelic army to deliver Jerusalem for the final time, as he did at the close of the Tribulation. Satan will be cast into the lake of fire and the curtain will fall:

> When the thousand years are completed, Satan will be released from his prison and will come out to deceive the nations which are in the four corners of the earth, Gog and Magog, to gather them together for the war; the number of them is like the sand of the seashore. And they came up on the broad plain of the earth and surrounded the camp of the saints and the beloved city, and fire came down from heaven and devoured them. And the devil who deceived them was thrown into the lake of fire and brimstone, where the beast and the false

prophet are also; and they will be tormented day and night forever and ever (Rev. 20:7-10).

I was fortunate to sit under the preaching of the Southern circuit-riding preacher, Vance Havner, who on one occasion said: "Beloved, the Bible is like a mystery novel. You don't have to wait until you read it through to find out who did it. All you have to do, real quickly, is turn over to the book of Revelation to find out that the villain, the Devil, gets his in the end." Truer words were never spoken. The last act of the drama, featuring Satan and the rogue nations, reaches its end and the angels and saints of all ages will, with one great applause, praise the God of heaven and earth.

Looking back over the history of Satan and his fall, his loss of authority is incremental: first, he as Lucifer "the covering cherub," loses his authority and is removed from his original position and limited to the middle heavens; second, he is removed by Michael from his position in the middle heavens and cast down to earth with limited authority for duration of the Tribulation; third, he loses his authority while bound for 1,000 years in the pit (the"*It*" that holds fast); and fourth and last, he is released for a little while and is allowed enough authority to marshal the nations toward their utter defeat, and his own. After losing all authority and power, he is rendered utterly impotent in the lake of fire.

Of all the abhorrent characteristics of Hell, the one that may particularly gall Satan the most will be his inability to exert his will over any other creature confined there with him. All will be equally miserable for the ages upon the ages. A dear friend and colleague, Lee Gore, presently with the Lord, wrote in his book of poetry, Confrontation:

A lake of fire and brimstone:
The place of the "Second Death,"
Is surely the habitat of the one
That snatches away our breath.
And all the liars whoever lived,
False prophets and all the rest,
Will feel the wrath of a Mighty God
In a terrible "Second Death."

The righteous will shine forever
Like the stars up in the sky
And none can ever sever
Those who never die.
Never again will there be strife
For those whose names are in the Book of Life.[1]

All of the foregoing deliverances of Jerusalem are either from threats of destruction or actual destruction, but other deliverances and one last destruction of a different nature await her.

II. THE DELIVERANCES AND DESTRUCTION OF JERUSALEM PRIOR TO THE AGE OF AGES

Once the great millennial age has come to a close and Jerusalem has been delivered from all earthly enemies, including Satan from whom all enemies originated, God will set about to deliver the city from this earthly scene. When one thinks of a city, locale and buildings come to mind, but a city is not a city without inhabitants. Citizenry characterizes and gives a city life, meaning, and purpose, otherwise; the architecture and aesthetics are meaningless (except, perhaps, to historians and archaeologists). The ages-old city of Jerusalem will become meaningless in light of what God has in store for its inhabitants. After the Millennium has run its 1,000-year course, and following the destruction of Satan and his forces, the Great White Throne Judgment will take place.

In contrast to those who are condemned to the Lake of Fire, the citizens of Jerusalem will be granted perfect freedom when she is delivered from the catastrophic destruction that is to follow the Great White Throne judgment.

1. DELIVERANCE OF JERUSALEM'S CITIZENRY INTO THE NEW JERUSALEM

God's people from the millennial age will be delivered into the heavenly city, New Jerusalem, to join those who will have been raptured prior to the Tribulation period. This deliverance will be both total and glorious.

Total Deliverance

Sinclair Lewis writes in his book, Jerusalem: The Endless Crusade, "Jerusalem is a quest as well as a place. It is a journey to a goal that may never be reached. Its founders hardly saw in it a heavenly city as the Christians were to do, because the ancient Jews believed that heaven was the house of God, while they would finish in Sheol, a form of mindless Hades or Purgatory, after their time on earth."[2] What a hopeless and untrue statement! Christians base their belief in an eternal and heavenly Jerusalem on the example of the faith of the great Jewish patriarch, Abraham (Heb. 11:8-10), and the prophet Isaiah (Isa. 65:17-18). Immediately following the Great White Throne Judgment or simultaneous to it, God will again rapture (catch away) His people (the citizens of old-and-worn-out Jerusalem) to a new place of residence, the new Jerusalem, where they will join the great family of God for the ages to come (Heb. 12:22-24). It is the same city for which Abraham looked and found to be a reality. "For he was looking for the city which has foundations, whose architect and builder is God" (Heb. 11:10).

Glorious Deliverance

Paul reminded the Roman Christians of the glorious deliverance and liberty awaiting not only God's people but also the whole creation (Rom. 8:18-25). The old creation will vanish and give way to the new, "Then I saw a new heaven and a new earth; for the first heaven and the first earth passed away, and there is no longer any sea" (Rev. 21:1). John does not explain the process of how the old heaven and earth pass from the scene, but we are not left to wonder about that event. Before further study of the wonderful city into which God delivers His people, it is important to digress and see just how God will bring about the destruction of the old heaven and earth and change them into a new heaven and earth. Since old Jerusalem is on the earth at that time when the old earth passes away, she too will be destroyed.

2. DESTRUCTION OF EARTHLY JERUSALEM

It is difficult to think of the ages-old Jerusalem passing from the scene. From the time of the first mention of the land where she would eventually be built (Gen. 12:1) to the close of her history at the end of the Millennium, she will have been the most remarkable of all the cities built by man. Most cities of Earth will still exist when Satan leads his hordes against Jerusalem at the end of the Millennium, but all cities will come to an end shortly thereafter, including Jerusalem. Throughout her history she has undergone many destructions, but she has not been completely annihilated because God has seen fit to allow her to continue until the close of the earthly phase of the kingdom of His dear Son. But, in God's good time she too will be erased, along with the earth and its works.

Before discussing the destruction of Jerusalem, along with the earth and its works, it is important to examine three passages that say the earth will last forever: Psalm 78:69; Ecclesiastes 1:4; and Isaiah 65:17. A look at each will prove that the earth is not eternal as to its present form. The idea of the old earth remaining forever is based on mistranslation of the Old Testament Hebrew word *olam*. A study of the word *olam* reveals that it means "age." Its meaning is the same as the New Testament Greek word *aion* (eon). *Olam* and *eon* mean age and their length depends upon the context in which they are used, e.g., the writer of the book of Jonah records that Jonah was three days and three nights in the stomach of the fish (Jonah 1:17). According to the most popular translations (KJV, ASV, NKJV, DB, NASB, RSV, NIV), Jonah was there forever (olam) (Jonah 2:6). If *olam* means eternity, as we understand eternity, Jonah is still in the stomach of the fish. It is obvious that *olam* in Jonah 2:6 means three days and three nights as stated in Jonah 1:17.

Returning to those passages that say the earth will last forever, each of the translations mentioned above translates *olam* as forever. This is found to be incorrect when each is examined in context, although on the surface, each gives the impression that the earth is here for eternity. (I have chosen to quote from the KJV because it is the most revered of the translations listed above.)

Psalm 78:69 states, "And He built His sanctuary like high palaces, like the earth which He hath established for ever (*olam*)." The translation rendered here is that the earth will last forever (*olam*) and it is implied that God's sanctuary will, too. Since transition from the Tabernacle (a temporary structure), God's sanctuary has been destroyed twice: Solomon's Temple (I Kgs. 5-9:9) was destroyed by Nebuchadnezzar in 586 B.C., and Zurubabel's/Herod's Temple was destroyed by the Romans in 70 A.D. The third temple, to be built before the Tribulation, in which the lawless one (the beast of Revelation 13) installs himself (II Thess. 2:3-4), also will be destroyed in God's time; it will be the last temple (Rev. 21:22).

Ecclesiastes 1:4 reads, "One generation passeth away, and another generation cometh: but the earth abideth forever." Here again, the KJV translates the word *olam* to mean forever, as though the earth is here to stay. Rotherham, however, renders *olam* correctly: "Generation cometh and generation goeth, but the earth unto times age abiding remaineth." The earth has a certain amount of time in which to exist; the longevity of that time is within an abiding age (*olam*), which will terminate following the Millennium.

The third and most convincing passage describing the earth's temporary existence is Isaiah 65:17: "For, behold, I create new heavens and a new earth: and the former shall not be remembered, nor come into mind." Here, the KJV contradicts those passages in which it translates the earth as lasting forever. It gives the impression that the earth will last for eternity, but God specifically says that He will create new heavens and a new earth. Obviously, *olam* and/or *eon* does not mean forever when used in context with either the temple or the earth. There is no confusion as to what God meant when He said that the present world will be destroyed.

Fiery Destruction

Jesus said that "heaven and earth shall pass away....(Matt. 24:35), but God has made it clear that man will have nothing to do with the process of earth's destruction. He has reserved that right to Himself. He who created something out of nothing will, in His Day, change its form by His own means of destruction. John said, "Then I saw a new heaven and a new earth; for the first heaven and the first earth passed away, and there is no longer any sea" (Rev. 21:1).

According to the words of the Apostle Peter, God will use fire to transform the heavens and the earth from the old to the new. That power is already stored within the interior of the heavenly orbs and the Earth itself. Peter writes:

> But the heavens and the earth, which are now, by the same word are kept in store, reserved unto fire against the day of judgment and perdition of ungodly men. But, beloved, be not ignorant of this one thing, that one day is with the Lord as a thousand years, and a thousand years as one day. The Lord is not slack concerning His promise, as some men count slackness; but is longsuffering to us-ward, not willing that any should perish, but that all should come to repentance. 10 But the day of the Lord will come as a thief in the night; in the which the heavens shall pass away with a great noise, and the elements shall melt with fervent heat, the earth also and the works that are therein shall be burned up. Seeing then that all these things shall be dissolved, what manner of persons ought ye to be in all holy conversation and godliness, Looking for and hasting unto the coming of the day of God, wherein the heavens being on fire shall be dissolved, and the elements shall melt with fervent heat? (II Pet. 3:7-12, KJV)

Whereas the two antediluvian worlds of which Peter wrote were destroyed by the volume of water contained in the earth's interior, on its surface, and in its atmosphere, the present heaven and earth "are reserved unto fire" (KJV), Rotherham's translation of "are reserved unto fire" is correct: "While the heavens and the earth that now are By the same word *have been stored with fire* [italics mine], Being kept unto the day of judgment and destruction of the ungodly men"[4] (II Peter 3:7). Within the interior of all heavenly bodies throughout the universe (all creation), there is enough fire stored up so as to cause each to explode at God's pre-arranged time. Such simultaneous explosions would cause a great noise-like sound throughout heavens. The late Dr. Kenneth S. Wuest comments on the passage above in his Greek word studies, In These Last Days:

> "Noise" is roizedon. The sound of the word suggests the meaning. The word was used of the whistling of an arrow, the sound of a shepherd's pipe, the rush of wings, the splash of water, the hissing of a snake and the sound of filing. "Elements is stoicheia, referring here to the four elements of which the universe is composed, fire, air, earth, and water. The words "pass away" are the translation of paraluo, "to loosen, dissolve." "Melt is luo "to dissolve." "Fervent heat" is kausoo, "to burn up, to set fire to." The word denotes a violent consuming heat. Literally, "the elements being scorched up, shall be dissolved." As to the original text back of the words "shall be burned up," authorities differ. The Nestle text gives the future of heurisko, "shall be found." Robertson suggests katakaesetai, "shall be burned up."[5]

As to the word "noise," *roizedon,* Nestle translates it as a "cracking sound"[6] Peter uses three other words relative to one another: *pareleusontai, lutheesetai,* and *luomenon*; the root word for each is *luo. Luo* means to loosen. "Elements," according to Wuest, refers to fire, air, earth, and water and he may be correct, but it is more likely that Peter's word for elements, *stoicheia,* has reference to the more basic principle elements that constitute fire, air, earth, and water—atoms. Peter's language is, no doubt, descriptive of the process of nuclear fission. Nuclear fission is "the process of splitting a heavy nucleus into two lighter nuclei. Spontaneous fission is a type of radioactive decay.... Considerable energy is released during the fission reaction...."[7] I understand the process to mean that radioactive decay is synonymous with radioactive disintegration, and as the nucleus of the atom splits (is loosed or unbound) the release of radiation creates tremendous heat, thus causing a dissolving (or melting) of the elements.

It is important to note what the Psalmist has to say concerning the heavens and the earth: "I say, 'O my God, do not take me away in the midst of my days, Your years are throughout all generations. Of old You founded the earth, And the heavens are the work of Your hands. Even they will perish, but You endure; "And all of them will wear out like a garment." But You are the same, And Your years will not come to an end; Like clothing You will change them and they will be changed'" (Psa. 102:24-27). The radioactive decay process could be what the Psalmist referred to when he said, "And all of them will wear out like a garment." The term "will wear out" could be the decaying process itself.

Only God knows the age of the heavens and the earth and when they will reach the old-enough stage at which they should be changed, when they will have accomplished the purpose for which He created them. He created them long before Lucifer and the angels rebelled against Him. The NKJV has for Hebrews 1:12, "You will fold them up like a cloak... " While the NKJV uses the word "fold," *kolpos*, it is not in the Greek text; *kolpos* is the fold of a garment forming a pocket for measuring, storing and or carrying something. The original Greek word, *elixeis*, "roll" is the textual and correct verb. It means to roll up something, such as a mantle (vesture, cloak), and/or scroll. The text should read, "And like a mantle You will roll them up; like a garment they will also be changed." Just how God will roll up the heavens and the earth relative to their change is difficult to imagine.

The Greek word for "change" is *allasso* and means that the heavens and the earth will be the same, but yet different. Lenski writes:

> The heavens and the earth as we now see them in the universe, grand and wonderful, indeed, yet sadly disturbed by sin and evil, invaded by the dragon, the beast, the lamb-beast, the whore, full of the kings of the earth and the dwellers on the earth (all having but anti-Christian earth thoughts), "went away," disappeared; "for, behold I create a new heaven and a new earth, and the former shall not be remembered nor come to mind" (Isaiah 65:17). The newness of the heaven and the earth shall be like our own. We shall be the same persons and

shall have the same body and the same soul that we now have; but these made entirely new. Our newness begins with regeneration. Already this the Scriptures call a creation of God, Ephesians 2:10; 4:24, so that we are "a new creation," 2 Corinthians 5:17; Galatians 6:15. After body and soul are glorified, we shall be new-created, indeed. The same will be true with regard to the new heaven and the new earth. This is more than an analogy, for man is the creature for whom the first heaven and earth were created, and if he is made new by creative acts without first having been annihilated, he the head of all this creation, shall God annihilate heaven and earth and create ex nihilo another heaven and earth.[8]

We will have new bodies and live in the new city New Jerusalem that will descend out of heaven from God and settle down upon a new earth. All things will become new. The promises and truth of God's Word shall have been brought to pass: "And He who sits on the throne said, "Behold, I am making all things new." And He said, "Write, for these words are faithful and true" (Rev. 21:5). The finished new state of the earth will be part of the process of "making of all things new." Just as it is not known how long God took to create the old heavens and earth, it is not known how long He will take to create all things new. It could be ages or less before the earth is fully prepared to accept the heavenly city, New Jerusalem, but one must remember that "one day is with the Lord as a thousand years, and a thousand years is as one day" (II Pet. 3:8).

Whenever God creates the new heavens and new earth to His satisfaction, a wonderful and perfect age will begin, an age unlike any the universe has known. Hebrews 1:2 reminds us that the ages were made by the word *hremati,* the spoken word of God, not the Logos, the Word made flesh, as in John 1:3. The ages that include the physical universe are great periods of time, each of different duration; God framed them (*katartisthai,* prepared boundaries to) when He began the creative process in Genesis 1:1. Within each age He accomplishes what He plans during that particular time period. The Millennium (1,000 years) and the present Church age (2,000 years and counting) are such ages. Imagine a string of parentheses where each represents an age, one overlapping or touching the other: (age)(age)(age)(age)(age)(age)(age). As Paul said in I Corinthians 10:11, "the ends of the ages have come upon us."

The Millennium will comprise all that God promised to David. He will set His Son, King Messiah, on the throne of David to rule the earth with enforced righteousness (Psa. 2). But it will not be a perfect age. Even with the Prince of Peace, the King of Kings and LORD of LORDS present on the earth, peace will not be real because the obedience of the nations will be feigned. They will be forced to "beat their swords into plowshares and their spears into pruning hooks," and commanded to accept the Lord's council and decisions on the administration of the Kingdom (Isa. 2:4). "As soon as they hear; they obey me; Foreigners submit to me" (Psa. 18:44). "Because of the greatness of Your power Your enemies will give feigned obedience to You" (Psa. 66:3). "Those who hate the LORD would pretend obedience to Him, And their time of punishment would be forever" (Psa. 81:15). The millennial age closes with the rebellion of Satan and the nations and their subsequent destruction. The purpose of reiterating the moral condition and nature of the Millennium is to emphasize that one can hardly describe it as God's future plan for the universe. His ultimate plan has to do with a perfect age, and the millennial age cannot be compared to that flawless age of complete and perfect deliverance.

III. DELIVERANCE OF JERUSALEM'S CITIZENRY DURING THE AGE OF AGES

The term age of ages refers to that age of which Paul writes in Ephesians 1:20-23; Philippians 2:9-11; Ephesians 3:21; and Hebrews 1:8-13. Ephesians 1:20-23 reads, " He raised Him from the dead and seated Him at His right hand in the heavenly places, far above all rule and authority and power and dominion, and every name that is named, not only in this age but also in the one to come. And He put all things in subjection under His feet, and gave Him as head over all things to the church, which is His body, the fullness of Him who fills all in all." I understand, "this age" to mean the Church age of which Paul was a part, and "the one to come," as an age beyond the Millennium.

Philippians 2:9-11 has, "For this reason also, God highly exalted Him, and bestowed on Him the name which is above every name, so that at the name of Jesus every knee will bow, of those who are in heaven and on earth and under the earth, and that every tongue will confess that Jesus Christ is Lord, to the glory of God the Father." Obviously, this universal worship will not happen during the Millennium. It can only refer to the heavenly age, the age of all ages.

Ephesians 3:21 is translated, according to Rotherham, "Unto Him be glory, in the assembly And in Christ Jesus—unto all the generations of the age of the ages; Amen."[9] The generations of which the Apostle writes are the multitudes that will be brought together in the New Jerusalem, the city of the living God (Heb. 12: 22-24). The "age of ages," spoken of here is that which is mentioned by Paul in the foregoing passages: "the age to come"—and the age of universal worship, beyond the Millennium.

Once the earth has been prepared, the New Jerusalem will descend out of heaven from God. Some scholars believe it already will have come down and placed in orbit around the earth during the Millennium. But how can that be if the new heaven and new earth do not come into existence until after the Great White Throne Judgment, which chronologically follows the Millennium? The conditions toward the close of the Millennium are sin, rebellion, and death. Those conditions will not exist in the New Jerusalem of the new earth for the inhabitants of the New Jerusalem will not remember them: "For behold, I create new heavens and a new earth; And the former things will not be remembered or come to mind" (Isa. 65:17).

God has a far-far better dwelling place for His people than earthly Jerusalem. Although Abraham looked and waited for this better city whose builder and maker is God (Heb. 11: 9), and Isaiah prophesied of it as being new (Isa. 65:17-19), God chose to reveal more details to John about the city than He had revealed to any individual throughout the Bible. Chapters 21 and 22 of Revelation cover in detail all that God was pleased to reveal to John concerning the city. Revelation 20:11-15 closes with, "And anyone not found written in the Book of Life was cast into the lake of fire" (Rev. 20:15). But immediately after writing those solemn words, it seems as though John can hardly wait to tell his readers about the particulars of the wonderful city, New Jerusalem. They are indeed more beautiful to behold than any scene ever described by human eyes. John was in the Spirit on the Lord's Day. The Spirit revealed details about the holy city, New Jerusalem, into which His people shall be delivered forever. Those details comprise the following blessings: (1) deliverance of Jerusalem's citizenry from death and, (2) deliverance of Jerusalem's citizenry into their inherited estate.

1. DELIVERANCE OF JERUSALEM'S CITIZENRY FROM DEATH

Death is the enemy of old; a discussion of deliverance from it must be dealt with before continuing with the joyous aspects of the New Jerusalem, into which God's people will be delivered. Deliverance from death is addressed almost from the outset in Revelation 21:1-4). John writes in verses 1-2, "Then I saw a new heaven and a new earth; for the first heaven and the first earth passed away, and there is no longer any sea. And I saw the holy city, new Jerusalem, coming down out of heaven from God, made ready as a bride adorned for her husband." And then he says, "And I heard a loud voice from the throne, saying, "Behold, the tabernacle of God is among men, and He will dwell among them, and they shall be His people, and God Himself will be among them and He will wipe away every tear from their eyes; and there will no longer be any death; there will no longer be any mourning, or crying, or pain; the first things have passed away" (Rev. 21:3-4). In chapter 20, he tells us about the Great White Throne, the dead being raised and cast into the lake of fire, which is the second death, but quickly he tells us that "there will no longer be any death" in the tabernacle of God, the new Jerusalem. It is as if God wants His people to know that this great enemy will be vanquished immediately.

Deliverance from death and the fear of death will be the release for which all souls have longed. Death has been with us since Adam, and can be classified as man's enemy in the following three ways: (1) death was man's first enemy, (2) death is man's worst enemy, and (3) death will be man's last enemy.

Death, Man's First Enemy

Death began in the Garden of Eden with Adam and Eve (Gen. 2-3). Eve was seduced by Satan to eat of the fruit of the Tree of the Knowledge of Good and Evil and Adam followed suit; but their conversion to death did not begin until each had eaten; when their sin was finished, they died. God told them: "Dying you will continue to die" (Gen. 2:15-17; James 1:14-15). Genesis 5 is a commentary on how devastating death was to Adam and his early descendants. "Therefore, just as sin entered the world through one man, and death through sin, and in this way death came to all men, because all sinned—for before the law was given, sin was in the world. But sin is not taken into account when there is no law. Nevertheless, death reigned from the time of Adam to the time of Moses, even over those who did not sin by breaking a command, as did Adam, who was a pattern of the one to come" (Rom. 5:12-14, NIV).

Death, Man's Worst Enemy

Death is man's worst enemy because it strikes without warning. It comes as a surprise—even when expected. No one knows the day or manner of one's death because it cannot be controlled. It is a power that strips everything away: wealth, health, and life. It pervades the lives of all living creatures and there is no defense against it.

Death, Man's Last Enemy

Last implies that other enemies precede death. Satan, sin's champion and man's archenemy, has inflicted war, global disaster, disease, and all their associated sorrows, upon man since Adam and Eve were expelled from the Garden. Every descendent of Adam must confront the consequences of Satan's evil influence over the first man; there is no choice. It has been so since man's beginning and will be so in the coming Tribulation period and millennial age.

Death during the Tribulation. Prior to the Tribulation, members of the Church (dead and living) will be raptured into the heavenly city, where there is no death (I Thess. 4:13-27; I Cor. 15:50-55). Following the

Rapture, Israel, along with people of "every tribe, tongue and nation" will remain on the earth to face a time of suffering and death (Rev. 7:13-17). Death will control them in the person of the beast. The covenant of false peace that Israel will make with the rider on the white horse (Rev. 6:2; Dan. 9:27) is known as the covenant with death, and Isaiah prophesied:

> Therefore hear the word of the Lord, you scornful men, Who rule this people who are in Jerusalem, Because you have said, "We have made a covenant with death, And with Sheol we are in agreement. When the overflowing scourge passes through, It will not come to us, For we have made lies our refuge, And under falsehood we have hidden ourselves." A Cornerstone in Zion Therefore thus says the Lord God: "Behold, I lay in Zion a stone for a foundation, A tried stone, a precious cornerstone, a sure foundation; Whoever believes will not act hastily. Also I will make justice the measuring line, And righteousness the plummet; The hail will sweep away the refuge of lies, And the waters will overflow the hiding place. Your covenant with death will be annulled, And your agreement with Sheol will not stand; When the overflowing scourge passes through, Then you will be trampled down by it. As often as it goes out it will take you; For morning by morning it will pass over, And by day and by night; It will be a terror just to understand the report." (Isa. 28:13-19, NKJV)

Death during the Millennial Age. Because of the covenant, the Jewish people will have feared death every day of their lives until the tried stone, the precious cornerstone, the stone the builders rejected, shall come (Dan. 2:31-35). That One will deliver them into the great kingdom age where death will be at a minimum; but even then, death will reign: "No more shall an infant from there live but a few days, Nor an old man who has not fulfilled his days; For the child shall die one hundred years old, But the sinner being one hundred years old shall be accursed" (Isa. 65:20, NKJV).

Following the millennial age, there will be an age into which Jerusalem's saved citizens, and the saved citizens of the nations of the world, will be delivered from death forever. They will join those who were raptured prior to the Tribulation and become part of the great family of God: "But you have come to Mount Zion and to the city of the living God, the heavenly Jerusalem, and to myriads of angels, to the general assembly and church of the firstborn who are enrolled in heaven, and to God, the Judge of all, and to the spirits of the righteous made perfect, and to Jesus, the mediator of a new covenant, and to the sprinkled blood, which speaks better than the blood of Abel" (Heb.12:22-24). "Therefore, since the children share in flesh and blood, He Himself likewise also partook of the same, that through death He might render powerless him who had the power of death, that is, the devil, and might free those who through fear of death were subject to slavery all their lives" (Heb. 2:14-15).

Paul writes: "For as in Adam all die, so also in Christ all will be made alive. But each in his own order: Christ the first fruits, after that those who are Christ's at His coming, then comes the end, when He hands over the kingdom to the God and Father, when He has abolished all rule and all authority and power. For He must reign until He has put all His enemies under His feet. The last enemy that will be abolished is death" (I Cor. 15:22-26). Over 1900 years have passed from the time Christ became the first fruits until the present. His coming will be followed by 1000 years, at the end of which all enemies except death will have been destroyed. Death will meet its death at the conclusion of the Great White Throne Judgment (Rev. 29:7-15). After that "comes the end," of which Paul writes. The end is not the terminus of the millennial reign; the end is "the dispensation of the fullness of times," the dispensation of the age of the ages. That age follows the death of death and begins with the new heavens and new earth, and the descent of the Holy City, New Jerusalem.

With John's glimpse of the holy city descending and his announcement that death would be no more, he proceeds to survey in detail things concerning the city of the ages. This is the last passage in the Bible relative to all the destructions and the deliverances of Jerusalem from her enemies. Scholars have been frustrated by Paul's statement: "I know a man in Christ who fourteen years ago—whether in the body I do not know, or out of the body I do not know, God knows—such a man was caught up to the third heaven. And I know how such a man—whether in the body or apart from the body I do not know, God knows—was caught up into Paradise and heard inexpressible words, which a man is not permitted to speak" (II Cor. 12:2-4). Was Paul prevented from divulging what was reserved for John to describe? John saw the following detailed scene of the holy city, New Jerusalem:

> "And he carried me away in the Spirit to a great and high mountain, and showed me the holy city, Jerusalem, coming down out of heaven from God, having the glory of God. Her brilliance was like a very costly stone, as a stone of crystal-clear jasper. It had a great and high wall, with twelve gates, and at the gates twelve angels; and names were written on them, which are the names of the twelve tribes of the sons of Israel. There were three gates on the east and three gates on the north and three gates on the south and three gates on the west. And the wall of the city had twelve foundation stones, and on them were the twelve names of the twelve apostles of the Lamb. The one who spoke with me had a gold measuring rod to measure the city, and its gates and its wall. The city is laid out as a square, and its length is as great as the width; and he measured the city with the rod, fifteen hundred miles; its length and width and height are equal. And he measured its wall, seventy-two yards, according to human measurements, which are also angelic measurements. The material of the wall was jasper; and the city was pure gold, like clear glass. The foundation stones of the city wall were adorned with every kind of precious stone. The first foundation stone was jasper; the second, sapphire; the third, chalcedony; the fourth, emerald; the fifth, sardonyx; the sixth, sardius; the seventh, chrysolite; the eighth, beryl; the ninth, topaz; the tenth, chrysoprase;

the eleventh, jacinth; the twelfth, amethyst. And the
twelve gates were twelve pearls; each one of the gates was
a single pearl. And the street of the city was pure gold,
like transparent glass. I saw no temple in it, for the Lord
God the Almighty and the Lamb are its temple. And
the city has no need of the sun or of the moon to shine
on it, for the glory of God has illumined it, and its lamp
is the Lamb. The nations will walk by its light, and the
kings of the earth will bring their glory into it. In the
daytime (for there will be no night there) its gates will
never be closed; and they will bring the glory and the
honor of the nations into it; and nothing unclean, and
no one who practices abomination and lying, shall ever
come into it, but only those whose names are written
in the Lamb's book of life . . . . Then he showed me a
river of the water of life, clear as crystal, coming from
the throne of God and of the Lamb, in the middle of
its street. On either side of the river was the tree of life,
bearing twelve kinds of fruit, yielding its fruit every
month; and the leaves of the tree were for the healing of
the nations. There will no longer be any curse; and the
throne of God and of the Lamb will be in it, and His
bond-servants will serve Him; they will see His face,
and His name will be on their foreheads. And there will
no longer be any night; and they will not have need of
the light of a lamp nor the light of the sun, because the
Lord God will illumine them; and they will reign forever
and ever (Rev. 21:10-22:5).

It is the place our blessed Lord promised prior to His death, burial,
resurrection, and ascension: "Do not let your heart be troubled; believe in
God, believe also in Me. "In My Father's house are many dwelling places;
if it were not so, I would have told you; for I go to prepare a place for you.
" If I go and prepare a place for you, I will come again and receive you
to Myself, that where I am, there you may be also" (Jn. 14:1-3). The place

He presently is preparing for His earthly people is a very special home, purchased with the sacrifice of His own precious blood.

2. DELIVERANCE OF JERUSALEM'S CITIZENRY INTO THEIR INHERITED ESTATE

This is the inheritance for which Peter praised God: "Blessed be the God and Father of our Lord Jesus Christ, who according to His great mercy has caused us to be born again to a living hope through the resurrection of Jesus Christ from the dead, to obtain an inheritance which is imperishable and undefiled and will not fade away, reserved in heaven for you, who are protected by the power of God through faith for a salvation ready to be revealed in the last time" (I Pet. 1:3-5). Peter was allowed to detail the destruction of the old heavens and earth (II Pet. 3:1-13), but as with Paul (II Cor. 12:2-4), Peter was prevented from fully describing the home of the redeemed; he only mentioned that it would not perish, that it was without sin, and that it was reserved. But John describes the inherited city in detail: (1) shape and size of the city, (2) substance of the city, (3) splendor of the city, (4) safety and security of the city, (5) stability of the city, (6) supernatural supply of the city, (7) society of the city, and (8) steady-state succession of the city.

Shape and Size of the City

After Cain murdered his brother Abel, God expelled him from Eden and he went to the land of Nod and there built the first city. Since then, man has constructed cities of every size and shape. The new city, reserved for the saints of God, is greater in size than all the cities of the earth combined.

Shape of the City. "The city is laid out as a square, and its length is as great as the width; and he measured the city with the rod, 1500 miles; its length and width and height are equal." (Rev. 21:16). Since John mentions height, we know that new Jerusalem is a cube.

Size of the City. ". . . and he measured the city with the rod, fifteen hundred miles; its length and width and height are equal" (Rev. 21:16). The area of the city totals 2,250,000 square miles. One writes:

"Did you ever think about the size of the city?" he asked, and without waiting for a reply he proceeded to reveal the significance of his statistics. "Man, it's amazing; it's astounding; it beats everything I ever heard of! John says that each of the walls of the city measures twelve thousand furlongs. Now, if you work that out"—he bent closely over his notebook—"it will give you an area of 2,250,000 square miles! Did you ever hear the like of that? The only city foursquare that I ever saw was Adelaide in South Australia. The ship that brought me out from the old country called in there for a couple of days, and I thought it a fine city. But, as you know, very well, the city of Adelaide covers only one square mile. Each of the four sides is a mile long. London covers an area of 140 square miles. But this city—the City Foursquare! It is 2,250,000 times as big as Adelaide. It is 15,000 times as big as London! It is twenty times as big as all New Zealand! It is ten times as big as Germany, and ten times as big as France! It is forty times as big as all England! It is ever so much bigger than India! Why, it's an enormous continent in itself. I had no idea of it until I went into the figures with my blue pencil here."10

If the new earth is to be the same size as the present earth, the land area covered by New Jerusalem would extend from San Luis Obispo, California on the Pacific coast eastward to the Mississippi River at Cairo, Illinois, northward to Nipigon on the Canadian border, westward to the Pacific coast, and southward to San Luis Obispo.

Size and Shape of the Walls and Gates of the City. "It had a great and high wall, with twelve gates, and at the gates twelve angels; and names were written on them, which are the names of the twelve tribes of the sons of Israel. There were three gates on the east and three gates on the north and three gates on the south and three gates on the west. And the wall of the city had twelve foundation stones, and on them were the twelve names of the twelve apostles of the Lamb. The one who spoke with me had a gold measuring rod to measure the city, and its gates and its wall. And he measured its wall, seventy-two yards, according to human measurements, which are also angelic measurements" (Rev. 21:12-15).

The measurements of the gates are not given, but their size will be in proportion to the size of the wall in which they are set. They are ornamental, not defensive; all sin and enemies will have been put away. They are equal in number, three according to each direction of the compass, giving dynamic symmetry to the appearance of the city as a whole. The names of the twelve tribes of Israel are written on them and I list them here in the same order as John did in Revelation 7: 4-8: Judah, Reuben, Gad, Asher, Naphtali, Manasseh, Simeon, Levi, Issachar, Zebulun, Joseph, and Benjamin.

The wall of the city has twelve foundations and on those foundations are the names of the twelve apostles of the Lamb. These are those Apostles who followed Jesus during His time on the earth, before the birth of the Church in Acts 2. They were handpicked by Jesus Himself and they are listed four times in the New Testament: Matt. 2:10-4; Mk. 3:16-19; Lk. 6:14-16; and Acts 1:13-26. Judas Iscariot is mentioned three times in the gospels' lists, but his name is dropped in the Acts' list and the name Matthias added in its place (Acts 1:26). Judas turned from the apostleship and "went to his own place," and in doing so lost the chance of having his name inscribed on one of the twelve foundation stones; therefore the names on the Acts' list are the ones John saw on the twelve foundation stones of the wall of the city: Peter, James, John, Andrew, Philip, Thomas, Bartholomew, Matthew, James, Simon, Judas (not Iscariot), and Matthias. The city for which Abraham searched had foundations (Heb. 11:10); those foundations are twelve in number, as John records.

The city that Abraham, John, and Paul described cannot possibly be the Church because the church of the firstborn is listed by the writer to the Hebrews as part of the citizenry of the city (Heb. 12:22-24). The bride that had made herself ready as seen in Revelation 19:7 will celebrate the marriage supper with Christ at which invited guests will be present: "Write, 'Blessed are those who are invited to the marriage supper of the Lamb.'" Even there, John does not identify the bride as the Church. But the "place" itself, which sat on twelve foundations, is termed by John as the bride, the wife of the Lamb. Paul identifies her as Jerusalem above, the mother of us all (Gal. 4:26), the representative of God's people all-inclusive. John said that "the holy city, new Jerusalem ... was made ready as a bride adorned for her husband" (Rev. 21:2).

Substance of the City

Men have constructed cities of mud, wood, stone, brick, and steel. Architects have dreamed of great cities and seen those dreams become reality: Nineveh, Tyre, Babylon, Rome, Jerusalem, London, Paris, New York, Chicago, and Tokyo. None can hold a candle to the Holy city, new Jerusalem, built by God, the master architect.

Substance and Strength of the Wall of the City. John says, "The wall was made of Jasper, and . . . the foundation of the city walls were decorated with every kind of precious stone. The first foundation was jasper, the second sapphire, the third chalcedony, the fourth emerald, the fifth sardonyx, the sixth carnelian, the seventh chrysolite, the eighth beryl, the ninth topaz, the tenth chrysoprase, the eleventh jacinth, and the twelfth amethyst" (Rev. 21:18-21). The strength of the wall is indicated by the hardness of the stones. The stones are beautiful and hard enough to last throughout the ages to come.

Substance, Stations, and Signifiers of the Gates of the City. "It had a great and high wall, with twelve gates, and at the gates twelve angels; and names were written on them, which are the names of the twelve tribes of the sons of Israel. There were three gates on the east and three gates on the north and three gates on the south and three gates on the west" (Rev. 21:12-13). Then in verse 21: "And the twelve gates were twelve pearls; each one of the gates was a single pearl . . ." Each gate is a single pearl.

Substance of the Street of the City. "The great street of the city was of pure gold, like transparent glass" (Rev. 21:21). Young has in his Modern Translation, "And the twelve gates are twelve pearls, each several one of the gates was of one pearl; and the broad-place of the city is pure gold—as transparent glass." The broad-place is the exact meaning of the Greek, plateia, and is, I assume, where each street ends, depending upon which gate one enters into the city.

Splendor of the City

John describes the city as being one great diamond, shining in splendor. The brilliance of a 2,250,000-square-mile diamond is unimaginable, but the eyes of the new body will see and be dazzled by the city and all its beauty.

Safety, Security, and Stability of the City

The walls and gates of the Holy City described above are, no doubt, symbolical of the protective characteristics of the city. In reality, all cities of antiquity were furnished with walls, gates, and foundations which were part of their character due to necessity; the walls and gates of old Jerusalem were for safety and security.11 The number of gates were kept to a minimum; the more gates, the weaker the wall. Old Jerusalem has had approximately eight gates during her history, but New Jerusalem has twelve, three in each wall, permitting freedom of movement in and out of the city.

Supernatural Supply of the City

A look at Revelation 22:1-3 reveals that the supply of the city is dependent on three sources: (1) the throne of God, (2) the river of life, and (3) the tree of life. Each is related to the other. "And he shewed me a pure river of water of life, clear as crystal, proceeding out of the throne of God and of the Lamb. In the midst of the street of it, and on either side of the river, was there the tree of life, which bare twelve manner of fruits, and yielded her fruit every month: and the leaves of the tree were for the healing of the nations. And there shall be no more curse: but the throne of God and of the Lamb shall be in it; and His servants shall serve Him . . ."

The Throne of God. Revelation 22: 3 tells us that the throne of God and of the Lamb shall be in it (the city), but it does not tell us exactly where. Since the river of life flows from the Throne (Rev. 22:1), it probably is positioned in a central-most place high above all else in the city. If the height of the city is measured to be part of its foursquare shape, the throne will set 1,500 miles high. The presence of God and the Lamb will be felt throughout the Holy city, and the saints of all the ages will receive nourishment from it. God has been the source of provision for His creation since its beginning in Genesis 1-3.

The River of Life. The river of life is crystal-clear and sparkles, and its flow is determined by the height of the throne. It may descend in a cascading fashion throughout the city until it becomes the great river that John says flows through the middle of the street, or broad place. (See Ezekiel 47, but keep in mind that Ezekiel's river will exist during the Millennium and lasts only for 1,000 years.) The river of the Heavenly city is after the Millennium and it is eternal. On each side of the river is the tree of life. "Tree" is a type rather than a number. Imagine standing at the river, facing it, and looking across to the other side; you would see the trees of life, and if you did an about-face, you would see the trees of life. Or imagine yourself in a boat on the river of life. Look to your left and you will see the trees of life; look to your right and you will see the same. The broad-place may be a great place where the citizens of Heaven fellowship with one another, and with God the Father and the Lamb. A river runs through it—the river of life! "There is a river whose streams make glad the city of God, The holy dwelling places of the Most High. God is in the midst of her, she will not be moved . . . ." (Psa. 46:4-5).

The Tree of Life. The trees of life bear twelve kinds of fruit. Every month the trees bring forth fruit. The leaves of the trees are for the healing of the nations. The word for healing in the Greek is, therapeian, from which comes the word, therapy. Since there will be no sin or death, God has chosen to maintain the mortality of His people by means of the leaves (Rev. 22:2). Since all sin, disease, and death will have been done away, the word health should be used rather than the word healing. Healing assumes that disease is still present, whereas, health does not. The fruit and leaves maintain the life and health of the citizens of Heaven. This is the way God has chosen to continuously nourish and sustain His people throughout eternity. God alone is immortal, our afterlife is in His hands, and whatever way he chooses to maintain our immortality is best for our eternal welfare.

God also had the same concern for our first parents; they had been given the right and access to the tree of life and could have maintained their lives forever had they chosen it over the tree of the knowledge of good and evil. God expelled them from Eden to keep them from eating of the tree of life and living forever in their sinful condition. Now, through Christ, God offers the tree of life, the water of life, and the Heavenly City to all the sinful children of Adam and Eve. Christ has restored what Adam and Eve took away from us (Psa. 69:4), and because of His work of redemption at Calvary, the saints of all the ages will be among the greatest society ever imagined.

Society of the City

As the writer of Hebrews wrote, "But you have come to Mount Zion and to the city of the living God, the heavenly Jerusalem, and to myriads of angels, to the general assembly and church of the firstborn who are enrolled in heaven, and to God, the Judge of all, and to the spirits of the righteous made perfect, and to Jesus, the mediator of a new covenant, and to the sprinkled blood, which speaks better than the blood of Abel" (Heb. 12:22-24).

Myriads of Angels. The number of this great company of angels may include all of those glorious beings God created from before the foundation of the world, excluding those who fell with Lucifer.

Church of the Firstborn. Every blood-bought believer in Christ since the birth of the Church at Pentecost, Acts 2, will make up this great body of Christ, who "is the head of the body, the church. He is the beginning, the firstborn [prototokos, brackets, mine] from the dead…." —ESV.

God. The Father of the Word, before the Word became incarnated as the person of Jesus Christ, will be there. He is the eternal Father of all who are named in Heaven and in Earth.

Spirits of Righteous Men Perfected. These were those throughout the Old Testament Period, Heb. 11:40, who were justified by faith in God. It has always been, "The just shall live by faith." (Hab. 2:4; Rom. 1:17; Heb. 10:38; 11:1-40).

Jesus. The Savior, Precious Lamb of God, Second Person of the blessed Trinity, the Word made flesh, the One in whom all the fullness of Godhead was expressed and explained to humanity, without whom this great celebration will not have transpired. He, the Creator who made the worlds, is mentioned last. It seems so unfair but not really; He is the last but not the least. He is in His rightful place. He said himself, "I am the Alpha and the Omega, the Beginning and the End, who is and who was and who is to come, the Almighty." (Rev. 1:8; 21:6).

All of the above will make up the society of New Jerusalem. The great body of angels will be there in great festal gathering celebrating this great coming together of the family of God. Never before will such an event have taken place since the founding of the universe. The eternal fellowship of Saints and Angels will have begun.

"But the cowardly and unbelieving and abominable and murderers and immoral persons and sorcerers and idolaters and all liars, their part will be in the lake that burns with fire and brimstone, which is the second death" (Rev. 21:8). The Lord says, ". . . and nothing unclean, and no one who practices abomination and lying, shall ever come into it, but only those whose names are written in the Lamb's book of life" (Rev. 21:27). These words are a promise to all who are washing their robes that they may enter the city and expect no harm from incorrigibles, ever again.

The New Jerusalem has been specially created by God to succeed earthly Jerusalem. Heavenly Jerusalem will continue to exist upon the new earth among the stars of the new heavens. She will be an ageless abiding place for His people; it is so because God and the Lamb will be in her midst (Psa. 46: 4-5; Rev. 21:3, 22; 22:3, 4). She will continue forever and ever, and will never cease to exist. But, while this beautiful and Holy City, New Jerusalem, will never cease to exist, the age in which it and its citizens abide will come to a close, and with its closure will come the city's last great deliverance.

IV. DELIVERANCE OF NEW JERUSALEM INTO THE HANDS OF GOD THE FATHER

1. DELIVERED AS A SOVEREIGN STATE

Of all the characteristics and descriptive terms of the New Jerusalem, it must be thought of as being a sovereign state.

The Sovereign State, a Kingdom

Sovereign state means that the city itself is the Kingdom that shall be delivered. While John is very detailed in describing the New Jerusalem throughout Revelation 21-22, he never mentions that the city is the Kingdom; but the writer to the Hebrews expresses it as such, "He has promised, saying, "Yet once more I will shake not only the earth, but also the heaven." This expression, "Yet once more," denotes the removing of those things which can be shaken, as of created things, so that those things which cannot be shaken may remain. Therefore, since we receive a kingdom which cannot be shaken . . . ." (Heb 12:26-28). These words follow those of Hebrews 11:8-16, and prove that the New Jerusalem is the kingdom, one and the same with the better country and city for which Abraham and the pilgrims of faith looked. This kingdom will not appear until well beyond the time period of the millennial kingdom—the old heavens and earth, and earthly Jerusalem. This, "the end" period, has an end and will conclude Christ's reign as the Son of Man. It is only during this period that the absolute Will of God will be done, as He taught His disciples to pray: "Your kingdom come. Your will be done, On earth as it is in heaven" (Matt. 6:10).

2. DELIVERED AS A SOVEREIGN STAGE

As we have seen, the kingdoms of this world and earthly Jerusalem will be delivered over into the hands of Christ when he returns to the earth at the close of the great Tribulation period, just prior to the beginning of the Millennium. The time of Jacob's trouble will have run its course, the nations and the kingdoms of this earth will have become the kingdom of our LORD and of His Christ (Dan. 7:13-14; Rev. 11:15-18), and He will begin His reign as the Son of Man. His reign will be in two phases: the first phase will last for 1,000 years, at the end of which, He will defeat Satan and the remaining rebellious nations, and thus, at the terminus of the Millennium, earthly Jerusalem will be delivered for the last time (Rev. 20:7-9). Just how long following this deliverance it will be before the citizens of old Jerusalem are delivered into the New Jerusalem, and the point at which the dead, small and great, stand before God to be judged and are cast into the lake of fire, and the last enemy, death, will be destroyed (I Cor. 15: 26; Rev. 20:11-15), it is difficult to tell. Nevertheless, whenever the saints of God are removed to their eternal home, the second phase of the Kingdom of the Son of Man will begin. This second phase, according to Scripture, is termed "the end" by the Apostle Paul.

Stage means a period of time in which the last stage of the Kingdom will be expressed. (The expression of the Kingdom is composed of all that John writes about it in Revelation 21-22.) This stage (period, or phase) is known biblically as "the end." Here, it is important to define exactly what Paul meant as "the end." The term can be defined in the light of Genesis 1:1: "In the beginning God created the heavens and the earth." The beginning was not the beginning of the creation process, but the great period of time in which the process of creation took place. Imagine "the beginning" as a parenthesis, like this: (The Beginning). Next, imagine God and Eternity before the parenthesis, like this: God and Eternity, then (The Beginning). Now, imagine "the end," as a parenthesis, like this: (The End). Next, imagine God and Eternity after "the end," like this: (The End), and then God and Eternity. Both, "the beginning" parenthesis and "the end" parenthesis illustrate, not the beginning or ending of something, but rather two great periods of time; the former period in which the old creation took place; and the latter period in which the new creation, the New Jerusalem (the Kingdom) will take place. Here is the whole scheme in a nutshell: God and Eternity, followed by (The Beginning); and then (The End) followed by God and Eternity.

Having defined the meaning of Paul's term, "the end," it is also important to delineate the following biblical concepts as representations of "the end," in order to get some idea as to the scope of the Kingdom, and just how long the Kingdom will last before it is delivered into the hands of God, the Father. Those concepts are: (1) the age-of-ages end, (2) the eighth-day end, (3) the better-end end, (4) the 1,000-generations end, and (5) the fullness-of-times end.

The Age-of-Ages End. This is a concept that represents "the end" as a great age that succeeds other ages. An age (Greek, aion, English, eon) has a beginning and an end. The age of ages is no exception to the rule, which means that the age under discussion is not eternity; eternity lies beyond. An age is a specific period of time that is marked off from other periods of time, either shorter or longer. The term, age of the ages, does not mean that it is to be greater than all other ages following it, but rather, will be greater than all ages preceding it. "The end," of which Paul speaks, may be just as long as the "In the beginning" age of Genesis 1:1. Yet, there may be hints in the following concepts that may indicate that "the end" age in which New Jerusalem manifests itself will be a shorter time period than the "In the beginning" age of Genesis 1:1.

The Eighth-day End. We are in the habit of thinking of our week as containing only seven days, but the Bible speaks of eight days. The concept is quite simple. Here, I must quote, at length, R.C. Trench:

> Without fixing any actual term to the present dispensation (as some have done, supposing that six thousand years from the creation will introduce the Millennium), we may certainly agree with all interpreters, that the Millennium is typified morally, if not chronologically, by the Sabbath, or seventh day.
>
> But Scripture points to an eighth day (see Lev. xxiii.16), "the morrow after the Sabbath"; and (verses 36 and 39) to eighth-day celebrations. The seventh day has to do with the old creation, for God rested upon it, and gave it to man for his rest and toil. It is the old creation rest, earthly, human and natural. It is also imperfect. So the Millennium will bring in an earthly, human, natural, and imperfect day, or period of rest for the world. For Israel chiefly, but for all nations if they will have it.
>
> But the eighth day, the first day of the week, the day of our Lord's resurrection, and the day of Pentecost too, points to the new creation rest. After the imperfect rest of nature on the seventh comes the supernatural and perfect rest of resurrection on the eighth day, the great closing festival" (see refs., p.92).
>
> So the perfect glory of the risen Christ in connection with a resurrection Kingdom will come in upon the morrow of the Sabbatic Millennium. (Examine Num. xxix. 35, with Lev. ix. 1; and xxxiii. 36-39).

Note, therefore, that this eighth day cannot point to the Millennium, which is represented by the seventh.

And it cannot be Eternity, for it is a day or definite period, like each of the preceding days.

And if anyone contends that the eighth day means Eternity future, I ask how it comes that Eternity past is not also represented by day? How simple it would have been, for example, to describe creation as beginning on the second day, the first representing the previous undivided age of Eternity past. Thus there would be harmony in this interpretation. But it is not so. The first division of time for man is called the eighth day. Eternity lies behind the first and the last. The eighth day must therefore be a dispensation lying between the Millennium and the subsequent Eternity.[12]

No doubt, this eighth day that follows the Millennium (the first phase of the Kingdom of the Son of Man), is the second phase of His Kingdom and corresponds to the preceding concept, the age of the ages.

The Latter Days End. This concept is to be found in the book of Job and is the same idea as that of Paul's, "the end." "The Lord blessed the latter days of Job more than his beginning. . . . After this, Job lived 140 years, and saw his sons and his grandsons, four generations. And Job died, an old man and full of days" (Job 42:12-17). The beginning of Job's life was not when it began at conception or birth, but was a period of time. Likewise, the latter end of his life was also a period of time (140 years). It can be illustrated like this: (the beginning = Job's life from his birth to the time of his second blessing), and like this: (the latter end = Job's life from the beginning of his second blessing to the end of his life = 140 years). The end of his life was better than the beginning. So it will be with "the end," of which Paul speaks in I Corinthians 15:24; the latter end of Christ's Kingdom (the New Jerusalem reign) will be better than the beginning of His Kingdom (the 1,000-year millennial reign). But the 140-year end of Job's life can, in no way, be compared to the length of "the end" of which Paul speaks, as will be seen in the following concept.

The 1,000-Generations End. In Deuteronomy 7:9 and I Chronicles

16:15, God tells Israel that He keeps His covenant made to Abraham, Isaac, and Jacob to a thousand generations, and He is faithful to perform every promise.

Even though the countdown toward the end of the 1,000 generations began when God made the promise to Abraham, it will not be fulfilled until the end of the Kingdom stage of the New Jerusalem, "the end," mentioned by Paul (I Cor. 15:24). Keep in mind that the New Jerusalem is not the Bride, the Church, although the Church is part its citizenry, but it is Israel completing the blessing of the promise, "The Lord did not set His love on you nor choose you because you were more in number than any of the peoples, for you were the fewest of all peoples, but because the Lord loved you and kept the oath which He swore to your forefathers, the Lord brought you out by a mighty hand and redeemed you from the house of slavery, from the hand of Pharaoh king of Egypt. Know therefore that the Lord your God, He is God, the faithful God, who keeps His covenant and His loving kindness to a thousandth generation" (Deut. 7:7-9). Israel is the city that has twelve gates, named for each tribe of Israel, and twelve foundations, named for the twelve apostles of the Lamb (Rev. 21:12-14). Obviously, the covenant made to Israel will not be fully realized until the end of the 1,000 generations. Those are the generations that will end the promise when the New Jerusalem is delivered over to the Father at the end of Paul's "the end." They are mentioned by Paul in Ephesians 3:21, "Unto Him be glory throughout all the generations of the aion of the aions." The generations of the aion of the aions (the age of the ages) correspond to the course of the 1,000-generations end.

The writer to the Hebrews made it clear that Abraham did not receive his full inheritance while here on earth because he did not find the city which has foundations, whose builder and architect is God, although he looked for it by faith (Heb. 11:8-10). Abraham's search for the city ended when he died at the age of 175 years and entered Sheol, which later became known as Abraham's Bosom. Later, the Lord Jesus was raised from the dead and emptied Abraham's Bosom, leading captivity captive (the souls of Abraham and Old Testament saints, and the spirits of the righteous men made perfect Eph. 4:7-10; Heb. 12:22-24). From the time the promise of the covenant was made to Abraham, his entrance into Sheol, to the time Abraham will have entered New Jerusalem, to the time of the covenant's completion, there are to be 1,000 generations. But there is no way of determining the length of time the 1,000 generations cover unless one knows the length of a biblical generation. This can be determined by referring again to Job 42:16, "After this, Job lived 140 years, and saw his sons and his grandsons, four generations" (Job 42:16). The writer of Job equates 140 years to four generations; on that basis, one must divide 140 by 4 in order to arrive at the correct number of years for one biblical generation, which is 35 years. There were 42 generations from Abraham to Christ (Matt. 1:17). Forty-two generations multiplied by 35 equals a total of 1,470 years. So, in order to know how long Abraham will be in the Holy City before the expiration of God's covenant with him, it is necessary to subtract 1,470 years (42 generations) from 1,000 generations, which equals 958 generations or 33,530 years. There are differences of opinion as to the length of a biblical generation; they range from 30-40 years, which would, if multiplied by 1,000, total 30,000-40,000 years. One would be unwise to be dogmatic on these figures, but at least it gives some idea as to approximately how long the New Jerusalem phase of the Kingdom will last before Christ turns it over to the Father.

The Fullness-of-Times End. One may not be absolutely sure how many years the heavenly city, New Jerusalem, will manifest itself during the latter phase of the Kingdom of the Son of Man, but one can be sure of the fact that during the Kingdom of the Son of Man, from the beginning and throughout the first phase of His Kingdom (the Millennium), to, and throughout the second phase of His Kingdom (the New Jerusalem), He will have brought all things into subjection. That is God's end-purpose. He will have brought into absolute subjection all opposing powers. This fulfillment of God's will was purposed in Christ by the Father Himself. "He made known to us the mystery of His will, according to His kind intention which He purposed in Him with a view to an administration suitable to the fullness of the times, that is, the summing up of all things in Christ, things in the heavens and things on the earth" (Eph. 1:9-10). The "administration suitable to the fullness of times" is, in fact, the dispensation that God has specifically tailored for bringing everything together in Christ. That whole period, the-fullness-of-times end, "the end," will indeed be a great time of reconciliation. Everything will be made right that has been wrong throughout all of the dispensations preceding it. "For it was the Father's good pleasure for all the fullness to dwell in Him, and through Him to reconcile all things to Himself, having made peace through the blood of His cross; through Him, I say, whether things on earth or things in heaven" (Col. 1:19-20). Once reconciliation has been accomplished through Christ, Christ will deliver the kingdom over to God, the Father. Paul writes of the deliverance in I Corinthians 15: 24-28. Trench makes the passage clear:

> The teaching of the passage will, I believe, be elucidated by the following transcript, with the explanatory words in brackets, and will show how carefully the apostle's words in brackets, are chosen to convey the leading thought in the mind of the Spirit.
>
> "Then the end [or final dispensation], when [that is, at the conclusion of which period] He shall deliver up the Kingdom to God, even the Father, when [that is, at the beginning of which period] He shall have brought to nought all rule and Authority and Power. For He [Christ] must reign till [and after] He [God] shall have put all enemies under His [Christ's] feet. The last enemy that shall be abolished is Death.
>
> "For He put all things in subjection under His feet. But when He [God] shall have declared, 'All things are put in [a settled state of] subjection to Him,' it is evident that He [God] is excepted, which did subject all things to Him [Christ]. And when all things have been subjected to Him [Christ], then shall the Son also Himself be subjected [that is, as to His reigning attitude] to Him that did subject all things to Him, that [even throughout the term of Christ's Kingdom, as always] God may be all in all."[13]

Trench leaves no doubt that by the time of the very beginning of the "dispensation of the fullness of times," Christ will have abolished all rule and authority and power, and death. His act of abolishment of His enemies does not mean that His reign comes to an end at the beginning of the dispensation, but will continue throughout that period. The continuance of His reign throughout that dispensation is based on Psalm 110:1: "The Lord says to my Lord: "Sit at My right hand Until I make Your enemies a footstool for Your feet " (Psa. 110:1). The preposition, "Until," is the Hebrew word, *ad*, and the Greek word is, *achri*; both mean "a point of time which is subsequent to a duration simultaneous with another point of time—'later, until after.'"[14] At His ascension, He sat down at the Father's right hand to become a priest forever (for the age abiding) according to the order of Melchizedek (Psa. 110:4). The phrase, for the age abiding, can only mean the millennial age because there will be no need for a priest afterward. The making of His enemies as a footstool will be a process beginning at His second coming, and continuing throughout the Millennium, to and through to the end of the "dispensation of the fullness of times."

Again, Trench: "For He [Christ] must reign till [and after] He [God] shall have put all enemies under His [Christ's] feet." He shall have put all enemies under His feet, beginning at the close of the Millennium through the close of the Great White Throne judgment. After that, He will continue to reign throughout the Kingdom stage of the New Jerusalem, during which time He will have brought all things into subjection to Himself. Once God shall have declared that all things have been put in a settled state of subjection, then Christ will subject Himself to God, the Father, and deliver the Kingdom, New Jerusalem, into His hands.

3. DELIVERED BY THE SOVEREIGN SON

Scripture reveals that the Son is God, "and the Word was God" (Jn. 1:1), and if He is God He is the absolute Sovereign One. But when did He become the Sovereign Son according to the flesh?

The Beginning of the Son's Sovereignty

"He hands over the kingdom to the God and Father . . . " (I Cor. 15:24), implies that it was handed over to Him (Christ), at one time in the past and now has come full circle. Christ said, "All things have been handed over to Me by My Father . . ." (Matt. 11:27; w/Matt. 28:18; Jn. 3:35; 13:3; 17:2), and now, at the end of "the end," He hands them back. He became the Sovereign Son according to Hebrews 1: 1-14: In that passage, Christ is presented as the Son who is heir of all things, who made the ages. He would be asked by the Father to sit at His right hand until later. At His second coming, He would be introduced into the world again as the Sovereign Son of Man and receive His throne unto times age-abiding. Daniel envisioned the beginning of that sovereignty, "I kept looking in the night visions, And behold, with the clouds of heaven One like a Son of Man was coming, And He came up to the Ancient of Days And was presented before Him. " And to Him was given dominion, Glory and a kingdom, That all the peoples, nations and men of every language Might serve Him. His dominion is an everlasting dominion which will not pass away; And His kingdom is one which will not be destroyed" (Dan. 7:13-14).

The End of the Son's Sovereignty

The "times age-abiding" ended at the close of the Millennium, but His Sovereignty would continue thereafter throughout "the dispensation of the fullness of times (Eph. 1:10, NKJV)," at the close of which, the Sovereign Son will relinquish the Kingdom that was given to Him by His Father. "And when all things have been subjected to Him [Christ], then shall the Son also Himself be subjected [that is, as to His reigning attitude] to Him that did subject all things to Him, that [even throughout the term of Christ's Kingdom, as always]. As Trench mentions above (also footnote 13), "that is, as to his reigning attitude," I believe what he means by attitude is that Christ's position, posture and way of thinking will be different than from the time He received the kingdom to when He delivers it back into the hands of the Father. His attitude will revert to what it was in His pre-incarnate state, before He would ever become the Son of Man, before the beginning of Genesis 1:1 began.

John informs us that "In the beginning was the Word, and the Word was with God, and the Word was God. He was in the beginning with God" (Jn 1:1-2). To paraphrase: When the beginning began, the Word was already present with God, the Father. The beginning of the ages came about through the Word. It was by the Word " . . . through whom also He made the worlds [ages, aionas]" (Heb. 1:2), and "All things came into being through Him, and apart from Him nothing came into being that has come into being" (Jn 1:3).

The Word, in His pre-incarnate state, not only framed the ages (the great time periods), but He also made all things that would fit within each of those periods. The beginning age was the great time period in which God (through and by the Word) created the heavens and the earth (Gen. 1:1). How long that age lasted is unknown, but it ceased when Satan led an angelic rebellion against the Creator (Ezek. 28: 11-19). Something dreadful and evil occurred that caused a split in the universe, and another kingdom came into being, the kingdom of Satan (Matt. 12:26). The age ended in judgment, resulting in utter chaos, confusion, and darkness. From the ending of that age to the beginning of "the end" age, creation will have known nothing but failure that brought each succeeding age to a close.

But just as there was an age that began all subsequent ages that ended in failure, so shall there be an age that will close those ages that have followed the beginning one. Thus, we have in Paul's statement: "then the end" (I Cor. 15: 24), at the end of which, we will have reigned "unto the ages of the ages" (Rev. 2:5). I understand John to mean by the phrase "unto the ages of the ages" (Greek, *eis tous aionas ton aionon*, English; *aions of the aions*) that we will not only reign with Christ to the point where He hands over the Kingdom, but we will also continue to reign on throughout the ages of the ages, which begins at the Kingdom's transference into the hands of the Father. Then, God shall become all in all in the Jerusalem that is the mother of us all (Gal. 4:26), and she shall be delivered for "the ages of the ages.

PART FOUR

The Name of Jerusalem:
A Poetic Incentive

INTRODUCTION

Not only is the name of Jerusalem an indicative that suggests a city of prophetic character, but the name also invokes and calls forth an incentive of a poetic nature. Of all the forms of literature having to do with Jerusalem, none have prompted the emotions of the heart like poetry. Poets, bards and song writers of every age have referred to Jerusalem with different appellations and have vented their feelings about the city's destructions and deliverances, e.g., as to the destruction of the city in 70 A.D., two lines from The Works of Lord Byron, On the Day of the Destruction of Jerusalem by Titus, reveal Byron's view of the city through the eyes of the General: "From the last hill that looks on thy once holy dome, I beheld thee, oh Sion! when rendered to Rome . . . ." In the same Works, he alludes to the city's deliverance in The Destruction of Sennacherib, upon his attempt to destroy Jerusalem: "And there lay the rider distorted and pale, With the dew on his brow and the rust on his mail: And the tents were all silent, the banners alone, the lances un-lifted, the trumpet unblown."

One would be remiss to present such a brief example of Byron's poems on Jerusalem without considering them in full along with many other poetic works that have stirred the hearts of God's people down through the centuries. The following chapter is a selection of those works.

CHAPTER X

Destructions and Deliverances of Jerusalem in Poetic Plaint and Praise

Jerusalem is unlike all other cities on the earth; none have been poeticized and hymned like she has. The following two modes of expression are indicative of her grief and glory.

I. DESTRUCTIONS OF JERUSALEM IN POETIC PLAINT

Plaint is a word seldom used anymore. The Greek has *plessein*, and means to strike ones breast in sorrow. It means to lament one's loss, hurt, and regretted actions or feelings toward another. Works of a lamentable nature include the following:

Psalm 137 is one of the great pieces of Hebrew poetry and describes the children of Judah as disconsolate, sitting by the streams of Babylon where Nebuchadnezzar, King of Babylon, had carried them into captivity. There they grieve over their beloved Jerusalem. The Psalm is presented in metrical form.

1. PSALM 137

By Babel's streams we sat and wept,
When Sion we thought on.
In midst thereof we hanged our harps
the willow-trees upon.

For there a song required they,
who did us captive bring:
Our spoilers called for mirth, and said,
A song of Sion sing.
O how the Lord's song shall we sing
within a foreign land?
If thee, Jerusalem, I forget,
skill part from my right hand.
My tongue to my mouth's roof let cleave,
if I do thee forget,
Jerusalem, and thee above
my chief joy do not set.
Remember Edom's children, Lord,
who in Jerusalem's day,
Ev'n unto its foundation,
Raze, raze it quite, did say.
O daughter thou of Babylon,
near to destruction;
Bless'd shall he be that thee rewards,
as thou to us has done.
Yes, happy surely shall he be
thy tender little ones
Who shall lay hold upon,
and them shall dash against the stones
— (Psalm 137 The Psalms of David in Metre, KJV)

While the children of Judah mourned Jerusalem by the rivers of Babylon, Jeremiah sat in the midst of the destroyed city and lamented. The book of Lamentations is a perfect example of plaint and consists of 5 Chapters/hymns in metrical form.[1] Each hymn is the Prophet's expression of deep sorrow for Jerusalem's plight and his own. The following excerpts are taken from each hymn.

2. THE LAMENTATIONS OF JEREMIAH

Hymn 1

How lonely sits the city
That was full of people!
She has become like a widow
Who was once great among the nations!
She who was a princess among the provinces
Has become a forced laborer!
She weeps bitterly in the night
And her tears are on her cheeks;
She has none to comfort her
Among all her lovers.
All her friends have dealt treacherously with her;
They have become her enemies.
—(Lam. 1:1-2, NASB)

Hymn 2

How the Lord has covered the daughter of Zion
With a cloud in His anger!
He has cast from heaven to earth
The glory of Israel,
And has not remembered His footstool
In the day of His anger.

. . . .

The Lord determined to destroy
The wall of the daughter of Zion.
He has stretched out a line,
He has not restrained His hand from destroying,
And He has caused rampart and wall to lament;
They have languished together.
Her gates have sunk into the ground,
He has destroyed and broken her bars.
Her king and her princes are among the nations;

The law is no more.
Also, her prophets find
No vision from the Lord.
—(Lam 2:1,8-9, NASB)

Hymn 3

All our enemies have opened their mouths against us.
Panic and pitfall have befallen us,
Devastation and destruction;
My eyes run down with streams of water
Because of the destruction of the daughter of my people.
My eyes pour down unceasingly,
Without stopping,
Until the Lord looks down
And sees from heaven.
My eyes bring pain to my soul
Because of all the daughters of my city.
—(Lam 3:46-51, NASB)

Hymn 4

The Lord has accomplished His wrath,
He has poured out His fierce anger;
And He has kindled a fire in Zion
Which has consumed its foundations.
The kings of the earth did not believe,
Nor did any of the inhabitants of the world,
That the adversary and the enemy
Could enter the gates of Jerusalem.
—(Lam 4:11-12, NASB)

Hymn 5

The joy of our hearts has ceased;
Our dancing has been turned into mourning.

The crown has fallen from our head;
Woe to us, for we have sinned!
Because of this our heart is faint,
Because of these things our eyes are dim;
Because of Mount Zion which lies desolate,
Foxes prowl in it.

. . . .

Restore us to You, O Lord, that we may be restored;
Renew our days as of old,
Unless You have utterly rejected us
And are exceedingly angry with us.
—(Lam 5:15-18, 21-22, NASB)

Lord Byron, an English poet of the 1800s, also mused about Jerusalem. He does not mention Jerusalem by name in the following work but he leaves no doubt that the vivid description is that of the city's would-be-destroyer's destruction just outside her walls.

3. THE DESTRUCTION OF SENNACHERIB

The Assyrian came down like the wolf on the fold,
And his cohorts were gleaming in purple and gold;
And the sheen of their spears was like stars on the sea,
When the blue wave rolls nightly on deep Galilee.

Like the leaves of the forest when Summer is green,
That host with their banners at sunset were seen:
Like the leaves of the forest when Autumn hath blown,
That host on the morrow lay withered and strown.

For the Angel of Death spread his wings on the blast,
And breathed in the face of the foe as he passed;
And the eyes of the sleepers waxed deadly and chill,
And their hearts but once heaved, and forever grew still!

And there lay the steed with his nostril all wide,
But through it there rolled not the breath of his pride;
And the foam of his gasping lay white on the turf,
And cold as the spray of the rock-beating surf.

And there lay the rider distorted and pale,
With the dew on his brow, and the rust on his mail:
And the tents were all silent, the banners alone,
The lances un-lifted, the trumpet unblown.
And the widows of Ashur are loud in their wail,
And the idols are broke in the temple of Baal;
And the might of the Gentile, un-smote by the sword,
Hath melted like snow in the glance of the Lord.[2]
—Lord Byron 1800s The Works of Lord Byron

I could find nothing written during or around the time of the Maccabees, but I did find, "The Banner of the Jew," by Emma Lazarus, a nineteenth century Jewish poet. "The Banner of the Jew" focuses on the Intertestamental Period, and Lazarus calls for her people to take a stand in the then present in which she lived.

4. THE BANNER OF THE JEW

Wake, Israel, wake! Recall to-day
The glorious Maccabean rage,
The sire heroic, hoary-gray,
His five-fold lion-lineage:
The Wise, the Elect, the Help-of-God,
The Burst-of-Spring, the Avenging Rod.*
From Mizpeh's mountain-ridge they saw
Jerusalem's empty streets, her shrine
Laid waste where Greeks profaned the Law,
With idol and with pagan sign.
Mourners in tattered black were there,
With ashes sprinkled on their hair.

Then from the stony peak there rang
A blast to ope the graves: down poured
The Maccabean clan, who sang
Their battle-anthem to the Lord.
Five heroes lead, and following, see,
Ten thousand rush to victory!

Oh for Jerusalem's trumpet now,
To blow a blast of shattering power,
To wake the sleepers high and low,
And rouse them to the urgent hour!
No hand for vengeance—but to save,
A million naked swords should wave.
Oh deem not dead that martial fire,
Say not the mystic flame is spent!
With Moses' law and David's lyre,
Your ancient strength remains unbent.
Let but an Ezra rise anew,
To lift the BANNER OF THE JEW!

A rag, a mock at first—erelong,
When men have bled and women wept,
To guard its precious folds from wrong,
Even they who shrunk, even they who slept,
Shall leap to bless it, and to save.
Strike! for the brave revere the brave![3]
—Emma Lazarus, The Poems of Emma Lazarus
*The sons of Mattathias—Jonathan, John, Eleazer
Simon (also called the Jewel), and Jonas, the Prince.

In the following work, Byron imagines and describes the emotions of Pilate as he looked out over the destruction of Jerusalem in A.D. 70, during the New Testament period.

5. ON THE DAY OF THE DESTRUCTION
OF JERUSALEM BY TITUS

On many an eve, the high spot whence I gazed
Had reflected the last beam of day as it blazed;
While I stood on the height, and beheld the decline
Of the rays from the mountain that shone on thy shrine.

From the last hill that looks on thy once holy dome
I behold thee, oh Sion! when render'd to Rome;
'Twas thy last sun went down, and the flames of thy fall
Flash'd back on the last glance I gave to thy wall.

I look'd for thy temple, I look'd for my home,
And forgot for a moment my bondage to come;
I beheld but the death-fire that fed on thy fane,
And the fast-fetter'd hands that made vengeance in vain.

And now on that mountain I stood on that day,
But I mark'd not the twilight beam melting away;
Oh.' would that the lighting had glared in its stead;
And the thunderbolt burst on the conqueror's head!

But the Gods of the Pagan shall never profane
The shrine where Jehovah disdain'd not to reign;
And scattered and scorn'd as thy people may be,
Our worship, oh Father, is only for thee.[4]
—Lord Byron, 1800s, The Works of Lord Byron

II. DELIVERANCE OF JERUSALEM IN POETIC PRAISE

The poetry and hymnody indicative of Jerusalem's permanent deliverance
and glory since the close of the New Testament period through the age
of the ages are innumerable. I have chosen the following as an example
of the love and longing expressed by the saints to stand within her walls

while, not only as an earthly city, but also when they shall stand in the heavenly one, the Holy City, New Jerusalem.

1. JERUSALEM THE GOLDEN

Jerusalem the golden, with milk and honey blest,
Beneath thy contemplation sink heart and voice oppressed.
I know not, O I know not, what joys await us there,
What radiancy of glory, what bliss beyond compare.

They stand, those halls of Zion, all jubilant with song,
And bright with many an angel, and all the martyr throng;
The Prince is ever in them, the daylight is serene.
The pastures of the blessèd are decked in glorious sheen.

There is the throne of David, and there, from care released,
The shout of them that triumph, the song of them that feast;
And they, who with their Leader, have conquered in the fight,
Forever and forever are clad in robes of white.

O sweet and blessèd country, the home of God's elect!
O sweet and blessèd country, that eager hearts expect!
Jesus, in mercy bring us to that dear land of rest,
Who art, with God the Father, and Spirit, ever blessed.

Brief life is here our portion, brief sorrow, short lived care;
The life that knows no ending, the tearless life, is there.
O happy retribution! Short toil, eternal rest;
For mortals and for sinners, a mansion with the blest.

That we should look, poor wanderers, to have our home on high!
That worms should seek for dwellings beyond the starry sky!
And now we fight the battle, but then shall wear the crown
Of full and everlasting, and passionless renown.

And how we watch and struggle, and now we live in hope,
And Zion in her anguish with Babylon must cope;
But he whom now we trust in shall then be seen and known,
And they that know and see Him shall have Him for their own.

For thee, O dear, dear country, mine eyes their vigils keep;
For very love, beholding, thy happy name, they weep:
The mention of thy glory is unction to the breast,
And medicine in sickness, and love, and life, and rest.

O one, O only mansion! O paradise of joy!
Where tears are ever banished, and smiles have no alloy;
The cross is all thy splendor, the Crucified thy praise,
His laud and benediction thy ransomed people raise.

Jerusalem the glorious! Glory of the elect!
O dear and future vision that eager hearts expect!
Even now by faith I see thee, even here thy walls discern;
To thee my thoughts are kindled, and strive, and pant, and yearn.

Jerusalem, the only, that look'st from heaven below,
In thee is all my glory, in me is all my woe!
And though my body may not, my spirit seeks thee fain,
Till flesh and earth return me to earth and flesh again.

Jerusalem, exulting on that securest shore,
I hope thee, wish thee, sing thee, ad love thee evermore!
I ask not for my merit: I seek not to deny
My merit is destruction, a child of wrath am I.

But yet with faith I venture and hope upon the way,
For those perennial guerdons I labor night and day.
The best and dearest Father Who made me, and Who saved,
Bore with me in defilement, and from defilement laved.

When in His strength I struggle, for very joy I leap;

When in my sin I totter, I weep, or try to weep:
And grace, sweet grace celestial, shall all its love display,
And David's royal fountain purge every stain away.

O sweet and blessèd country, shall I ever see thy face?
O sweet and blessèd country, shall I ever win thy grace?
I have the hope within me to comfort and to bless!
Shall I ever win the prize itself? O tell me, tell me, Yes!

Strive, man, to win that glory; toil, man, to gain that light;
Send hope before to grasp it, till hope be lost in sight.
Exult, O dust and ashes, the Lord shall be thy part:
His only, His forever thou shalt be, and thou art.[5]
—Bernard of Morlaix, 12 Century

Next are three passages selected by George Fredrick Handel for his immortal oratorio, Messiah; consisting of those that specifically mention Jerusalem and the appellation, Zion.

2. HANDEL'S MESSIAH

Comfort Ye

Comfort ye, comfort ye my people, saith your God. Speak
ye comfortably to Jerusalem, and cry unto her, that her
warfare is accomplished, that her iniquity is pardoned.
The voice of him that crieth in the wilderness, Prepare ye the way
of the Lord, make straight in the desert a highway for our God
(Isaiah 40:1-3, KJV)

Rejoice greatly, O Daughter of Zion
Rejoice greatly, O daughter of Zion; shout, O daughter
of Jerusalem! Behold, thy King cometh unto thee;
He is the righteous Saviour, and He shall speak peace
unto the heathen.
—(Zecharaiah 9:9-10, KJV)

Lift up your heads, O ye gates

Lift up your heads, O ye gates; and be ye lift up, ye everlasting doors; and the King of Glory shall come in. Who is this King of Glory? The Lord strong and mighty, the Lord mighty in battle. Lift up your heads, O ye gates; and be ye lift up, ye everlasting doors; and the King of Glory shall come in. Who is this King of Glory? The Lord of Hosts, He is the King of Glory.

— (Psalm 24:7-10, KJV)

3. JERUSALEM! HIGH TOWER THY GLORIOUS WALLS

Jerusalem! high tower thy glorious walls,
would God I were in thee!
Desire of thee my longing heart enthralls,
desire at home to be;

wide from the world out leaping,
o'er hill and vale and plain,
my soul's strong wind is sweeping
thy portals to attain.

O gladsome day and yet more gladsome hour!
When shall that hour have come
when my rejoicing soul its own free power
may use in going home,

itself to Jesus giving in trust to his own hand,
to dwell among the living in that blest fatherland?
Unnumbered choirs before the Lamb's high throne
there shout the jubilee,

with loud resounding peal and sweetest tone,
in blissful ecstasy:
a hundred thousand voices take up the wondrous song;
eternity rejoices God's praises to prolong.

4. THE HOLY CITY

Last night I lay a-sleeping, there came a dream so fair
I stood in old Jerusalem beside the temple there
I heard the children singing and ever as they sang
me thought the voice of angels from heaven in answer rang
me thought the voice of angels from heaven in answer rang
Jerusalem, Jerusalem, lift up your gates and sing
Hosannah, in the highest, hosannah to the king.

And then me thought my dream was changed the
streets no longer rang
Hushed were the glad hosannahs the little children sang
the sun grew dark with mystery, the morn was cold and chill
as the shadow of a cross arose upon a lonely hill
as the shadow of a cross arose upon a lonely hill
Jerusalem, Jerusalem, lift up your gates and sing
Hosannah, in the highest, hosannah to the king.

And once again the scene was changed, new earth there
seemed to be
I saw the Holy City beside the tide-less sea
the light of God was on its streets
The gates were opened wide,
and all who might enter, and no one was denied.
No need of moon or stars by night, nor sun to shine by day
it was a new Jerusalem that would not pass away.
It was a new Jerusalem that would not pass away
Jerusalem, Jerusalem, lift up your gates and sing
Hosannah, in the highest, hosannah to the king.
—Fredrick Weatherly

The last words of the above hymn call for the New Jerusalem herself to sing, "Hosannah, in the highest, hosannah to the king." A city is not a city without its citizenry. The writer to the Hebrews lists the different groups comprising the citizenry of New Jerusalem: "But you have come to Mount Zion and to the city of the living God, the heavenly Jerusalem, and to myriads of angels, to the general assembly and church of the firstborn who are enrolled in heaven, and to God, the Judge of all, and to the spirits of the righteous made perfect, and to Jesus, the mediator of a new covenant, and to the sprinkled blood, which speaks better than the blood of Abel." (Heb. 12:22-24). Jerusalem will sing while the ages roll throughout the ages of the ages.

CONCLUSION

I have presented a concise analysis of the fulfilled and unfulfilled prophecies of Jerusalem's deliverances and destructions throughout the Old and New Testaments. I have traced how Jerusalem's progression as city of prophecy began with her name; how she has continued through history from the time of her deliverance from the Jebusites by David; how she will continue as an earthly city; and how her existence will culminate in the transformation and transfer of her citizenry into the holy city, New Jerusalem. My study ends with an arrangement of the great hymns that have kept her memory alive in the hearts of God's people from ancient times.

Examination of the derivation and descriptive names of Jerusalem has revealed that the name definitely is a prophetic indicative. I have explained the different appellations of Jerusalem and how they shed light on the certainty that the city is, undeniably, the outstanding city of prophecy among all the cities of the earth. Every name attached to her proves her prophetic character and foretells her destiny.

Fulfilled prophecies of the deliverances and destructions of Jerusalem during the Old Testament period range from the reign of Shishak, monarch of Egypt, through the Babylonian monarchy of King Nebuchadnezzar. I have identified the time of Nebuchadnezzar as the beginning of the times of the Gentiles and the end of the times of the Gentiles as the second coming of Christ, when He defeats the beast just prior to Jerusalem's entrance into 1,000 years of blessing.

Fulfilled prophecies of the deliverance and destruction of Jerusalem during the Intertestamental Period include the accounts of the sparing of Jerusalem by Alexander the Great and the cruelties of Antiochus Epiphenes toward her during the Maccabean revolt, bridging the 400 year gap of silence between the Old and New Testaments, and allowing a view of what transpired between Jerusalem and her enemies when no prophecy was heard.

Prophecies having to do with the destructions and deliverances of Jerusalem during New Testament times reveal that the destruction of the city by the Roman General Titus is typical of the destruction of the city, and that Titus is a forerunner of "the prince who is to come" (Dan. 9: 26). These prophecies look ahead to the prince who is to come (the beast of Revelation 13 and 17) and his destruction.

I have shown that present-age prophecies of the destructions and deliverances of Jerusalem include the destruction of the city by Hadrian and the closing of the New Testament period. Events of this present age, i.e., actions against the city not cited in Scripture but prophetic in general, cover the period cited by Luke, "... Jerusalem will be trampled underfoot by the Gentiles until the times of the Gentiles are fulfilled" (Lk 21:24).

Unfulfilled prophecies of the deliverances and destructions of Jerusalem during the time relative to the Tribulation dramatize and vividly describe the destruction of the Godless forces of Russia and her allies, who will try to annihilate the city in the not-too-distant future. I have provided sufficient evidence to demonstrate that the attempted invasion will occur at a time impinging upon, but not in the middle of, the Tribulation; sometime before, after or simultaneous to the Rapture, or at the beginning of the seventieth week of Daniel. It is my personal belief that the invasion will occur sometime before the Rapture.

The Excursus of II Thessalonians 2: The Restrainer Recast, offers the co-contextual, grammatical-component, and contextual arguments which prove beyond a reasonable doubt that the Restrainer of the "lawless one" in II Thessalonians 2:1-12 is the pit of Revelation 9 and not the Holy Spirit. The pit holds "the lawless one" (the beast [Nero]) in check until the time of his revealing — at the middle of the Tribulation when Satan opens it.

My treatment of the unfulfilled prophecies of the deliverances and destructions of Jerusalem during the Tribulation period has revealed the identity of Satan's men: the Antichrist of Revelation 6:2 and "the lawless one" (the beast) of II Thessalonians 2. I clearly show that while each is a separate man during their short careers, they will, at the end, take on a composite character as one and the same person and, as the beast, will set out to destroy the city and be destroyed at the return of the Lord Jesus from Heaven.

Prophecies unfulfilled having to do with Jerusalem's deliverances and destructions during the Millennium and the ages of the ages look forward to the very end of all prophecy, at which point the Son of Man will deliver the Kingdom into the hands of God the Father, beyond which there is no revelation, except the revelation of the beginning of the ages of the ages that will never end.

In the final portion of this study I provided an arrangement of many of the great well-known and loved poems and hymns of plaint and praise about Jerusalem's destructions and deliverances, ranging from the writing of the Psalms to the present era. These works have brought much comfort and hope to the hearts of God's people from ancient times to the present.

It is my sincere hope that I have accomplished what I set out to do — shine the light of prophecy on Jerusalem, thereby revealing not only her past darkness but also her bright and eternal day of the future, after which, when her Messiah, the Son of Righteousness will have arisen with healing in His wings. Until that blessed time, pray for the peace of Jerusalem.

AFTERMATH

After one has written a body of work there are still words yearning to be expressed, especially since it has to do with one's study of God's great plan of the ages relative to Jerusalem, Israel, the Church, and the saved out of every nation of the world. W. E. Blackstone, a fervent lover of Jerusalem and Israel, wrote in his little book, Jesus Is Coming:

> It will be noticed . . . that the aions are not the same duration, but each marks a change in God's dealing with mankind. Probably the aions of the past, the Hebrew olams of the Old Testament mark the geological periods of the earth and the various eras in the development of the universe. And as the past has been an orderly unfolding of creation and revelation of the Creator, so shall the future be, not a limitless aion called eternity, but a limitless succession of aions measuring infinite duration. Time is the measurement of eternity and eternity is the continued measurement of time. Take for instance a yard stick, and it measures only three feet. But turn it over and over and over, and you pass around the world, out to the moon, the sun, the stars, the farthermost nebula, and all the limits of imagination, and still the little measure goes on and on into the unthinkable. In like manner the Scriptural succession of *aions* measures eternity.[15]

The measure will go on and the people of God will be with God the Father, and His Son the Lamb our Savior. Those for whom the Lamb shed His blood in order to provide eternal salvation from sin, death, Satan, and Hell shall enjoy the pleasures of eternal life and fellowship with the family of God while the ceaseless ages continue to roll on, and on, and on.

> "Then He who sat on the throne said to me, 'Behold, I make all things new.' And He said to me, 'Write, for these words are true and faithful.'" (Rev. 21: 5). God's people will live in new bodies, in a new world, on a new earth, in a new and beautiful city called the New Jerusalem where "there shall be no more curse, but the throne of God and the Lamb shall be in it, and His servants shall serve Him. They shall see His face, and His name shall be on their foreheads. There shall be no night there: They need no lamp nor light of the sun, for the Lord God gives them light. They shall reign forever and ever." (Rev. 22: 3-5).

After the old earthly city of Jerusalem will have ceased to exist. She will have served her purpose well, for it was outside her city walls where Jesus, the Lamb, was slain from before the foundation of the old world. All glory to the Lamb that was slain!

The New Jerusalem is still in the future. God invites all to enter. "And the Spirit and the bride say, "Come!" And let him who hears say, "Come!" And let him who thirsts come. Whoever desires, let him take the water of life freely." (Rev. 22:17).

Pray for the peace of Jerusalem: may those who love you be secure (Psa. 122:6).

ABOUT THE AUTHOR

Don Bailey was born and raised in the Appalachian-Blue Ridge Mountain area of southeastern Kentucky and West Virginia. At the age of 17, he served in the Korean War (1950) with the U.S. Army's 24th Division Medical Battalion, and is a recipient of the Distinguished Service Cross. He accepted Christ as his personal Savior at the age of 22. He is a graduate of Moody Bible

Photo by: Bailey Fantino

Institute, Chicago, Illinois; and holds a B.A. Degree from Arizona Bible College, Phoenix, Arizona; an M.A. Degree from Kansas City Bible College (Kansas City University), Kansas City Missouri; and the Doctor of Ministry Degree from Trinity International University at Deerfield, Illinois. He is an ordained minister and has served as guest speaker at churches throughout America. He was instrumental in the healthcare field for thirty-eight years–thirteen as a surgical assistant and twenty-five as Chaplain of Bethesda Hospital, Chicago, Illinois. He assisted a medical team in Guatemala during the 1976 earthquake. He is the author of *The Challenge of Euthanasia: An Annotated Bibliography on Euthanasia and Related Subjects*, and has written numerous biblical articles, and pamphlets. He has a burning love for the Jewish people, Israel, and the city of Jerusalem. He has sat as a panelist on Holocaust discussions, and has taught seminars on Dialogues with the Jewish People. He is an accomplished soloist and holds copyrights to four songs. Through the years, his hobbies have been backpacking annually through the Grand Canyon, inline power skating, biking, and running marathons.

ENDNOTES

Preface

1. Wilbur M. Smith, "Jerusalem in Prophecy," Moody Monthly, 60:43-54, June 1960.

Chapter 1. Derivation and Descriptive Names of Jerusalem

1. The Concise Columbia Encyclopedia, (Bookshelf 1995 [software]).
2. Howard J. Kitchen, *Holy Fields,* 124-125.

Chapter 2. Fulfilled Prophecies of the Deliverances and Destructions of Jerusalem during the Old Testament Period

1. Wilbur M. Smith, Egypt in Biblical Prophecy, 69.
2. T. Nichol, "Shishak, "The International Standard Bible Encyclopedia, V. 4, 2778.
3. Albert Barnes, The Prophet Isaiah, V. 1, 168.
4. Charles Lee Feinberg, Is the Virgin Birth in the Old Testament?, 47-48.
5. Wilbur M. Smith, "Jerusalem In Prophecy," Moody Monthly, 60:43-54, June 1960.
6. William Whiston, Josephus' Complete Works, 213.
7. M. G. Easton, M.A.D.D., "Sennacherib," Eastman's Bible Dictionary, 1996.
8. Henry H. Halley, Bible Handbook, 209.
9. Chaim Herzog, Mordechai Gichon, Battles of The Bible, 213.
10. Wilbur M. Smith, "Jerusalem In Prophecy," Moody Monthly, 60:30-33, June 1960.

11. S. Fisch, Rabbi Dr., Ezekiel, Chapters 19-24. This work presents excellent comments on Ezekiel's imagery.
12. See Note 10,60:30-33, June, 1960.
13. (Dictionnaire des sciences médicales, par une société de médicins et de chirurgiens, Paris, 1818, V. 29, 246).

Chapter 3. Fulfilled Prophecies of the Deliverances and Destructions of Jerusalem during the Intertestamental Period

1. David Baron, The Visions and Prophecies of Zechariah, 298.
2. William Whiston, The Complete Works of Josephus, 243.
3. H. A. Ironside, Daniel, 147.
4. John F. Walvoord, The Nations in Prophecy, 81.
5. Robert Anderson, The Coming Prince, 42.
6. Oxford University Press, The Apocrapha, 211-13, n.d.
7. See Note 2, 257.

Chapter 4. Fulfilled Prophecies of the Deliverances and Destructions of Jerusalem during New Testament Times

1. John Walvoord, The Nations in Prophecy, 83-84.
2. Edward J. Young, The Messianic Prophecies of Daniel, 71-73.
3. See Note 2.
4. A. C. Gaebelein, The Annotated Bible, V. 5, 34.
5. Lewis Sperry Chafer, Systematic Theology, V. 5, 119.
6. Wilbur M. Smith, "Jerusalem in Prophecy," Moody Monthly, 60:34, August, 1960.
7. George Adam Smith, Jerusalem from The Earliest Times to A.D. 70, V. 2, 578.
8. Dean Millman, The Fall of Jerusalem, 63.
9. See Note 6, 61:31, September, 1960.
10. William Whiston, Josephus, 562-563.
11. Ibid., 578.
12. Ibid., 588.
13. Ibid., 578-79.
14. Ibid., 588.

Chapter 5. Fulfilled Prophecies of the Deliverances and Destructions of Jerusalem during the Present Age

1. Frederick G. Owen, Abraham to Allenby, 18.
2. A. C. Gaebelein, The Annotated Bible, V. 5, 182.
3. Richard Wolfe, Israel, Act III, 52.
4. George Adam Smith, Jerusalem from The Earliest Times to A.D. 70, V. 2, 580.
5. See Note 1, Owen, loc. cit.
6. Ibid.
7. Arnold T. Olson, Inside Jerusalem, City of Destiny, 14-15.
8. Wilbur M. Smith, World Crisis and the Prophetic Scriptures, 158.
9. Michael Mols, "The War, Astounding 60 Hours," Life, 62:81-82, June, 1967.
10. See Note 7, 102.
11. See Note 8, 171.

Chapter 6. Unfulfilled Prophecies of the Deliverances and Destructions of Jerusalem during the Time Impinging the Tribulation

1. The Stuttgart Edition of The Biblia Hebracia and The Septuagint Version of The Old Testament, Ezekiel, Chapters 38-39.
2. Wilbur M. Smith, World Crisis and the Prophetic Scriptures, 181-182.
3. James D. Price, Rosh: An Ancient Land Known To Ezekiel, Grace Theological Journal, V6, 1, Spr., 85-68. A brief descriptive of what the piece purports: "Extensive evidence from ancient Near Eastern texts and from normal Hebrew syntax supports the view that Rosh is a toponym in Ezek. 38:2, 3; 39:1. The syntactical support involves a detailed examination of instances where some scholars posit a break in a construct chain. These hypothetical breaks are not convincing for several reasons. Therefore, Rosh in Ezek. 38:2, 3; 39:1 should be translated as a proper noun ("the prince of Rosh, Meshech, and Tubal" [NKJV]), not an adjective ("the chief prince of Meshech and Tubal" [KJV].
4. Josephus, Josephus, (Garland, Texas: Electronic Edition by Galaxie Software),1999.
5. Easton's Bible Dictionary, Oak Harbor, WA: Logos Research Systems, Inc., 1996.
6. Josephus, Josephus, (Garland, Texas: Electronic Edition by Galaxie Software), 1999.
7. The Popular Critical Bible Encyclopedia, V. 2, 1680.
8. Unger's Bible Dictionary, 845.

9. International Bible Encyclopedia, V. 4, 2510.

10. Dwight J. Pentecost, Things to Come, 351.

11. See Note 3, 342-351.

12. CIA World Fact Book 2007, [Search] Guide to Country Profiles (Military), Internet-https://www.cia.gov/cia/publications/factbook/.

13. Rabbi Dr. S. Fisch, Ezekiel, 259.

14. (http://www.geocities.com/pleides61-hailstones.html).

15. M. G. Easton, M.A.D.D., Easton's Bible Dictionary, (Oak Harbor, WA: Logos Research Systems, Inc.), 1996.

Chapter 7. Excursus of II Thessalonians 2: The Restrainer Recast

1. E. W. Bullinger, Commentary on Revelation, 408.

2. _____, Word Studies of the Holy Spirit, 167-173.

3. Gresham J. Machen, New Testament Greek for Beginners, 105-106.

4. H. E. Danna, and Julius R. Mantey, Manual Grammar of The Greek New Testament, 222.

5. Henry Morris, Biblical Eschatology and Modern Science, Part IV, 299, B Sac-V125 #500 Oct. 68.

6. Laird R. Harris, Gleason L. Archer, Jr., Theological Word Book of The Old Testament, 847.

7. R. H. Charles, The Book of Enoch, trans. S.P.C.A. Holy Trinity Church: London, 42-44.

8. Arthur W. Pink, The Antichrist "The Antichrist in the Gospels and the Epistles," 142.

9. Scott Peck, People of the Lie, 206.

10. Endnotes, Enhanced Strong's Lexicon, (Oak Harbor, WA: Logos Research Systems, Inc.), #2411.

11. Ibid., #3485.

12. J. B. Smith, A Revelation of Jesus Christ, 245-246.

13. Are "Babylon" and "Diaspora" Literal or Figurative? JETS 17:3 (Summer 1974), 175, Multiple, Journal of The Evangelical Theological Society, (Lynchburg, VA: JETS (Electronic Edition by Galaxy Software), 1998.

14. J. B. Smith, A Revelation of Jesus Christ, 207.

15. Ibid, 207.

16. Jerome R. Corsi, The Late Great U.S.A., Introduction, 1-7.

Chapter 8. Unfulfilled Prophecies of the Deliverances and Destructions of Jerusalem during the Tribulation

1. Keil-Delitzsch, Commentary on the Old Testament, V. 9, 470.
2. Endnotes, Enhanced Strong's Lexicon, Oak Harbor, WA: Logos Research Systems, Inc., 1995.
3. Simple to Remember.com, Judaism On Line: Jewish Population Statistics.
4. Keil-Delitzsch, Commentary on The Old Testament, V. 10, 403.
5. P. L. Tan, (1996, c1979), Encyclopedia of 7700 illustrations: [a treasury of illustrations, anecdotes, facts and quotations for pastors, teachers and Christian workers], Garland TX: Bible Communications.

Chapter 9. Unfulfilled Prophecies of the Destructions and Deliverances of Jerusalem during the Millennial Age and the Age of Ages

1. Lee A. Gore, Confrontation, 23.
2. Andrew Sinclair, Jerusalem: The Endless Crusade, 1.
3. Stephen Weinberg, The First Three Minutes: A Modern View of the Origin of the Universe, 1-6.
4. Joseph B. Rotherham, Rotherham's Emphasized Bible, New Testament, 244.
5. Kenneth S. Wuest, In These Last Days, 72-73.
6. E. Nestle, P. R. McReynolds, (1997, c1982). Nestle Aland 26th Edition Greek New Testament with McReynolds English Interlinear. Includes the Nestle Aland Greek New Testament with morphology, lemmas, glosses, and interlinear translation in modern English; The Greek New Testament c1982 by United Bible Societies, Oak Harbor: Logos Research Systems, Inc., 2 Peter 3:10-11.
7. Scientific Digital Visions, Inc., The Language of the Nucleus, On-Line Edition. The world's largest nuclear glossary.
8. R. C. H. Lenski, The Interpretation of St. John's Revelation, 614-615.
9. See Note 4, New Testament, 198.
10. Wilbur Smith, The Biblical Doctrine of Heaven, 246.
11. For a detailed study of the gates of Jerusalem see The International Standard Bible Encyclopedia, V. 3, 1602-1608.
12. R. C. Trench, After the Thousand Years, 93-94.
13. See Note 12, 117-118.
14. J. P. Louw & E. A. Nida, (1996, c1989). Greek-English Lexicon of the New Testament: Based on Semantic Domains (electronic edition of the 2nd edition), V. 1, 634.
15. W. E. Blackstone (W.E.B.), Jesus Is Coming, 224.

Chapter 10. The Destructions and Deliverances of Jerusalem in Poetic Plaint and Praise

1. The International Standard Bible Encyclopedia, V. 3, 1824.
2. The Wordsworth Poetry Library, The Works of Lord Byron, 82.
3. Emma Lazarus, Online Text © 1998-2007 Poetry X. All rights reserved. From The Poems of Emma Lazarus, Vol. II, Jewish Poems: Translations.
4. See Note 2, 81-82.
5. A. Ewing, Hymns Ancient and Modern, #228, 239.

BIBLIOGRAPHY

A. BOOKS

Anderson, Robert. *The Coming Prince*. Grand Rapids, Michigan: Kregel Publications, 1963.

Baron, David. *The Visions and Prophecies of Zechariah*. London: Hebrew Christian Testimony to Israel, 1951.

Bullinger, E. W. *Number in Scripture*. Grand Rapids, MI 49501: Kregel Publications, 1967.

Chafer, Lewis Sperry. *Systematic Theology*. 8 Vols. Dallas, Texas: Dallas Seminary, 1948

Comway, Joan. *The Temple of Jerusalem*. New York: Holt, Rinehart and Winston, 1975

Conder, C.R., *Tell Amarna Tablets*. London: Alexander P. Watt, 1893

Corsi, Jerome R., *The Late Great U.S.A*, Los Angeles, CA. Published by World Ahead Media, 2007.

Easton, M. G., M. A. D. D., *Easton's Bible Dictionary*, (Oak Harbor, WA: Logos Research Systems, Inc.) 1996

Feinberg, Charles L., *Is The Virgin Birth in The Old Testament?* Whittier, CA: Emeth Publications, Inc., 1967

_____, *Premillennialism or Amillennialism*. Grand Rapids, MI: Zondervan Publishing House. 1936

Fisch, S., Rabbi Dr., *Ezekiel*, Hebrew Text & English Translation With An Introduction And Commentary, London: The Soncino Press, 1950

Fruchtenbaum, Arnold G. *A Review of the Pre-Wrath Rapture of the Church*. Tustin, CA: Ariel Ministries. n.d

Gaebelein, A.C. *The Annotated Bible*. Vol. 5. New York: Publication Office, Our Hope, n.d

Gentry, Kenneth L., and Thomas Ice. *The Great Tribulation: Past or Future?*. Grand Rapids, MI: Kregel Publications. 1999

Gentry, Kenneth L., and Thomas Ice. *The Great Tribulation: Past or Future?*. Grand Rapids, MI: Kregel Publications. 1999

Gore, Lee A., *Confrontation*. Georgia: Brentwood Christian Press. 1990.

Halley, Henry H., *Bible Handbook*. Chicago: Henry H. Halley.

Han, Nathan E. *A Parsing Guide to the Greek New Testament*. Pennsylvania: Herald Press. 1972

Herzog, Chaim; Gichon, Mordechai. *Battles of The Bible*. Pennsylvania: Stackpole Books, 1997.

Hope Publishing Company. *Worship and Service Hymnal*, 1957.

Horton, Fred L. Jr., *The Melchizidek Tradition*. Cambridge: Cambridge University Press, 1976

Hull, William L, *The Fall and Rise of Israel*. Grand Rapids, Michigan: Zondervan Pub. Co., 1954

_____., *The Struggle of a Soul*. Garden City, New York: Doubleday, 1963

Ice, Thomas, and Timothy J. Demy. *The Return*. Grand Rapids, MI: Kregel Publications. 1999

Ice, Thomas, and Timothy J. Demy. *When the Trumpet Sounds*. Eugene, OR: Harvest House Publishers. 1995

Ironside, H. A. *Daniel*. New York: Loizeaux Brothers, Inc., Bible Truth Depot, 1960.

Kobelski, Paul J., *Melchizedek and Melchiresa*. Washington, DC: The Catholic Biblical Association of America, 1981.

LaHaye, Tim, and Thomas Ice. *Charting the End Times*. Eugene, OR: Harvest House Publishers. 2001

LaHaye, Tim. *Revelation Unveiled*. Grand Rapids, MI: Zondervan Publishing House. 1999

LaHaye, Tim, and Thomas Ice, eds. *The End Times Controversy*. Eugene, OR: Harvest House Publishers. 2003

LaHaye, Tim. *The Rapture*. Eugene, OR: Harvest House Publishers. 2002

Lenski, R.C.H., *The Interpretation of St. John's Revelation* (Columbus, OH: Lutheran Book Concern, 1935).

MacArthur, John. *Revelation 1-11 : The MacArthur New Testament Commentary.* Chicago, IL: Moody Press. 1999

MacArthur, John. *Revelation 12-22 : The MacArthur New Testament Commentary.* Chicago, IL: Moody Press. 2000

Massie, Robert K., *Peter the Great*, New York, NY: Ballantine Books, 1981.

Millman, Dean. *The Fall of Jerusalem.* London: Nelson and Sons, 1870.

Morris, Henry. *The Revelation Record.* Wheaton, IL: Tyndale House Publishers, 1983.

Pentecost, Dwight J. *Prophecy for Today.* Grand Rapids: Zondervan Publishing House, 1966.

_____. *Things to Come.* Findly, Ohio: Dunham Publishing Company, 1958.

Pink, Arthur Walkington. *The Antichrist.* Oak Harbor, WA: Logos Research Systems. 1999, 1923

Price, Randall, *In Search of Temple Treasures.* Eugene, OR: Harvest House Publishers, 1994.

_____. *The Coming Last Days Temple.* Eugene, OR: Harvest House Publishers, 1999.

Pritchard, James B., ed. *Ancient Near Eastern Texts Relating to the Old Testament.* Princeton: Princeton University Press, 1969

Ryrie, Charles C. *Come Quickly, Lord Jesus.* Eugene, OR: Harvest House Publishers. 1996

Ryrie, Charles C. *Dispensationalism.* Chicago, IL: Moody Press. 1995

Showers, Renald E. *Maranatha, Our Lord Come.* Bellmawr, NJ: The Friends of Israel Gospel Ministry. 1995

Showers, Renald E. *The Pre-Wrath Rapture View.* Grand Rapids, MI: Kregel Publications. 2001

Sinclair, Andrew. *Jerusalem: The Endless Crusade.* New York: Crown Publishers, Inc., 1995.

Smith, George Adam. *Jerusalem From The Earliest Times to A. D. 70.* 2 Vols. London: Hodder and, Stoughton, [n.d.].

Smith, Wilbur. *The Biblical Doctrine of Heaven.* Chicago: Moody Press, 1968.

Trench, R.C. *After the Thousand Years*. London: Morgan and Scott, Paternoster Buildings, E. C., [n.d.].

Unger, Merrill F. *Unger's Bible Dictionary*. Chicago: Moody Press, 1966.

Walvoord, John F. *The Millennial Kingdom*. Grand Rapids: Zondervan Publishing House, 1974.

_____. *The Nations in Prophecy*. Grand Rapids, Michigan: Zondervan Publishing House, 1967

Walvoord, John F. *Daniel: The Key to Prophetic Revelation*. Chicago, IL: Moody Bible Institute. 1971

Walvoord, John F. *Every Prophecy of the Bible*. Colorado Springs, CO: Chariot Victor Publishing. 1990, 1999

Walvoord, John F. *The Rapture Question*. Grand Rapids, MI: Zondervan Publishing House. 1979

Walvoord, John F. *The Revelation of Jesus Christ*. Chicago, IL: Moody Press. 1966

Weinberg, Stephen. *The First Three Minutes: A Modern View of the Origin of the Universe*. New York: Bantam New Age, 1977.

Whiston, William, *Josephus' Complete Works*. Grand Rapids, Michigan: Kregel Publications, 1960.

Wuest, Kenneth S. *In These Last Days*. Grand Rapids, Michigan: WM. B. Eerdmans Publishing Company, 1957.

Young, Edward J. *The Messianic Prophecies of Daniel*. Grand Rapids, Michigan: WM. B. Eerdmans Publishing Company, 1954.

B. COMMENTARIES

Keil-Delitzsch, Commentary on the Old Testament.10 Vols. Grand Rapids, Michigan: WM. B. Eerdmans Publishing Company, 1975.

The New Bible Commentary. Grand Rapids, Michigan: WM. B. Eerdmans Publishing Company, 1954.

The Penteteuch and Haftorahs, London: Soncino Press, 5722-1962.

C. CONCORDANCES

Englishman's Hebrew and Chaldee Concordance. Grand Rapids: Zondervan, 1970

Strong's Exhaustive Concordance on the Bible. New York: Abingdon
Press, 1970

D. DICTIONARIES

Easton, M. G., M. A. D. D., *Easton's Bible Dictionary*, (Oak Harbor, WA:
Logos Research Systems, Inc.) 1996.
Dictionnaire des sciences médicales, par une société de médicins et de
chirurgiens, Volume 29 Paris: 1818,
Unger, Merrill F., Unger's Bible Dictionary. Chicago: Moody Press, 1973

F. ENCYCLOPEDIAS

Fausset, A. R., Bible Cyclopedia. New York: Funk & Wagnalls
Company, n.d.
The International Standard Bible Encyclopedia. 5 Vols. Grand Rapids,
Michigan: WM. B. Eerdmans Publishing Company, 1939.
The Popular Critical Bible Encyclopedia. 3 Vols. Chicago: The Howard
Severance Company, 1907.

F. LEXICONS

A Greek-English Lexicon of the New Testament. Chicago: The University
of Chicago Press, 1957.
Analytical Hebrew and Chaldee Lexicon. London: Samuel Bagster and
Sons, 1966.
Hebrew and Chaldee Lexicon, Gesenius. Grand Rapids: WM. B.
Eerdmans, 1969.
Hebrew and English Lexicon of the Old Testament. London: Oxford
University Press, 1907.
Index to the Arndt and Gingrich Greek Lexicon. Santa Ana: Wycliffe
Bible Translators, Inc., 1966.

G. NEWSPAPERS

Jerusalem Post. Jerusalem, 1967-2007.

H. PERIODICALS

Bibliotheca Sacra. (Dallas, Texas: Dallas Theological Seminary (Electronic edition by Galaxie Software), 1999.

Grace Theological Journal. (Winona, IN: Grace Seminary (Electronic edition by Galaxie Software), 1999.

Journal of the Evangelical Theological Society. (Lynchburg, VA: JETS (Electronic edition by Galaxie Software), 1998.

Life. 62:81-82, June, 1967.

Master's Seminary Journal. (Sun Valley, CA: Master's Seminary (Electronic edition by Galaxie Software), 1999.

Moody Monthly. Chicago: May, 1960.

REFERENCE LIST FOR SUGGESTED STUDY

Anderson, Robert. The Coming Prince. Grand Rapids, MI: Kregel Publications, 1957.

Ankerberg, John, John Weldon; Dave Breese and Dave Hunt. One World: Bible Prophecy and The New World Order. Chicago: Moody, 1991.

Armerding, Carl E., and W. Ward Gasque (editors). Handbook of Biblical Prophecy. Grand Rapids: Baker, 1977.

Barker, Kenneth (General Editor). The NIV Study Bible. Grand Rapids: Zondervan, 1985.

Baron, David. Zechariah: A Commentary On His Visions And Prophecies. Grand Rapids, MI: Kregel Publications, 1951.

Benson, John L., Who is The Antichrist. Schaumburg, IL: Regular Baptist Press, 1978.

Benware, Paul N., Understanding End Times Prophecy: A Comprehensive Approach. Chicago: Moody, 1995.

Bullinger, E. W., Commentary On Revelation. Grand Rapids, MI: Kregel Publications, 1984, 1935.

Couch, Mal (general editor). Dictionary of Premillennial Theology. Grand Rapids: Kregel, 1996.

Feinberg, Charles. Premillennialism or Amillennialism. Grand Rapids, MI: Zondervan Publishing House, 1936.

____. Israel: At the Center of History and Revelation. Portland: Multnomah, 1980.

Ferguson, Sinclair B., and David F. Wright, and J. I. Packer (editors). New Dictionary of Theology. Downers Grove: InterVarsity, 1988.

Fruchtenbaum, Arnold G. The Footsteps of the Messiah: A Study of the Sequence of Prophetic Events. Tustin, CA: Ariel Press, 1982.

___. Israelology: The Missing Link in Systematic Theology. Tustin, CA: Ariel Press, 1993.

___. A Review of the Pre-Wrath Rapture of the Church. Tustin, CA:

Printed in the United States
By Bookmasters